Life Has A Way

Life Has A Way

created and written by
DWAYNE JENKINS

Acknowledgement

I'm known to be a bit of a verbose fellow (through written text), so I'm going to do my best to keep this as brief as possible. First and foremost, I'd like to thank everyone who is going to read this who may be battling their own demons. As someone who has dealt with depression for a good chunk of my life, stemming as far back as early childhood, I've been there. It's still something that I struggle with, but know that your pain isn't exclusive. There are others out there who share your plight, be it depression, anxiety, bi-polar disorder, or many other mental disorders that we, as a people, need to prioritize as a serious topic of discussion.

I wrote this not just as a catharsis for myself, but for those who feel like there's nothing else out there for them. It's an uphill battle, but not an impossible one to overcome. If I can sit here and type out this little message for you, someone who's had his fair share of debilitating, harsh lows, I want you to know that there's always a chance for you too! Remember, you never have to suffer alone. There's always someone out there that you're able to reach out to for a meaningful connection that may completely change your outlook, as well as potentially save your life. Hopefully, I can keep you sufficiently entertained with this sweet, literary child of mine! Now, for the other important people that deserve to be lauded for everything they've done in making a formerly lost soul's dreams come true!

I'd like to give a huge kudos to my publisher, BlackGold

Publishing, for seeing something in me that I started to believe wasn't there. After a difficult, heartbreaking publishing journey, they took me in and made fantasy a reality. For that, I'll always tout them to anyone with an open ear! Specifically, I'd like to first thank Tiffany, who was my first point of contact with BlackGold when I reached out to them. I pitched her the premise of this book, and she became the lynchpin to what would be an amazing partnership between myself and my publisher!

Of course, that leads me to BlackGold's lovely, multi-talented CEO, Ms. Tahara Saron! She read my manuscript and decided to bring me into the fold, even championing me against some initial rough currents and a few pockets of skepticism. She's been nothing but supportive, kind, and generous. Beyond our obvious partnership, I'm also proud to call her a friend who has talked me through some of my own doubts and insecurities during the preparation of this novel. Needless to say, she's awesome, and if there were more people willing to put themselves out there for the underrepresented and worked as hard as she has, the world would be a more vibrant, beautiful place.

Next, there's Noelle, my observant, sharp editor. It's funny because we initially butted heads when she took me on as we went back and forth regarding certain characters and plot points. However, she ultimately challenged me and made me a more astute writer when it came to the more minute intricacies of storytelling. It's true that an author needs a strong editor to be empowered to tell them if something is wrong, or if they can make certain elements more cohesive, and that's precisely what Noelle has done for me. "Life Has A Way" is much stronger due to her dedication! I also need to quickly acknowledge everyone else at BlackGold who made this as powerful a final product as it is because I was certainly a brat on more than one occasion. I love the entire team and know that nothing but great things are on the horizon for all of us. Ashleigh, Ty, Whitley, Wes, Blakely, Justin, Krys, Qualita, and all the other talented BlackGold authors... This is only the beginning for us. Our voices will never be silenced.

Brenda, my wonderful grandmother. You helped me through some very hard, painful moments. I don't know if I'd still be here if it weren't for you. I love you so much, and you're one of the only people that I've been able to consistently depend upon. You've kept me sane, and we've been through hell and back together. For everything you've done for me, I promise that I'm going to continue living a life that you'll always be proud of. I'll be the man that you've raised me to be, and I'll strive to be as good of a mentor to someone as you always were to me.

I'd like to thank everyone at the library, my fellow co-workers, who have been nothing but supportive since learning about my literary aspirations. Despite my incredible secrecy, I was met with nothing but warmth and joy when I finally gave them the news. That's another family that I have an enormous amount of admiration for. I couldn't ask for a better team of hard-working, determined colleagues that always keep me engaged, grinning and hopeful! I'd especially like to thank Robbie, who was the first real friend I made at the library and proved to be an invaluable part of my confidence in sending out the manuscript in the first place! He was the very first person to read it, love it, and encourage me to never give up when trying to get published!

All the friends that are watching from the wings and cheering me on, you know I love all of you. Asia, Jeran, Theo, Todd, Jeff, Mike, Larry, every single one of you. You saw the kid at his worst, and now you get to see him start to show off his best! Also, I have to single you out, Dom, simply because you're you.

Last, and certainly not least, I must recognize my muse. I don't know if you're entirely cool with me putting your name out there, but you already know who you are. You're an amazing, beautiful, talented human being who pulled me out of the darkness and made me see the light within myself. I love you selflessly and infinitely, and I want you to know that none of this would've been possible if you hadn't taught me how to love myself at a time where I was convinced that I never would. I can only hope that I'm able to grant you a fraction of what you've given me. There will always be nothing but love between us. Alright, I think that covers everything! By now, you've either skipped over this or are just skimming, and either way is fine with me! As long as you enjoy what you're about to read, you ignoring the acknowledgements are the least of my concerns.

Now, go on, read away!

Chapter 1

A hush of anticipation fell over the restless crowd as the sharply-dressed woman finally sauntered to the head of the bright, colorful section of the crowded bookstore, the space temporarily given to her client as a reward for his toilsome journey. She stood directly in front of the long table stacked with his books, perfectly aligned in neat rows and columns. With a smile, she addressed the audience, their energy palpable, almost electric.

"Good afternoon, all! My name is Christine York, and I'm the agent representing Mr. Earl Veares—"
She could barely get his name out before the frenzy that had been simmering amongst the congregation of people exploded, roaring with rabid cheers. Christine smirked and made a gesticulation indicating that she wanted the crowd to quiet down, which they did shortly afterwards.

"Don't worry, I'm going to get him out here. Believe me, he's just as excited to see all of you as you all are excited to see him!" Christine said happily, brushing a loose strand of hair away from the front of her face. "Now, this is a moment that is suspended in literary history. Not only is Mr. Veares the youngest African-American to ever top the New York Times Best-Sellers list at the age of twenty-three, but his debut novel, 'Voyage of a Nascent Soul' sold over a million copies in its first week! Numbers like that are nearly unprecedented for any author, let alone someone so new with such a unique, meticulous style!" Following that sentiment were hoots, whistles and celebratory shouts from the horde of passionate fans. "As a literary agent, I've obviously worked with my fair share of aspiring, as well as established, authors. I can easily say, however, at the cost of revealing a certain degree of bias, that working with Mr. Veares has been one of my best experiences yet. It's rare that you see such passion and stick-to-itiveness, and I'm privileged to have the opportunity to represent his brand of talent. I'd go into detail about his journey to get here, but that's something that he'd be more equipped to tell you than I could!"

As Christine continued speaking, a head poked out from behind a door quietly, just out of the line of sight from the people sitting on the far-right side of the room. From this perspective, all he could nervously identify was Christine's back as she touted his accomplishments. He quickly snatched his head back to safety and closed the door, unable to get a head-count of how many people had attended his first book signing. There was a mirror to his immediate right, and he looked himself over one more time as he'd done once every few minutes, making sure that not a single thing was out of place. "Earl, calm down! You look fine; you're going to go out there and kill it, baby!" a voice from behind him proclaimed. Earl turned around into a pair of lips meeting with his own. They kissed briefly, and she squeezed his shoulders in reassurance, feeling his entire body quivering.

"I'll be right out there with you, E! Just be yourself, stop overthinking it! They're here for support! They aren't out there to judge you, they're here to celebrate with you!" "I'm shaking," Earl retorted, speaking more to himself than to her. "Did you hear them? How can I sign anything if I can barely keep my hands steady?!" She put her hands on the back of his neck and stared at him with her eyes of deep mahogany. She waited until she could see in his eyes that he'd calmed down enough to hear her, enough to receive the pep talk that she was gearing up for him.

"Alright, here's what we're going to do," she said, turning his head in the direction of the mirror he'd looked away from.

"Do you see that person?"

Earl's adam's apple threatened to drop into his stomach as he gulped, nodding at her query.

"That's a true artist. It took over a year for you to perfect that manuscript. You had a lot of potential agents not 'understand' your work because it was so unlike anything they'd ever read, you busted your ass and look at where you are now," she said as she grabbed both of his hands from her position behind him and held them, using her thumbs to caress his palms in an effort to stop them from shaking. "There were definitely a few bumps in the road on the way here, sure. Remember when you had writer's block for about two weeks and I had to stop you from throwing your laptop out of my window, potentially smacking someone walking down the street? I didn't want you to go to jail, I know how much you hate the idea of dropping the soap in the shower."

This caused Earl to snicker as she giggled with him, recalling the parts of the process that Earl only entertained due to hindsight. "It wasn't all sunshine and roses, but now you get to stand in front of people who adore your work! You even listened to me when I told you to rock the black and purple combo to match the cover of the book! Do you think your agent is out there pumping you up just for shits and giggles? No, she's out there because she gets a percentage of your royalties and I know you're making her really happy on that side of things, but even then, she believed in you! I believed in you! Everyone is here because of your brilliant writing, to honor the man behind the words, and you know what? You deserve to have the story behind your novel heard, so go on out there and tell them! Allow them to see what I see, the amazing, thoughtful, determined man beneath the surface! This is your moment, and you deserve to bask in every second of it."

He could feel his tense body slowly loosen as he took a deep breath and turned around to his girlfriend's smiling face. She always had that effect on him, that soothing calmness that persisted despite the typhoon of his over-active mind. He suddenly hugged her, feeling his anxiety melt away as they embraced lovingly. After a minute, Earl broke the hug to lean in and kiss her with the fervor that she rightfully deserved.

When they finally separated from one another, Earl looked upon his biggest supporter and couldn't help but grin widely, noting the dimples that always made themselves known whenever she'd felt her happiest

"Thank you for everything you've done for me, Saniya. If it wasn't for you, I don't know what the hell I'd have done or where I'd be today. I'm not entirely convinced that there would've even been a 'Voyage of a Nascent Soul' without your love and care," Earl stated warmly, using his thumb to outline her dimples as she closed her eyes, enjoying his touch. "That's what I'm here for! I support you in everything that you do because I know what kind of heart you have. Plus, you always do the same when it comes to me and my artwork, and I'm grateful to have someone as amazing as you in my life to grow with. We're equals, and that's why we've spent a wonderful six years together with many more to go! Plus, it doesn't hurt that you're damn near a millionaire now, so be on the lookout for my pickaxe because this humble girl is definitely about to be mining for gold soon."

Earl frowned and shot her an unamused glare as Saniya cackled at her own joke with Earl eventually succumbing to her infectious laughter. Their mutual mirth lasted for a moment before they began to hear Christine's cue to bring out the budding novelist himself. "—my distinct pleasure to introduce to you, the author of the best-selling 'Voyage of a Nascent Soul' novel, and one of literature's most promising prospects, Earl Veares!" The deafening roar of the crowd prompted Earl to take a deep breath before looking to Saniya, who nodded proudly and opened the door leading to the culmination of her trepid lover's hard work. With only a second of hesitation, Earl strode out of the door and walked up to the ornate table where

Christine was standing. She put down the microphone she was holding and applauded Earl's emergence with the rest of his zealots, standing off to the side as she let Earl and Saniya take their place at the front of the table. As Earl got closer to the display tailor-made for him and his novel, he just stood, awestruck, and stared into the mass of excitement. Mouth agape, he blinked twice, unable to believe he was living the fantasy he'd envisioned on occasion while hunched over his keyboard. His eyes went from scanning his supporters to the table in front of him. On the left side, there were stacks of his novel, both hardcover and paperback. On the right side were shirts, keychains, caps, necklaces and many other manners of merchandise; all bore the purple-colored theme, in some shape or form, of the cover of his novel.

He felt a gentle brush against the back of his hand, and he looked over to see Saniya, beaming at him, more thrilled than he's ever known her to be, a difficult triumph to supersede. He could feel his eyes begin to sting with tears of utter joy, and as he reached out to grab the microphone and address the crowd, they began to chant his name. This public demonstration adoration pushed Earl over the edge and he began to cry, no longer able to withhold his bliss. As he sobbed, the only thing he could think was "I've done it."

He'd spent his entire life dreaming, of a purpose, of a goal, of belonging to something. Here he was, being cheered, not ignored. The sensation was too much for him, and he wept for a solid minute before being able to take the microphone on the table. Saniya turned away, not wanting to risk Earl seeing her tears too, feeling the burden of the colossal weight he'd been carrying being lifted from his shoulders all at once. After wiping his eyes and regaining his composure, he finally willed himself to speak, hoping that the words came out coherently and clearly.

"…Thank you. This—this means more to me than all of you could ever know. This is, without a doubt, the happiest day of my life," Earl said, his voice croaking between words. He sniffled and cleared his throat, Saniya handing him two tissues to blow his nose and wipe his tear-streaked face before continuing.

"Uh, so I know that you guys didn't take time out of the day to watch a grown man cry, so I'll get right to it. I want to give out the warning now: I'm nowhere near the speaker that you're probably expecting from the way that I write. This is my first time really speaking publicly, so go easy on me if I fumble and stutter over a few words," Earl joked, garnering a few laughs for his efforts. "Let me take this time to give my sincerest thanks to a few people before I start ranting because it's important that I let them know how significant they are to this moment. First, though I already did, I'd like to thank not only those that attended my signing today, but also everyone that bought a copy of 'Voyage of a Nascent Soul.' Thank you from the bottom of my heart. I wouldn't be standing here if it wasn't for you guys." The audience applauded Earl's humble gesture as he took a second to consider the next recipient of his gratitude.

"I'd like to thank my literary agent, Christine York, for helping me achieve my dream. She opened the door to a whole new world for me; editors, publishers, she helped me understand the ins-and-outs of the publishing process, and for that, I'm immensely grateful. Obviously, my book wouldn't be on the shelves for anyone to buy if it wasn't for her. I didn't have the most... accessible novel with my original manuscript being over 180,000 words, but she stuck with me, and she introduced me to a lot of people that assisted me in fine-tuning my first book! I have quite a few novels cooked up in my head that I hope she sticks around for, if she plans on representing me long-term." Earl shot a look to his agent standing next to a row of people sitting down, and she gave him a thumbs-up to confirm the continuation of their partnership. "Oh, and in that same vein, I want to thank everyone involved in the publishing world that helped me refine and publish my work! A special thanks to David Ortenga, who illustrated the eye-popping cover!" Earl gestured over to a stand to the right of the table that had a big poster of the novel's cover adorned for all to see.

"Next, I want to thank my grandmother, Charlotte, who raised me for as long as I can remember! Without her, I'd have lost my mind years ago! She was consistently there for me when I was down, out and didn't think I'd ever be happy. I was... difficult growing up, so for her to be so dedicated and loving was a godsend. She'd be here, but she said that planes make her nauseous. The flight from the state of Washington to New York is a little long, as you could imagine, so maybe I can convince her next time! Last, and certainly not least..."

Earl looked over to Saniya, who blushed at his impending sentimentality.

"My muse, my lady love, and my gift from the Gods. I sure as hell wouldn't be standing here, color-coordinated, without this beautiful woman by my side! Saniya has been my rock and the light that shines on me when my world is dark. We've been through a lot together, especially considering that she's been putting up with me since high school! She read my book first, she told me when things didn't make sense or scenes needed to be fleshed out, and she comforted me when I was sure that I'd never get published. I wish I had the time or the words to describe the impact she's had on my life. Ironic, as I stand in front of a book I've written, but some things in life are beyond simple, or even complicated, language or vocabulary. The love I have for this girl is endless and she's hands-down the person that has reinforced and reinvigorated my dormant authorial soul to enrich this book, which I hope enriches the lives of so many more people like me who think that they don't have a place in the world." Whistles and whoops filled the room as Saniya hugged Earl and whispered 'I love you' into his ear, and Earl returned the phrase affectionately as he waited for the clamor to pass.

"All that being said, I think before I get into the act of signing books for you lovely people, I suppose I'll tell you guys a little bit about myself because I know that I kind of came out of nowhere. It won't take too long, I promise. Up until this point, I've lived a very

9

uneventful, boring life. I'll try to hit some of the bigger questions some of you might have before you come up here though, just to save time."

Earl tapped the microphone against the table in contemplation, the feedback echoing against the walls of the bookstore. Realizing what he was doing, he apologized and then awkwardly fidgeted with the microphone before speaking again. "I mean, honestly, prior to writing, I was a blank slate for most of my life. Even as a kid, I didn't have a lot of friends. I was bullied on and off, and I spent a lot of my time playing videogames to fuel my need for escapism. I was sensitive, the news, in particular, used to upset me a lot. People would suffer, day after day, and I was powerless to do anything about it. That, combined with my inability to make friends, led to me falling into these deep bouts of depression. I was also disgustingly thin and had a huge head, so the word 'alien' was thrown around frequently on the playground, or in gym when I got older. My body eventually evened itself out, but I never exactly learned how to socialize. I'd have a few friends, but the conversations would never go too far, and we'd always end up going our separate ways. I'm terrible at maintaining contact, don't get me started on that. I don't 'understand' small talk, and, as you can see, I can have small moments of being incredibly awkward despite that probably needing to be addressed when I was still going to school, so…"

Bursts of laughter rang throughout the audience as Earl took a swig from one of the three water bottles that were lined in a row at the bottom-left section of the table. He was navigating the maze well, knowing that as long as he kept his anxiety from cornering him, he'd make it through this.

"But, yeah, I was the shy, quiet, weird kid. I never went to parties; I didn't see a point in them. I coasted through school with grades generally ranging from 'Eh,' to 'Adequate,' though I excelled, of course, in Reading and English. History was cool too, but I was a part of the five percent of students who actually enjoyed summer reading projects and assignments tailored around the books that I'm sure everyone remembers being forced to read. I loved that. My literary idol is Epsen Knight, I love his books. I wish I had dedicated more time growing up to reading, but that was difficult to endear myself to when I've lived a life playing videogames and watching movies and TV. It took me a while, but Epsen was the first author who captured my attention that I read completely of my own volition. The way he writes horror is frightening, and his characters always have such depth and feel so authentic. There's a reason why he's one of the best and almost everything he's ever written has been adapted to the screen in some capacity." Earl's voice, as he was hearing it, began to grate on his senses. He'd decided that he'd wrap up the summary of his life and transition to his book, quickly, inwardly hating talking about himself.

"Never mind all of that, though, I want to talk about my paper-borne son, or maybe daughter. I guess there's nothing wrong with my book being whatever gender you want it to be! So, the idea of 'Voyage of a Nascent Soul' came from an episode of an old anthology television series that Saniya and I were watching late one night. It was about a father dying in a construction accident, and his soul remained tethered to earth as a spectator. He's stuck in this limbo with his soul unable to 'move on.' He watches his daughter and wife suffer the consequences and ramifications of his death, and to abridge an hour of awesome television, he helplessly witnesses the sorrow and degradation of his family for years, decades, until they died. In a bold twist, it turns out that the father used to be a serial killer that stopped killing because he 'found the Lord,' and his version of 'Hell' is watching his family unravel for all eternity."

He drank another swig of water to pause, clear his throat again and grade himself on his performance. So far, minus a few hiccups here and there, he thought he was doing alright. He smirked, pleased by his abandonment of his stage fright for an occasion where freezing up or losing his nerve was absolutely unacceptable. "I don't know if it was because I was in the presence of my muse or if the content of the episode did something to my sleep-deprived mind. I can't tell you what sparked the sudden deluge of unrefined creativity. As the end credits rolled, idea after idea popped into my head, and I remember turning to Saniya and saying, 'I want to write a book.' For those of you who popped into the bookstore just to see what the commotion was about or haven't heard of my book, I'll give you a quick, spoiler-free synopsis! Nineteen-year-old Lamont Webb gets into a car accident on his way home from community college, and unfortunately, he dies almost instantly. For him, the world goes dark for a second, only for him to suddenly be looking upon the scene of his death.

Twisted metal, gnarled car parts, glass everywhere, a vision of utter horror. He slowly comes to the understanding that he's a spirit and can't interact with anything or anyone, only able to watch life progress without him. He attends his own funeral, and his parents are beside themselves with grief. The night of his funeral, he sees his mother sobbing in her bedroom and she cries herself to sleep. Lamont then realizes that he's not as powerless as he thinks, he's able to interact with his parents in their dreams. In the dreams, he can speak to them, touch them, he's essentially 'alive' when he enters their dreams.

Knowing this, he tries to help them cope with his death, but the more he interferes, the worse that things get. He starts to learn about who his parents really are, how they truly feel about their marriage amongst other things in their lives, and he makes some unexpected discoveries, both good and bad. His mother, Tonya, is a church administrator, and his father, Marlon, is a cop that wants to change the negative image of the police force in his town, inside the precinct and out. Between Lamont's frequent intercessions as he tries to maintain his parents' marriage and respective occupations, a lot of dark corners in the family's history gets light shined upon them. Lamont goes on a journey to discover his own values and ideals after his death and attempt to keep his mother and father from falling into complete turmoil. Overall, I'm extremely happy about my novel, especially as it pertains to handling grief, religion, opening discussions on what it means to be black in our modern societal landscape, and the difference that

13

perspective makes. I firmly believe I've done my people proud and created something timeless in the process!"

Earl took an exaggerated bow as laughter broke out and thunderous applause erupted amongst his devotees. Saniya ran up to Earl and practically leapt into his arms, a seal of her approval for his presentation. He let out a heavy exhale, glad to be done with the bulk of his ranting. He put Saniya down, and she handed him a fanciful pen, signaling that it was time to start the book signing proper.

"Alright, so rather than keep you guys waiting by listening to me babble forever, how about we start signing some books?!"

"Wait!" Christine suddenly said from the side of the room. She walked up to Earl and Saniya, both of whom wore expressions of complete confusion. She nonverbally requested the microphone, which Earl handed to her, his thick eyebrows furrowed in bewilderment.

"Before we get to that, I pulled some strings and put in a few phone calls, and I arranged something that I think you'll really appreciate!"
She gestured to the door that Earl had come out of earlier, and Earl followed Christine's smirk to the direction her gaze was fixed in. As soon as the figure emerged from behind the door, Earl's eyes nearly popped out of his head and his jaw almost hit the floor, trapped between disbelief and delight.

"That's... that's..."

Earl couldn't find the words as the grinning, bespectacled figure, revealing himself to be an older man that Earl knew to be seventy years of age from being so enamored with his line of work, strode up to him with his hand outstretched. As soon as the realization hit everyone else, the crowd could've shattered the windows of the bookstore with how loudly they were screaming. Cameras flashed as Epsen Knight, the beloved, contemporary master of the horror genre, shook the hand of Earl Veares, whose hand mechanically met his idol's.

"You did good for yourself, kid. You got a promising career in front of you if you keep the quality of your writing as crisp and detailed as it is now!"

Earl looked at his hand afterwards, which shook even more than it did before he himself had walked out to meet his readers. The only thing that was keeping him on his feet was the adrenaline he'd felt for coming face-to-face with someone he couldn't have ever guessed he'd remotely come into contact with. "...Thank you, Mr. Knight," Earl meekly managed to chirp out. "It's a huge honor." "Ah, don't be so modest, kid! It's bright, impressive minds like yours that keep reading entertaining and the art of literature everlasting! How about you do me an honor and allow me to be the first person you sign a book to?"

Saniya shoved the pen she was holding out into Earl's chest and then broke out into a sprint away from Earl and Epsen.

"...Sure, I-I would love to," Earl said as he slowly opened one of the hardcover books and scrawled his signature along the inside cover of the page, handing it to a person he considered a living legend in the world of fiction. "I thank you kindly, Mr. Veares!" Epsen said as he nodded his head in respect of Earl's accomplishments. Just then, Saniya reemerged with a camera. "Mr. Knight, would you mind getting a picture with Earl?!" Saniya shouted, already in the act of prepping the camera before Epsen had a chance to respond. "Of course! The pleasure would be mine!" Epsen said as he faced Saniya with a huge smile plastered on his face. Earl turned to Saniya as well as Epsen stepped closer to Earl, making it easier for Saniya to capture them into the frame of the imminent flash of the camera.

"Alright, guys," Saniya said, smirking to herself as she adjusted the settings of her camera to her exact specifications. She raised the camera at the two authors, readying herself to snap a photo that Earl would never forget for as long as he lived.

"Say *'Legendary'*!"

This can't be real, Earl thought. Epsen played along, but even as the flash threatened to blind Earl, his face was still stuck in a state of euphoric shock.

It was the fresh barrage of light, not her voice, that wrested Earl from his deep slumber. He could feel the crust at the corners of his eyes as he blinked rapidly, trying to adjust his eyesight to the illumination of a brand-new morning. "Wake up, E! Your meeting is in an hour and a half! You didn't forget that you told me to wake you up at exactly 7:30, did you?"

Earl sat up in the king-sized bed and rubbed his eyes, shaking his head to orient himself to his surroundings. When he finally got his bearings, he looked around, seeing nothing but Saniya's studio apartment. From where he sat, he could see the kitchen, the "entertainment space," as Saniya affectionately called it, and the table where they'd eaten on many an occasion. There was only one other "room," and that was the bathroom, the door to which was directly across the expansive room from his seated position. Outside of the essentials, the rest of the open area was dedicated to her schoolwork, or to her art. There was an easel with a fresh canvas and various painting materials surrounding it in one corner of the room, and in the opposite corner, she kept a "photography station" to indulge her side-interest of photography.

Next to him was a nightstand where he kept his phone face-down, afraid of what would show up if he checked it for messages or emails. Earl groaned, lamenting the destruction of the teased actualization of his desires. As bubbly as Saniya had been, she'd inadvertently ruined

17

one of the best dreams he'd ever had, one that he wished he hadn't woken up from.

Here, there isn't any cheering, just silence. No progression, just stagnation. No success, just failure. Endless failure and wasted potential.

"You want me to make you some breakfast before your meeting, baby?" Saniya asked, as she kissed Earl after crawling to him playfully. "No, but thanks anyway, Sans. I'll eat when I come back," Earl responded, trying to mask his disappointment. Saniya's smile turned into a look of melancholic acknowledgement. She'd known her boyfriend long enough to know when he wasn't feeling his best. Some days, it was best to let him come to her with his issues or her keen concern would cause him to sink deeper within his own mind; she knew this due to the trial and error approach that she had to endure early in their relationship. Other days, she'd known that he needed her to actively try to make him feel better, and she'd gotten adept when it came time to discern between which of the two options she'd have to implement.

"Do you want to talk about it, E? I know that you kind of rushed here last night because of Ms. Charlotte, but we didn't get a chance to say much to each other." That was the diplomatic way of saying that Earl, as he was prone to doing, showed up unannounced at her apartment while she was doing homework and, rather than confiding his problems to her, the two of them had sex. Not that she minded, she loved Earl more than anything, and knew that the fondness she harbored for

18

him was mutual. That aside, she wished, after all this time, that he wouldn't close himself off from her when he knows he needed her.

"No. I'll be fine, baby," Earl said plainly as he got up, kissing Saniya on the forehead as he walked past her and made his way to the bathroom. She glanced in the direction at Earl's face-down phone, hoping that today was the day that a prospective literary agent answered one of his queries positively. As she heard the toilet flush, she sighed, inwardly hoping for the best. She'd genuinely believed that what he'd written was worthy of publication, having read over it twice, but knew that the road to becoming an author was paved with many rejections, Earl having seen many more than either of them had hoped for.

"Maybe this time, it'll be different," she said quietly, a small smile etching its way onto her freckled face.
Earl came out of the bathroom and made his way across the room where Saniya was standing but stopped midway as he turned his attention towards the speakers mounted on the wall joined by a huge flat-screen television in the entertainment space. As he took note of the music he'd ignored up to this point, his slightly saddened features turned to mild disgust, and he raised an eyebrow at Saniya. Unfortunately, he knew exactly who the "artist" was that was rapping through the current track because Saniya had been listening to a lot of his music as of late, and a part of him didn't get how someone so creatively-inclined could listen to someone so vulgar and hollow. "…Lil Grande? You still listen to

this trash?" Earl said with a slight chuckle, causing Saniya to glare at him defiantly.

"I told you, I fully admit that his music isn't exactly 'good.' Those beats, however? Phenomenal, and it helps me focus while I draw! We both have our 'happy place' mediums to get into our artistic grooves. You have those weird ambient rainforest videos, and I have garbage music! If I want to dumpster-dive every so often to feel alive, then let me do me, E!"

This caused Earl to guffaw and nod as he was reminded of his own quirks compared to that of one of his girlfriend's many eccentricities.

"I can't argue with that," Earl yielded, "but in my defense, those videos aren't weird, they're soothing! Plus, they're a nice break in the event that I get tired of listening to Beethoven or Pavarotti," Earl said, pantomiming a musical conductor as Saniya laughed at his antics. "Yeah, I forgot you had the tastes of a spoiled white boy who grew up thinking that he was better than his friends because he attends the opera every month." "Oh!" Earl exclaimed mockingly, "and I forgot that you have the tastes of a disgruntled 16-year-old teen whose dad never loved her, so she sleeps around hoping that one of the boys that tell her what she wants to hear will validate her existence one day. It's alright though because you have a promising career of pole-riding and welfare-collecting ahead of you once you pump out your fifth child!"

"...Wow," is all that Saniya was able to say after hearing the loud cackling that emanated from Earl after seeing her dismayed expression. "Every time, you turn the dial up way past one-hundred when I'm sitting at a cool fifty," Saniya said, shaking her head regretfully. "Your mind is way more diabolical than mine. My comedy is light-hearted, yours is just dark and terrible!" "Ah, you were one of the lucky ones, Sans! You had both of your parents, so you don't have to worry about that situation! Plus, you already know I'm not going anywhere, and the idea of children before I'm exactly where I want and need to be freaks me out!"

Saniya's smile faded only slightly. She knew that sometimes; Earl would say things in jest that turn out to be unresolved tensions later. In that regard, she was unsure, sometimes, if Earl's alleged jokes were attuned more to his morbid sense of humor, or his internal strife. His mood tended to shift on the fly some days. He'd be laughing and joking one moment, and then lock himself away from the world the next. The only thing that she could do was err on the side of optimism and assume that he was simply being funny rather than pessimistic.

"There's a girl just like the one I described drinking herself into a stupor somewhere in the world right now. She probably used to be a cheerleader; now she's a little older, a little wider, and wondering where she went wrong." "...Baby, when was the last time you've taken your medication?" There it was, the deafening silence. Earl looked at her warily, and she looked back, eyes alight with worry. "I feel like I don't need it, honestly. The dips and downs are a lot less frequent, and I'm

21

slowly on the course to becoming more of a glass half-full kind of guy regarding my daily circumstances!" Avoiding the question, a staple of Earl's. Saniya looked at him with a countenance riddled with disapproval. Earl, knowing that he now had no choice, sighed and came clean with her.

"…I haven't taken them in about a week and a half."
Earl saw Saniya's eyes close and her chest rise and fall slowly, knowing that she was searching herself for the tact she needed to speak earnestly to him. Earl, not wanting to be a burden, beat her to the obvious conclusion that she, undoubtedly, was prepared to articulate.

"I promise that I'll go back on them, baby. I'll take one as soon as I get back home," Earl said. "I know that it was stupid of me to stop taking them in the first place, but I don't know, I've been feeling… good about my chances of being published lately."

Saniya's lip curled in appreciation of Earl's thoughtfulness, and just when she was about to speak, Earl's phone blared a sound akin to a police siren. As if on cue, the two of them both turned their heads towards his phone, knowing that it likely meant that he'd received another response from a potential agent. Apprehensively, Earl walked around the bed and to the nightstand where his phone had rested. He slowly lifted the phone to meet his face, and Saniya waited with bated breath as he muttered through the email he'd received. Earl's shoulders drooped sadly, and Saniya put a hand to her forehead, knowing that Earl had, again, gotten yet another rejection. Earl put his phone back onto the nightstand and sat at the edge of the bed. He buried his face into his hands, shaking his head as he took an elongated breath in, and then exhaled it back out after holding it for a few seconds. Saniya scooted close to Earl and wrapped one arm around him while cradling her head in the nook of his shoulder. She said nothing, opting to let him speak when he was ready, if he was ready. Neither of them compromised their positions for a minute or two, almost as still as two statues. Finally, Earl took his hands away from his face and placed them on his lap, but his eyes remained glued to the floor in front of him.

"Well, I think I've hit a new record," Earl said sadly. "I got three of them, and it isn't even 8:30 yet."
"…I'm sorry to hear that, E. I know that it's far from what you were hoping for."

"Yeah," was all that Earl said afterwards before getting up and starting his morning routine of showering, brushing his teeth and putting on his clothes. During this process, he spoke not another word to Saniya, his eyes glassy and unfocused. As he gathered up his things and prepared to leave for his meeting, Saniya finally spoke to him, hoping to break through his introspection, if only briefly. "E, can I speak to you for a quick second?" He stopped short of the small partition that led to the door that allowed egress from the apartment and his eyes met Saniya's, breaking his deeply involved self-reflection to address his lover.

"Yeah. What is it?"

23

Saniya knew she was going to feel bad about what she had to say next, not wanting to add insult to injury, but knew that he'd understand once it settled within him.

"I know this isn't the best time to say it, but… you may not be able to come back over until the middle of next week. You surprised me last night, and I actually had a lot of work I needed to catch up on, so I need a couple of days to regroup and get caught back up. I promise that it has nothing to do with you. I have exams in a month, and I need to ace these final few weeks of classwork. We'll be able to hang out a lot more afterwards, but I need to focus so I can get this MA degree."

Another silence. Earl's eyes glossed over nearing the end of Saniya's explanation, and he let her finish completely before saying one of things that Saniya disliked the most.

"That's fine."

With that, Saniya heard Earl's footsteps head towards the exit from the other side of the partition, then heard the door close. Saniya sighed, hating that she had to say that to him, but knowing that she'd make it up in full sooner rather than later

Chapter 2

As Earl sat there in the circle formation with the rest of his emotionally or mentally unstable kin, he pondered the significance of having a support group for depression anyway. Sure, it meant that none of them would kill themselves anytime soon, though a tragedy had hit the group in the form of an attempt at one point, but still. The person who'd talk the most was Dr. Tommen, but at least he was an accredited expert in psychology and mental health and not some sympathetic soccer mom or a guy who looked up a few technical terms on the internet to make himself seem smarter than he was. Earl had been through those sorts of "leaders" in a support group, but when he came across Dr. Tommen's, something clicked. Unlike others, who seemed to be in the business of making people feel better temporarily to satisfy their own ego or suppress their own mental deficiencies, Dr. Tommen wasn't for himself, he was for them. "There is no satisfaction in temporary contentment; there is, however, in the extended nourishment of the whole."

Perhaps his talents here were wasted with us. Twenty-somethings circling the drain; Dr. Tommen only delaying the inevitable. He should be somewhere changing the world, not stuck with the ones that are beyond any kind of help. I admire him; he wasn't arrogant enough to capitalize on the fact that he's better than us, but he's subjected himself to this lost battle of trying to put a sheet of paper together after it's been shredded, sullied and ripped into nearly microscopic bits. Noble.

Earl desperately needed to keep his mind off his latest batch of rejections, so he kept himself distracted until it was his turn to speak. As he listened to Sean, a chubby 19-year-old who was trying to stop himself from eating every time he felt bad, he realized how insensitive he'd grown during these meetings. When he first started attending, he'd listen to them, even chirp in every now and again to help his mournful brothers and sisters cope with their situations. Lately though, he's been trapped in his own pit of quicksand, feeling his body sinking, slowly.

Mouths moved, but sounds never came out.

He'd wanted to assist, he really did. Obviously, he knew how it felt, or else he wouldn't be there. But he'd taken a more cynical approach to his support group in the last couple of months. The third Saturday of every month became harder to wake up for.

What was the point?

The pitch of the noise he was only vaguely conscious of had changed, which meant that Sean had finished speaking. The focus had shifted to Jenna, the one sitting to Earl's immediate left. He'd accidentally placed himself in the circle in a way that meant that he would be the last one of them to speak before they disbanded until next month. *Great.*

26

They all had a thing; Earl came to realize after the fourth month. A central cause to the "voice" only they could hear. Dr. Tommen talked about that extensively once, that depression and anxiety was like a malevolent, toxic shadow trying to take root inside of the mind, independent of the self. The dark, detrimental thoughts weren't your own; your body is simply the host to an intruder, and you must take the steps necessary to evict this intangible saboteur. It was a way of telling them that their sorrows didn't control them, they controlled their sorrows. Assume ownership of yourself and disown the voice, he'd say.

How well has that worked out for you?

Earl began to mentally go around the circle, refusing to acknowledge his inner turmoil. He decided to start from his right. Jack was one of the survivors of a school shooting that happened almost a year ago. Understandably, it messed him up quite a bit. One of the most heartbreaking things that Earl recalled Jack saying was along the lines of, "I wish Victor had killed me too. At least I'd be able to sleep."

To Jack's right was Travis, someone closer to Earl's complexion, but not by much. Travis had been planning to marry his long-term girlfriend, but one night, they got into a terrible argument. His girlfriend stormed out of the house, citing that she needed to take a walk and clear her head, and a drunk frat boy swerved onto the sidewalk and ran her over. She was rendered comatose and had to be put on life support to keep her lungs from completely collapsing. Her parents didn't have the money to cover the insurance required to maintain their daughter, and Travis turned to selling drugs to try and keep his girlfriend alive. He got busted and sent to jail during a drug raid from the DEA, and his girlfriend died while he was in prison. He's felt responsible for her death ever since, repeatedly saying that if he hadn't argued with her over something as trivial as a cell phone charger, she'd still be there.

Saniya's going to get tired and leave you too if you don't get your shit together. She can only be supportive and doting for so long.

Carly was interesting, to say the least. She'd been a child actor, notable for her role in 'Daring Darcy,' where she played the titular, intrepid adventurer that would explore far-off, fictional lands. She'd "interact" with starry-eyed kids watching her show by claiming that they obtained the artifact of the week together at the end of every episode. She even had a lasso for safely incapacitating potential threats.

Earl loved that show growing up. It'd fuel his imagination and he envisioned himself as an explorer too, fantasizing about being brave instead of timid, adventurous instead of content with his comfort zones.

An insignificant speck of a person that sent out a total of 170 queries and got back 53 rejections. Well, now 56, and those are only from the ones that felt sorry enough to respond to you. It's just not going to happen. It's

28

*been eight months and you've contacted nearly every
literary agency available. You aren't meant for—"*

Sadly, the producer of 'Daring Darcy' liked Carly more
than her young fans did. Her parents knew about the
producer's predatory inclinations, but due to the money
involved, turned the other cheek. Carly grew up full of
unmitigated rage and had a severe case of OCD,
needing to always control her surroundings. If you so
much as dared to mention Darcy around her, she'd make
you regret it. Their anti-celebrity. The three next to
Carly, including Sean, were all fairly unremarkable in
terms of intrigue. Marcus, Westley and Sean all suffered
from either negligent, reckless or abusive parenting, and
Earl didn't see much of a purpose in delving deeper into
the origin of their unique voices. Jenna, however, was
worthier of attention than everyone else. To put it
nicely, Jenna wasn't what one would refer to as
"conventionally attractive," as Earl came around to
describing her appearance forced a lifetime of jeers and
outlandish assumptions. It consumed her, and feeling as
though she'd given her existence as much positivity and
meaning as it was ostensibly going to have, she marked
a date on her calendar to commit suicide. Earl's second
month in, and he'd seen Jenna nervously walk into their
circle sporting a white patch over her right eye. Dr.
Tommen explained to the group that Jenna had sliced
her arms up with a razor blade, but stopped short of her
wrists, seized by the sudden fear of dying. Impulsively,
she instead took the razor to her eye, and her parents
were quickly alerted by her blood-curdling, horrific
screams. The doctors couldn't save the eye in time, and

while Jenna was sitting in the hospital bed, one eye completely unavailable to her, she had a revelation.

She had been terrified of herself. She didn't recognize the girl that had wanted to die that day, saying that it almost felt like she was put under a spell and coerced into desiring death. Since then, she made a promise to never try to do anything so radical ever again regardless of how she's feeling. In a way, Jenna became the martyr of the group, almost choosing to leap into the abyss that followed them all very closely. She told everyone that suicide isn't a glamorous escape, it's an indifferent darkness that swallows you whole and doesn't care about your well-being if you choose to opt out at the last second.

She isn't you. A higher purpose didn't enter her life. You have, or had, great things to look forward to. You had delusions of greatness and leadership, wanting to save people like Jenna, like Carly, like Travis, from themselves. That's why you like Dr. Tommen; he inspires hope, and you're just another broken, battered soul that exists to be nothing but a reminder to others that can still be their own heroes. Suicide may be the freedom that you've always wanted. There's no more pain, no more overthinking, no more false dreams of a better—

"Earl? Are you alright?"

The wise, sympathetic voice brought him back to reality, and Earl looked around the circle, everyone's eyes landing squarely upon him. "It's okay, Earl. You know that there's no judgment amongst us. Take your time if you need to, but I want you to say what's on your mind," the older man in the middle of the circle implored. *Pitiful. He pities you because you're so fucking pathet—*

Earl hadn't noticed that Dr. Tommen had reentered the circle, inwardly hoping that they'd skip him and go right to the end of the meeting. That was their time for "final thoughts" before everyone left, Dr. Tommen oversaw the circle from a distance as they updated each other about what they were up to and encourage conversation amongst one another. Dr. Tommen made new members to his group share contact information, even providing his own. That way, if anyone was going through something extremely trying, they could reach out to someone, anyone. Dr. Tommen only got in the middle of the circle when the situation called for it, and Earl supposed that he'd zoned out for longer than he'd thought. "You don't have to speak if you don't want to, but I deeply encourage you to do so. What about your book? Anything to update us on regarding that?" He had such a calm, disarming voice.

"Uh…" Earl paused, not knowing where to begin. Suddenly, the intruder, as Dr. Tommen called it, spoke on his behalf. "So, I got three more rejections this morning," Earl started, getting a benign nod from the doctor. "How are you feeling about the whole process, Earl?" *Stupid. Like I never should've done it in the first place. Why give someone a dream and then snatch—*

"Disillusioned," Earl said, attempting to fight the intruder off. "I don't even have any more agencies to query. I've run through all of them. Truthfully, I don't know what I'm doing wrong. It's not the actual letter I sent out because I feel as though I did a good job telling agents what 'Voyage of a Nascent Soul' was about in a general sense. Maybe I'm just not as good of a writer as I thought. It's one of the worst feelings, knowing that you've coasted through life. You're floating in a void, existing instead of living, feeling like you have nothing to contribute." The other members of the group did things such as fidget, look anywhere else but at Earl, or nodded along with his story. Some understood, profoundly, but Earl didn't exactly view it in that light.

You're even a burden to them.

"Finally," Earl continued, "you have a purpose, you have an endgame, you have a *something*. You have an answer to that question that employers like to ask their potential employees when hiring them: 'Where do you see yourself in five years?' that isn't 'I don't know,' or 'I don't care.' You try and cultivate this gift that you earnestly believe that you have, and you pour every ounce of every emotion across the spectrum into it. From the womb of your brain comes what you see as a beautiful child created by that person inside of you that's screaming to get out, that nobody but you know exists. I outlined, I typed, I spent weeks with writer's block, wanting to perfect a story. Then, the impossible happened. I completed it. Sure, it took me about a year. I had to split my time between that, my girlfriend, my grandmother, and the job I hate. But, I did it. I was frustrated as hell during it at some moments, but writing that book was the only time that I felt truly alive, working towards something I wanted so badly. Nothing else had a sense of wonder or discovery anymore, not video-games, not movies, not television, nothing. I'd felt so helpless and beaten down that I didn't complete anything I'd ever tried to do before that because I didn't see a point. I was a failure; that's all I was, and a part of me accepted that."

Earl began to develop a headache from the outpouring of information he was giving his group. Charlotte never knew how to take on Earl's introspection when he tried to vocalize it to her, and he felt as though he put Saniya through too much and didn't want to inundate her with his problems after a while. This group was the only time he got to freely express himself and he took advantage of it. "This book brought color back to a world that had lost it from my perspective years ago. Imagine, then, how I felt when I crafted a query letter after finishing my manuscript, making sure I made every word of it count, scrutinizing over grammar and punctuation marks. Then came the time when I had to put myself out there to agents. The first 'no' was disheartening, but that made me want to continue, it put the fires of determination in me to see my book succeed. But I kept getting them, day after day, without a moment to recover. Sometimes a week or two would pass before I heard anything from anyone, and when I excitedly picked up my phone, it was just another 'no.' It became so frequent that I could tell if it was bad news just from the text preview of my phone that only shows you the first line or so of a text or an email before you open it.

I'd learned the 'rejection diction,' and I would go from sad to angry, wondering what the hell it was about my book where *nobody* wanted to represent it. Was it too long? Am I just a bad writer? I even concocted this insane idea that because most literary agents were white, that they could somehow intuit that I was black from my writing style and I legitimately believed that there was some kind of racial conspiracy against me! The ones that pissed me off the most were the instances of 'no' that went on for too long. I get that there's a certain tact if you're going to respond to aspiring authors, but after a while, I felt insulted. The last line, which usually goes something like 'Keep querying other agents though, and good luck!' starts to read as an empty platitude rather than a sincere gesture." Earl had taken a moment to calm himself down as he almost started shouting nearing the end of his impassioned tirade. He took a few deep breaths to regain his composure, and everyone in the circle waited patiently, even Dr. Tommen. Earl leaned back in his seat, futilely, as he absently looked around for answers to his own questions.

"...I don't know," Earl said, addressing himself more than the others. "I felt it, you know? I just knew I was going to get that one 'yes.' That was all I needed, for someone to at least read the whole manuscript, then I know that they'd understand what my story meant to me. Maybe the opening chapter is full of amateur writing mistakes and I simply can't see it because I'm not a 'classically-trained' writer like an Axlam Suleman. Axlam's this... new, young, amazing talent, and she's only a year younger than I am. She was born and raised in America, but her mother and father are both from Somalia. She graduated from Stanford, of all places, with an honors in English Literature. She went to Somalia for a summer and she came back inspired, using the culture and their traditions to create this beautiful novel, 'The Desperate Sails of Somalia.'

I read an excerpt online, and I was hooked. I can see why she's getting all the accolades she's gotten this past month or so. I rooted for her not only as a burgeoning writer, but she opened the gateway for people like me, young, black authors who want to prove themselves. The publishing world is difficult, and I try my best not to make it a racial thing, but there aren't a lot of black writers that top the New York Times Best-Sellers list. She did it, and I was proud as hell, hoping to reach that level. ...I can't even buy a copy of her book for myself. Charlotte has me give her half of my paycheck for 'rent,' then I have to feed myself, and then I have to deal with—"

Earl stopped himself, realizing the tangent that he'd went on. He looked directly at Dr. Tommen, who nodded and gestured for him to continue. "...People treat depression these days like a buzzword, like something that they think they can easily simplify, and can't. It depends on the individual; it's like a cancer, there are too many variables for it to be an isolated concept that's so simple to deal with or explain. They make bracelets, shirts, and create cute little anti-depression phrases and mascots. You know what kind of people say 'You can beat depression by choosing to have a good outlook on life instead of being negative'?

People who have never been depressed a single day of their lives. If it were that easy, none of us would be here right now. Do you know how many days I wake up and wished I hadn't? How many times it's taken me hours to get out of bed because I didn't feel like it? That's depression. For me, it comes in two forms. The first is the fog, where you walk listlessly, not knowing where you're going. It's passive; it doesn't interfere with you directly, but it does affect the way you see the world. You're in this trance, unable to snap yourself out of it. You can feel its weight, not quite enough to crush you, but enough to make its presence known. The second form is a rope. This is the active, aggressive one that is way more direct in how it deals with you. It wraps itself around your neck, and depending on the day, it tightens, sometimes suffocating you silently. You want to yell, but you can't. All you can do is hope that the rope does the job it sets out to do. It never does, even on its worst days. It wants you to suffer so that it can repeat the torment all over again."

Earl fell silent, as did the rest of the circle. Earl, noticing the awkward, almost tangible silence, did what he does best: distanced himself from everything. Dr. Tommen said a few words to the group, and then began the process of ending their meeting for the month. Before everyone left, Dr. Tommen took a minute or two to talk to the group individually as they walked out. Earl was frozen in his seat, experiencing something of an out-of-body occurrence. He could see himself, sitting there, self-pitying.

Just like you. You'd rather sit on your ass and accept that everything is fucked up rather than do something about it.

"What can I do?" Earl desperately mused to himself. "Earl? Did you say something?" Dr. Tommen inquired. Earl realized that they were the only two people left in the room, and he acknowledged the doctor with a pensive nod. "I was thinking out loud, that's all," Earl reassured. "I have to admit, Earl, the recounting of your mentality today was haunting, but eloquent. It's clear that there's a writer burrowed inside of you," Dr. Tommen said, giving Earl a small, sincere smile.

"At least my flowery way of saying things impresses somebody. They used to call me 'Oreo' in middle school," Earl said with a mirthless half-smile. "I was laughed at for being as… verbose with the way I articulate things. I thought that would help me in my writing, but I guess not." Dr. Tommen gave Earl a reassuring pat on the shoulder, an indication that Earl was in good company that held no judgmental intentions. "You've never been open about your internal dialogue since you've been with us. I know it may not seem like it, but you've made a lot of progress today simply by vocalizing your distress and acknowledging it." "It doesn't feel like it," Earl said, mentally kicking himself for disregarding the sentiment. "Have you considered taking writing courses of any sort?" Dr. Tommen asked.

"Can't afford it. Between the mortgage on the house and bills, Charlotte can't afford to fund anything like that.

I'm at work thirty-six hours out of a week, and after Charlotte takes a chunk of my money, I don't have a lot to work with. I understand that she keeps the roof over our heads, but she spends some money taking care of her deadbeat boyfriend, Randall, and that's not a can of worms I want to open right now."

There it is, you can see it in his eyes. Pity. Does that make you angry, the fact that you're either ignored, ridiculed or pitied?

"How about a new hobby, at least for the time being?" the doctor suggested. "I don't know what I'd do." "It doesn't have to be anything too strenuous or time-consuming, just do something to keep yourself occupied. It's not over for you, Earl, I need you to understand that. Inspiration can come from the most unlikely of places, and sometimes, you must be willing to open yourself up to new possibilities in order to obtain a fresh perspective. I believe that you've been through these trials to prepare yourself for the next big step of your life. Who knows, you may find the motivation to work on a second book; I'd certainly desire to be the basis of a character in one of your novels!"

This self-help bullshit is getting annoying.

He smiled, grateful for Dr. Tommen's kind words. Just then, the quick sounds of a police siren caused Earl to dig into his pocket and retrieve his phone, seeing a text from Ben. "You won't believe what I just had installed into the basement. You gotta come as soon as you can!"

38

What does this fucking idiot want?

"I have to go, Dr. Tommen," Earl said, standing up and shaking the doctor's hand for all his hard, generous work for today's session. "Remember, Earl, I'm just a phone call away! This will pass, I promise you." With as big a smile as he could muster without it seeming too disingenuous, he nodded at the doctor and began to make his way out of the building and to the parking lot. He rummaged around in his pocket for his car keys as he strode up to an old, brown sedan that looked like it came directly from the dying gasps of the 20th century, a relic of an older era. Earl sighed and plopped into the driver's seat, grateful for Charlotte giving him her old car, but wishing that he'd had something a bit more modern to cruise around in. He closed his eyes as he put the key into the ignition and muttered a silent prayer as he turned the key. The engine clanked and clunked, but the car sprung to life, much to Earl's relief. It didn't happen often, but on occasion, the car would refuse to start, and he'd have no choice but to call Randall to help him jumpstart it. He hated depending on Randall, but it was better than having to call roadside assistance and pay out of pocket for it.

Whatever Ben has planned…
it'd better be worth my time.

Chapter 3

Earl could hear the faint guitar riff as he pushed in the doorbell to Ben's townhouse, suppressing the urge to roll his eyes. *It's almost hilarious. His online presence alone earns him enough money to maintain his own house and do whatever he wants to do. Meanwhile, a pure, creative mind like yours gets swept under the rug.* The front door flung open in the flash of an instant and Ben stood before him, shining with absolute glee. "Dude, come in!" Ben said, practically pulling Earl inside of his home.

"Quick, I need someone else to see this!"

Earl noticed early on in their friendship that Ben wore whatever suited him, even if it looked like he'd just woken up in it. As Ben maneuvered him around his house, the remnants of his many sexual conquests strewn about wherever Earl turned his head, all Earl could think about was what was so important that Ben had to take him to it with such urgency. "Where's the mark of your latest, Ben?" Earl asked dryly, knowing that Ben hated the implication that he used women and then ditched them a month later, if they were lucky enough to make it that far. Ben stopped in his tracks a few feet outside of his basement door and gave Earl a look indicating his lack of amusement at Earl's jest.

"...Jaylin was a sweetheart, dude. I told you, she just had too many hang-ups over her ex. I knew I had to end it when she called me by his name when we were making lemonade."

Earl's face contorted into one of distaste, prompting Ben to laugh at his misfortune. If Earl knew how to get under Ben's skin, then the opposite was as, if not more, applicable. Earl's dry snark was no match for Ben's bizarre euphemisms. "You win, take me wherever you want. As long as you never say anything like that to me ever again." Ben put his hands on his hips and smirked triumphantly, the temporary victor of their unspoken game. "Since you asked though, she actually showed me how to style my own hair, which saves me some money. I think that my viewers get bored if I maintain the same style or color for too long. That's the way of the internet!" Earl knew too well about Ben's propensity for upholding his own lofty standards as it pertained to his image. If it wasn't a trip to the salon, it was a spa day. On top of being popular for playing his acoustic guitar or indulging himself by engaging in various pranks and other silly antics, Ben was also known for his videos regarding men not properly taking care of their bodies, offering them many tips regarding self-care and beautification. Ben's comfort with what many viewed as an embarrassment to masculinity was one of the reasons, he'd been so popular amongst women, and Earl had long-since accepted Ben's many oddities.

"Now, follow me!"

With that, Ben opened the basement door and excitedly scurried down the steps. Earl took a moment to look around the kitchen, seeing many tokens of Ben's lascivious past. Earl could remember, vividly, which item correlated to a gift or suggestion that Ben received from his former flings. To his defense, Ben genuinely seemed to care about every girl he's been with lately, but he had a tendency to be extremely particular when it came to determining whether a girl had "long-term potential," as he liked to call it.

And you make fun of him for it, though you like to live vicariously through him.

Earl stuffed down the invasive thought and made his way down the basement stairs, slowing down and becoming more awestruck as he saw the cause of Ben's delight. Microphones, mic stands, headphones, speakers, a technological marvel sat before his eyes. "Isn't it awesome?!" Ben chirped, nudging Earl's ribs as he said it. "The people finished installing it about an hour ago. Oh, it's a musician's wet dream!"

The room that they were standing in contained elaborate machinery, most of which Earl couldn't begin to comprehend, leading to a huge console with nothing but dials, levers and buttons. To say that Earl was overwhelmed was a grand understatement as he gaped at the equipment in stunned disbelief.

"...How did you—"

"Trust me, I've been putting some money aside for a while for this!" Ben interrupted. "A couple of generous donations from my followers in the past month put me *way* over my goal! It's not the best recording studio that money could buy, obviously, but it's a damn good start! Did you see the live room I set up?!" Ben pointed at the window ahead of them leading to a room full of musical instruments and a microphone stand with a long cord that looked like it was fed through the floor and into the console in front of them. "I can finally play around with beats and sound editing like I've always wanted to! All those years in school that my mom forced me to play a bunch of instruments is about to pay off! So, what do you think?! Tell me how you're feeling about it!"

Envious.
A pretty boy trying his best to be something he's not.

"I'm happy for you, Ben! It's cool!" Earl said, disregarding the intruder that threatened to poison his pleasure at Ben's genuine happiness. "At least *someone* is getting close to achieving their hopes and dreams."

Couldn't resist, could you?

Noting the change in Earl's tone, Ben's face went from joyful to curious. Ben liked to help, almost to the point of prying, and Earl struggled to lead the conversation anywhere else that wasn't the accidental slip of his one of his many pieces of internal dialogue. Unfortunately for Earl, he wasn't quite swift enough to prevent Ben's inquisition. "Is it the book again?" Ben asked, his face bereft of any semblance of humor. "...Yeah," Earl

43

replied, his eyes drifting to the floor. "I got three more rejections this morning, man. I don't know, maybe I'm just not cut out for writing."

That's right, do what you always do. Give up. You're always going to be second-rate or unappreciated. You don't have the balls to take what you want, you never did. After a weighted silence, Ben finally spoke, finding the adequate string of words to best convey his message. "Dude, you have a gift, trust me. You forget that I read a chapter of your book, and I thought it was cool! I'm sure that eventually, someone will want to represent it! Give it a little time, E!"

This is coming from someone who owns all of, what, three books? He doesn't have the capacity to understand your work, so he should save his rah-rah "You can do it!" nonsense for whichever mindless slit enters his bedroom next time.

Earl opened his mouth to respond, and simultaneously, the familiar alert from his phone caused him to quickly snatch the device from his pocket. As soon as he looked at the new message, he dropped his phone back from where he'd pulled it. Disappointment gripped him and he felt heavier, as if he were made of stone.

"There goes another one," Earl bitterly stated, causing Ben to regard his best friend sadly.

Ben looked away for a second before his eyes lit up in realization. He couldn't hide the almost mischievous smirk that had crept onto his face. "They say that artists are at their best when they can reach into the darkest parts of their minds and use that negativity to create their finest work!" Ben said encouragingly, causing Earl to give him a look that demanded he get to the point. "Now, I want to suggest something to you, but you have to promise me that you're not going to say 'no' immediately afterwards. I'd like for you to let the idea marinate for a second!" Earl tilted his head downwards with his eyes trained on Ben, almost giving him a look of condescension.

"…I can't guarantee anything, but go for it."

"So, maybe you can use that negative energy you've got to spit a few bars for me! It'll give me a good chance to use the new software and test how deep I can go into editing!" Earl blinked once, then again. He was so taken aback by the request that he was rendered speechless for a few seconds. "…What?"

The word came out without the usual cynical undertones, almost childlike in its bewilderment. Soon enough, Earl's stony countenance returned, and Ben could distinguish the caliber of answer he was preparing to receive. "That's one of the most ridiculous things you've ever asked me to do. Do I look like Lil Grande, Big Buckz, or whatever terrible 'rapper' is popular these days?" "No," Ben said in a matter-of-factly tone, "but it's not like I'm asking you to drop your book and become a rapper. It's just a fun little thing for us to do! I know how you feel about 'fun' or 'enjoyment,' but you gotta live a little, my dude! You can be stuffy as hell sometimes! I get that you're upset about the book, but come on, humor me! Please?"

"No," Earl said quickly, wanting to end the conversation then and there. "I'm a writer, not a lyricist." "Look," Ben began, "I know that you think that modern-day rap is 'puerile, meaningless garbage,' you've been very good on making that known to me. But the fact that you use words like 'puerile' and are so in-tune with the English language, a skill that I just don't have, it could lend itself to being a fun side project! You can be the words, I can be the sounds, and together, we can have a good time! Where's the crime in that?!" Earl glowered at Ben, but Ben knew that the lack of a response meant that Earl was at least yielding some of his stubbornness, which was promising.

"At the very least, go in there, rhyme a little, and then boom, you're done! You never know, it could make you feel better! Nobody else will hear it but me, I promise. Please?"

Ben flashed a row of teeth at Earl, batting his eyes at his friend to try to make him complicit in his scheme. Earl sighed heavily and considered Ben's absurd proposal. After shaking his head and muttering to himself, he looked back at Ben and shrugged his shoulders. "Fine. I'll do it. But I swear to God, if anyone hears this recording, I'll kick you square in the balls." Ben let out a celebratory hoot and did a little dance, prideful of his well-earned victory. "My balls are willing to take that risk, good sir!" Ben joked, causing Earl to roll his eyes. "You'll need them for your next victim, so you'd better

46

not pull the unpredictable shit you usually like to do."
"You're hilarious, E," Ben said with a chuckle.
Suddenly, Ben snapped his fingers, Earl's sarcasm
seemingly jogging his memory.

"That reminds me, I have to introduce you to Imani next
time you're over! I met her a week ago at the bar
downtown, and we hit it off! I have a good feeling about
her, man, she's into yoga and channeling energies! You
know, that meditation stuff!"

The countdown begins. How long will this one last?

Earl bit his sharp tongue and instead opted to go down a
different channel of inquisition rather than derision.
"'Imani'? Ben, can I ask you a question that the two of
us have always skillfully circumvented before now?"

"Sure, partner!" Ben said, smiling.

"Imani is… black, correct?"
"Yeah, why do you ask?"

"You've really been putting your spoon into the
container of chocolate ice cream lately, huh?" Earl
commented, using Ben's penchant for euphemisms
against him. Ben laughed and ran an embarrassed hand
through his well-coiffed hair. "I like all flavors of ice
cream, E, you know that! There's nothing wrong with a
little chocolate-vanilla swirl, is there?"

"No, I guess not," Earl said as he shared a laugh with
his longtime friend.

"Anyway, get your ass in the live room, E! When you get in and you think of something, give me a nod. I'll point at you to tell you when the recording has started, and you say whatever you got! No music, no pressure, just speak your mind, make it rhyme, and I'll see what I can do in post-production!" Earl sighed, already regretting his decision, but nodded and walked through the door to the live room. He stepped in, closing the door behind him, and beheld the instruments surrounding him. Ben had a good selection to choose from: A saxophone, piano, guitar, violin, a set of drums and even a pair of cymbals had their own spot. If Earl were honest with himself, he was impressed. Extremely impressed. *Jealous.*

"Most people like my saxophone covers, but I'm also trying to relearn the piano," Ben's voice assaulted Earl's ears through the speakers at the front of the room, startling him. "My bad, I didn't realize the volume was up that high," Ben said, trying to suppress his amusement. "You asshole," Earl muttered.

"The acoustics in there are pretty good, so I heard that, E," Ben said mockingly, a sneer being his reward. "Alright, step on up and let's hear what you got! I'd tell you to put on the headphones on that stand next to you, but we aren't using any beats, so it'd be kind of pointless. One thing I should tell you is that when you start, make sure you speak into the pop filter in front of the microphone. You know, that metal thing in front of the mic. It'll ruin the recording otherwise."

Earl nervously strode up to the microphone in the middle of the room, making sure to adjust the filter in front of his face as Ben instructed. When he thought he had the correct alignment, he looked up at Ben for reassurance, and Ben gave him a thumbs-up and a wide smile. "Alright, actually, let me try and mess with this for a second and make sure everything sounds okay. Say something into the mic, E, anything."

"Fuck you," Earl said without hesitation. Earl gave his disappointed friend an evil grin, proud of himself.

"Shameful," was all that he received as a response as Ben messed with a few dials on the console in front of him, his headphones on as he listened to the recording back to himself. "Okay, we're good! Whenever you're ready... smart-ass." Earl's mind drew a blank as he searched around the depths of his brain, trying to think of something to say. He looked up and saw Ben's eager face, which didn't help his mental block. "...Could you turn around or something? You're staring me in my goddamn face and making me nervous." "Okay, okay! Sheesh... you artistic types can be rude!" Ben joked as he spun his chair around, facing away from Earl.

After another minute of deliberation, Earl's mind settled on something, and he'd hoped that it sounded as good coming out of his mouth and it did in his brain. "Alright, let's get this over with," Earl said, prompting Ben to turn around and tinker with his console again. When he was finished, he went back to facing away from Earl and held his left hand up. Earl realized that

49

Ben was counting him down, and when Ben got to his last finger, Earl took a prolonged, deep breath.

Now or never.

♪ Kicked while I was down, call it misstep,
A failing chef without the sous, no chance, no prep.
Embittered with the fact that I'm not published yet, pissed off. Got me in a studio, rapping, making me want to scoff. I don't gel with this life, trying to live without strife. It makes me want to scream, makes me want to grab a knife. ♪

And end it
.

With that, Ben spun back around and pushed a button, presumably ending the recording.

"Was that good enough for you?" Earl asked dryly, stepping out of the live room and back into the control room with Ben. "That was actually kind of awesome, dude! ...It got a little dark, but it was still cool!" Ben retorted. Just then, a scratching at the basement door alerted the two, and Ben ran up the stairs and opened the door. A black cat bolted down the stairs and sat right at Earl's feet, prompting Earl to kneel and run his hand along the cat's back. "Hey, Miles," Earl said as he stroked the purring cat. "I wish I could have a pet, but I feel like I can't give a pet my commitment. At least, not now," Earl said as Miles, content with the attention, ran off into a corner of the room and laid down.

"Yeah, I guess we woke him up," Ben said, sitting back down at the console. "So, what's your endgame with all of this?" Earl inquired. "I told you, I want to make beats! Not just any kind of beats, but I want to combine live instruments with some of the modern stuff! I figure you out of anybody would appreciate an attempt to add some class to the mix! I don't share your hate for modern day music, but I do think that it could use something that makes it stand out a little more. I think I can give it that freshness! Who knows, maybe a big label will notice. I do have the following to potentially have something like that happen!" *Cute.*

"I hope it works out for you!" Earl said, wanting to say the right thing. "I think I have a solid foundation for it, so we'll see where it goes!" Ben responded, puffing out his chest. "I hope you get the response you're looking for about your book, E. Seriously. I know how much work you put into it, and it deserves to get noticed."

No, you don't and no it doesn't.

"Thanks, Ben. A man can dream, right?" "Of course! You gotta believe!" Ben said with a wide, encouraging smile. *Great.*

"How's Saniya?" Ben asked.
"She's fine."

Earl kept topics regarding Saniya brief around Ben. He wasn't allowed to mention Ben in his girlfriend's presence without her getting irritated; that's how much she disliked him, believing him to be a bad influence.

Earl appreciated Ben asking about her, knowing that he usually only inquired out of respect. "That's good. Your six-year anniversary is coming up soon, right?"

"In a few months, yeah."

"Man," Ben said with a dreamlike admiration, "I can't imagine being with someone for that long. I got to hand it to you, that's something to be proud of, E. It doesn't seem like people our age like the whole... what's the word for it when you're just with one person?" "Monogamy," Earl answered. "Right," Ben said, embarrassed. "It feels like that's just not the thing to do anymore. It takes a strong couple to keep the flame burning for that long; I hope we're still here six years later talking about how amazing it is that your twelve-year anniversary is coming up! Maybe I'll be celebrating something like that one day!" *Doubtful.*

"Honestly, I just want the semester to be over for her so that we can see each other a lot more this summer. The past few months, I've only been able to see her once a week. Twice, if I'm lucky. I know she's working hard for what she wants, but still," Earl said, drumming his fingers restlessly along the pocket of his pants. "You have to wait it out, dude, and then she'll be done! She's probably just as ready to make up for lost time with you too!" Ben reassured.

Earl's phone began to ring, and he took it out, seeing "Home" pop up on the screen. Hesitantly, he answered it, mentally preparing himself for the demands that were sure to follow. "Hello?"

"Boy, get your ass back here!" the familiar screech of his grandmother commanded. "I need you to run me a quick errand because Randy didn't come back home from his lunch break! Where are you anyway?!" "I'm at Ben's," Earl replied, looking away from Ben and focusing on the sleeping cat nestled gently in the corner of the room. "Well, I need you here now. Whatever goofy shit ya'll got going on, stop it and hurry on home!" "Yes, ma'am," Earl said, almost dejectedly. The call ended, and Earl slid the phone back into his pocket. He'd been summoned away from Ben so many times that Ben already knew what Earl's somber disposition meant. "Ms. Charlotte?" Ben inquired.

"Yeah."

"Alright, well, I'll let you out," Ben said, getting up from his chair as he began to lead Earl back to his car. They walked outside, Ben making sure that the door was fully closed so that Miles couldn't make any sort of emboldened escape. "I'll see you later, dude. Oh, and don't forget, you'll most likely be meeting my new lady, Imani, next time you're here!" "I look forward to meeting her," Earl said, his usual snark or mild intrigue replaced with the unhappiness that had become harder to ignore as the days continued. "Alright, man," Ben said, noting the lack of biting commentary from his friend. Ben extended his fist to Earl, who returned the gesture as they did their typical farewell fist-bump.

"I'll drop by again soon," Earl promised as he started walking to his car. When he was sure that Ben had gone back into his house, Earl closed his eyes and rubbed his temples with his middle finger and thumb. A headache had begun to stir, and Earl did his best to curtail it before it fully materialized.

Just like always, it's us against everyone.

Chapter 4

Earl sat in his car with his head against the steering wheel, parked in the driveway of Charlotte's house. He hadn't moved an inch for over fifteen minutes, prepping himself as best as he could for the elderly, but boisterous woman. Already, he could hear her voice bouncing around in his head.

"Where the fuck have you been at!?"

"How come you just left last night without telling me?" "I need you to go here and get me this, then go there and get me that!" He dreaded it.

Earl loved Charlotte to death, but she had her moments where he had to take a break from her, if only for a day or two, so that he could recharge.

Finally, he stepped out of his sedan and closed the door as gingerly as possible, recalling the time that the door got stuck when he closed it too swiftly. He fumbled around in his pocket for his keys and unlocked the front door, stepping into the house which had been his prison for as long as he could remember. No sooner had he closed the door and locked it back up that Charlotte poked her head out from the kitchen, making direct eye contact with Earl. "There you are. It's about goddamn time!" the elderly woman remarked, barely taking her eyes off her favorite game show. "Hey, Charlotte," Earl said, attempting to mask his exasperation. "Why didn't you come home after your shift yesterday, Earl? Where were you? You know that Randy is getting too old to be running around the streets doing what you should be doing!"

Earl suppressed a groan and prepared to recite the speech he'd spent the time in his car crafting to address as many of the questions that she was sure to throw at him so that he could get whatever menial task she wanted him to do over with and have a moment to himself. "I did come home that night; I changed out of my uniform and went over to Saniya's. You were asleep. I'm sorry, I didn't think that—"

"You usually don't think, Earl," Charlotte interjected. "Instead of focusing on that girl and distracting her from school, you should be speaking to Ron about giving you either Saturday or Sunday for extra hours. You need that money, Earl, I need more help around the house." Between the rent Charlotte made Earl pay, his car insurance, needing to feed himself and having a small chunk of money saved away in case of emergencies, it was true that he rarely had enough money to do much else. Outside of the occasional treat, like a video-game, he'd never used his money in any other capacity aside from keeping himself afloat. On a particularly bad week of work where he'd only get around twenty-five hours, he had to pick and choose which days he could eat a full meal. Micromanaging his bank account had become so rote to him that he'd be lucky to have even fifty dollars that he could spend freely. "I'll talk to him about it when I go back on Monday," Earl said, "but I do need at least some time to myself."

"To do what?" Charlotte inquired, giving him a look of incredulity. "You don't do anything other than write that goddamn book, and you won't even let me or Randy read it! Have you heard anything back from any of the people you reached out to lately?" "…No," Earl lied, knowing that the lecture would go on for much longer if he'd told her about the rejections he'd gotten recently. "Then maybe you should focus on work. You didn't want to go to college like I told you to, so now you have to deal with the consequences. That's life, Earl, you just need to get your head out of the clouds and get real."

He didn't have the energy to argue with Charlotte; he never did. She had good intentions, he knew, but her blunt, unapologetic tone and diction frustrated him to no end. Even though the two of them were considered the black sheep of the family, she didn't try to give him any sort of outward encouragement, only telling him the ramifications of his bad decisions. She wasn't wrong, but she lacked the tact to make her point in a way that didn't make Earl want to pack his things and leave for good.

"Okay. What did you need me to do?" Earl asked, having had enough of the conversation. Charlotte got up, reached into her purse, and pulled out a twenty-dollar bill.

"Go get me my wine coolers. The sangria ones, you know I like those. You can get yourself a sandwich or something from the market afterwards with the change if you want." Earl took the money from Charlotte and stuffed it into his empty wallet. Charlotte's eyes briefly softened up as she looked at her grandson, and she let out a brusque huff. "...I worry about you sometimes, boy. When you aren't fooling around with Saniya or Ben, you're cooped up in that room. You rarely even come out to speak to me. You don't need to see your doctor again, do you?" "No," Earl said with a little more force than he'd intended. "I'm fine. I need to figure a few things out, that's all." "Well, maybe you need to give that book a rest and do something else. If you won't let me see it, maybe it isn't something that should be out there in the first place."

Something about the way that Charlotte had stated her comment had gotten under Earl's skin, and against his usual judgment, he couldn't hold back the rebuttal resting at the tip of his tongue. "...Don't take this the wrong way, but what opinion could you give me? You wouldn't understand it; you aren't a critic." "And you aren't a writer," Charlotte retorted, making Earl's face warm with anger.

"Alright, Charlotte, I'll be right back," Earl snapped, almost slamming the door shut behind him as he left to fulfill Charlotte's task.

--

Why do you let her undermine you? Like the fucking bitch that you are, you allow her to walk all over you. Twenty-three years old, and you're still living with your grandmother? Instead of making excuses like "I'd feel guilty if I left her here alone," or "We need each other," how about you man the fuck up and go out on your own? Saniya did, she's killing it, and here you are, your dreams about four more rejections away from crumbling. Then what? You move in with Saniya and watch her soar while you become a stay-at-home father who forces his dead ambitions on his children because you didn't have the fortitude or the talent to make them happen yourself? Do yourself a favor and put that miserable, old bitch in a home like she always claims you're going to do.

"Shut up," Earl muttered to himself, trying to block out the encroaching intruder.

"...I'm sorry, sir?" the cashier said as she rung up the 12-pack of wine coolers that Earl had placed on the counter. "Nothing, I was thinking out loud," Earl responded.

Maybe you're more than simply depressed. Maybe you're insane.

59

"That'll be thirteen dollars and nineteen cents, sir!" the cashier said with a cheeriness that Earl didn't feel was appropriate for her occupation. He reached into his wallet and pulled out the twenty-dollar bill, thinking about what he could get to eat from the supermarket just around the corner from the miniscule amount of change he was going to receive. As he handed the cashier
the bill, he'd realized that he hadn't really noticed her until he looked up to hand her the money.

She's gorgeous. What's a chick like this doing in a rinky-dink liquor store? "...I'm-I'm sorry, did you start working here recently?" Earl stammered out.

Smooth. You never knew how to organically speak to people. It's like an alien trying to mimic human speech patterns. "Yeah! This is actually my second week! I used to work at a check-cashing place about ten minutes away from here, but this job pays a little more and is a lot less stressful." That's what Earl figured. The liquor store had been right down the street from where he lived, and Charlotte sent him there, the market, the mall and her bank so frequently that he learned the faces of many of the employees.

Too bad you have zero awareness when it comes to people skills and social interaction.

"Besides, there are certain benefits to working at a liquor store, especially for someone like me who likes to experiment with different drinks! I still have to pay full-price for the high- end shit, but you know how that goes! What's your preference?" the cashier asked jubilantly as she handed Earl his change. "I, um, I actually don't drink. This is for —" *Go on, tell her what a joke you are.* "—someone else." "Oh! I'm sorry, it's just that it's rare to find someone who doesn't drink *something* these days," the cashier said with a giggle.

Is she being nice or is she flirting with you?
Surely the former, I mean, look at you.

You're a hard five, and she's about an eight-and-a-half to a nine. She doesn't want your dopey- looking ass. "So, are the coolers for a girlfriend then?" "N-No, just for a friend of mine," Earl stuttered, hoping that the cashier hadn't noticed that his eyes wandered to her low-cut shirt, revealing a good amount of the top of her breasts. The weather certainly permitted for the attire, as Earl saw all manners of clothing that lent itself to a spring that was mid-way through transforming into summer. He'd become mesmerized by the perfectly symmetrical perkiness that rose from the top of her shirt.

I guess that gentle artist angle is bullshit too, huh? Just a pig like the rest of them! I'm sure Saniya would love this; the only thing that's missing is a line of drool dangling from the side of your mouth.

"Aww, that's a little boring!" the cashier said with a smirk. "Yeah," Earl awkwardly responded as he grabbed the wine coolers from the counter and shambled out of the building, quickly putting the wine coolers in the backseat of his sedan parked directly in front of the large glass panes of the store. He could practically hear the intruder laughing at him as he made his way to the supermarket on foot, trying to use the other parked cars to hide himself as he wasn't sure whether the cashier was looking at him or not. He hadn't planned on finding out either, finding the option of turning his head to check to be too risky.

--

"Thank you, Earl," Charlotte said as her grandson opened the box containing her wine coolers and began arranging them in their sparse refrigerator. Despite her recklessness, Earl was still conscious of the minor tasks that helped Charlotte, especially concerning her arthritis. "I know that you're mad at me, but I don't want you to take what I said earlier the wrong way," Charlotte said, remembering Earl's reaction to what she'd told him before he stormed out of the house. I don't want you to take the process too personally. We've been down this road already where you just… aren't here. Your body is, but your mind is gone. Dr. Evans did the right thing by giving you those pills, which I hope you're still taking." "I am," Earl said, closing the fridge as he put in the last wine cooler and turned himself so that he was facing Charlotte. "Good. I don't want you to go to that place where I can't reach you, not again. I want you to be happy, I want your relationship with Saniya to work, and of course I want your book to be published. I told you that I had a dream about your name on the cover of a book a week or so ago."

"You did," Earl said with a small smile, pleased by Charlotte's sentiments. A tiny comfort to the maelstrom of thoughts clashing chaotically within him, but still a much-needed relief, no matter how small. "Did you have enough to get yourself something to eat?" "Yeah," Earl stated, "they were having a sale on chicken tenders and fries, so that should keep me nourished for the day." "There you go with those fucking words again," Charlotte said with a chuckle. "Nobody can tell you that you're not a writer." The two of them shared a laugh, and then Earl started to leave the kitchen and head to his room with his food. "Oh, before you go, I wanted to tell you that Randy called, asking me if I had ten dollars to spare. I'm all tapped out, Earl. I just paid the gas and electric bill, and it was higher than I was expecting. Could you please give him ten dollars for me? I know the money is tight, but give the motherfucker what he wants so he doesn't come in here complaining later."

Not for that junkie. He has a full-time job, gets paid a hell of a lot more than you do, and he still finds a way to spend it up on drugs. Charlotte shouldn't keep enabling him. If anything, she should kick him the fuck out.

"Sure, I got you," Earl said, his displeasure written in his face. "Thanks, Earl," Charlotte said, turning her attention back to her television.

With that, Earl grabbed his bag of food and migrated to his room. He opened and closed his door behind him and flopped onto his bed, embracing the silence. He closed his eyes, enjoying every second of solitude that he was allowed. He found his over-active imagination revisiting the dream he had the night prior, and he smiled. It had changed slightly, however. Instead of Saniya, he imagined the cashier from the liquor store being by his side. The dialogue had been the same, just from the mouth of his newest admirer, and his adoring fans were enraptured with her momentarily as Earl prepared to sign copies of his book for them.

He imagined the aftermath of his book signing, where he and the cashier go back to her apartment and have wonderful, torrid sex, collapsing next to each other in utter bliss. Earl reopened his eyes, seeing nothing but the white of the ceiling. He moaned wistfully, the daydream being nothing more than a bittersweet fantasy.

Earl loved Saniya endlessly, but after almost a full six years of being together, he'd see an attractive woman out and about while he was running errands for or with Charlotte, and he'd occasionally replace Saniya with them. In his mind, they were always different, and he was more than what he truly was. He was suave and charming, able to hold and incite many different forms of conversation. Sometimes, he envisioned himself as an entirely different person altogether, giving himself a fictional backstory and life, and he'd be more engrossed with the fantasy of that than with the starkness of reality. Not here. Here, in reality, Earl was awkward, clumsy, and only really opened up to people he'd known for a while. He relished the peace of silence, but he sometimes wished that he were more capable, in many different regards.

To Earl, there was nothing wrong with fantasizing about a better life. It allowed him the escapism he needed to function where any other means of distraction such as television, games and other things of that nature stopped being able to fulfill that purpose as he got older.

Why don't you admit that you're boring? You're boring, you're bored of Saniya, you resent Charlotte for babying you and Ben gets on your last nerve. Call it what the fuck it is and stop being so feeble and weak. Earl's nerves got the better of him, and he knew that the "intruder" had done enough damage for the day. He reached out to the headboard at the front of his bed, which contained open spaces for his books and other assortments of items, and retrieved the medicine bottle of anti-depressants that he was ordered to take daily.

He saw an unopened bottle of water strewn

Life Has A Way

haphazardly onto the bed, probably something he'd done absent-mindedly in his rush to leave last night. He placed it next to him. He shook a single pill loose from the container of medicine onto his hand and stared at it.

This could all be over if you chug the whole bottle. It'll be like taking a nap, except you'll never wake up. You can drift away *into the nothingness.* Tired of the plague that was his vitriolic thoughts, he shoved the pill into his mouth, not giving himself another second to contemplate the horrific suggestion. He opened the water bottle and washed the pill down into his esophagus, ending the action with an emphatic gulp. It wouldn't stop the intruder long-term, but it'd silence him for a while. he looked around at his room, earnestly. What he saw afterwards was nothing less than disturbing. Earl couldn't remember the last time he vacuumed, seeing crumbs and specks of dirt all over his floor. He was stunned that his room didn't have rats occupying it. If a surface could have it, dust rested upon it. His cabinets, the oscillating fan, his books, the majority of which only seemed to serve as decorations, his game systems, the chairs he could barely squeeze into the diminutive area, it was nothing short of embarrassing. He hadn't properly made his bed up in about a month, letting sheets cascade over the edge of the bed and onto the floor. If he hadn't had taken the pill with its high number of milligrams, he'd have been hard on himself for a little bit, then ignored whatever his inner musings had to contribute. He'd instead tried to use his capricious headspace as a crutch to excuse himself, but knew that laziness combined with a lack of motivation made him more than slightly inert.

"I don't know how to fix it," he said, almost as an apology to himself.

Chapter 5

Earl sat in his car with his head against the steering wheel, parked in the driveway of Charlotte's "How the hell does this work?" Earl asked, trying to get the keycard that they'd gotten from the front desk to acknowledge the keycard lock next to the door. The number emblazoned directly in front of the pair indicated that they were assigned the 13th room on the fifth floor of the lavish hotel.

"Give me that, E," Saniya said, playfully snatching the keycard from her boyfriend and rotating the card in front of the lock in a way that Earl hadn't tried yet. A subsequent click later, Saniya opened the door, giving Earl the smuggest expression that her face could conjure. "…Look, this is my first time in a hotel, Ms. Clements. Let me live!" Earl begged as they both entered the hotel room.

"Well, what better occasion for a first-time hotel experience than us being free from the muck that was high school?!" Saniya said excitedly as she made sure that the hotel door was locked. "Holy shit," Earl said as his head swiveled from left to right, trying to capture every detail of the magnificent room. A far cry from anything that he'd known, the hotel room contained a kitchen area, a fully-stocked refrigerator, a regal king-sized bed with purple sheets that looked like it belonged to royalty, and last but not least, the biggest flat-screen television that Earl had ever set his eyes upon. "Yeah, my parents must *really* like you," Saniya commented, an allusion to the fact that her parents paid out of pocket for their celebratory excursion tonight.

"Mrs. Shirley made a deal with me that if I attended graduation, she'd be alright with the two of us getting a hotel room afterwards!"

"That makes sense," Saniya said while examining every square inch of the room to ensure that everything was in order. "She knows your asocial ass was ready to bow out of one of the biggest milestones of our lives! Plus, I killed it this year when it came to grades, so it was hard for her to say 'no' when I initially asked if the two of us could do this about a month ago! Top three out of everyone in our graduating class is nothing to be ashamed of!" Saniya even checked under the bed, which got a suppressed snort out of Earl. She gave him her signature evil squint, and he defensively raised his hands in response.

"Honestly, I'm still kind of shocked that she let us do this," Saniya said as she checked the bathroom, opening cabinets and analyzing every nook and cranny. Earl smiled, noticing when her astute attention-to-detail and perfectionist tendencies flared up. It was no wonder that she was so good at what she did. It was almost annoying to him how much she ended up hating most of her work for their art class that school year, one of the few classes they'd had together. Her "worst" work was so much better than anything he'd ever done, believing that he'd only passed the class because Ms. Tremayne liked him so much. "I mean, we've been together for a year and a half now. I guess she's already accepted the fact that the two of us are—"

"Fucking?" Saniya exclaimed, finishing Earl's hesitant thought. The smile that followed seemed almost demented in its glee of Earl's discomfort for her boldness. "…Yeah," Earl confirmed, looking away from her and scratching the back of his head nervously. "This is better than us having to sneak in a decent fuck while everyone is sleeping when you'd stay over, or waiting for the rare opportunity where everyone left and we didn't know when they'd be back. Besides," Saniya purred as she strode up to Earl and lovingly caressed his crotch through his jeans, "I can be as loud as I want in here." Saniya gave Earl a sly wink before finishing her scrutinization of their living quarters for the night. Earl gulped, somehow managing to be jittery despite the fact that he brought condoms in his backpack. "How is Ms. Shirley's lawsuit coming along?" Earl asked, trying to quell his own nerves while Saniya turned on the television and made sure that they had all the services that they were promised. Upon hearing the question, Saniya's eyes darted to Earl's and remained, the underlined sultriness in her light brown eyes now shifted to steely and focused.

"The next court date is July 25th, about a month and a half from now," Saniya stated. "Can you believe that the son of a bitch managed to get the vice principal to stand up for him to say how great of a person he was? As if that excuses the fact that he was running around smacking teachers' asses in the break room and making disgusting jokes about them, trying to pass it off as something normal," Saniya said, her eyes smoldering as she recounted her mother's case against her boss.

"I'm still shocked that Mr. Pechello did all of that," Earl said, remembering his time in the elementary school where Saniya's mother now taught. He'd cross paths with the principal in the hallways quite frequently, recalling a time where he got to talk to Harmon Pechello about bullies, he was having an issue with. Of course, as a child, he hadn't caught on to Pechello's alleged crimes, but now, hearing about the incident between his former principal and Ms. Shirley made his decision to back his girlfriend an easy one.

"My mom thought that she'd be more respected here than in Virginia. At least when she was teaching over there, it was only one of the other teachers that tried her with the racist remarks. Some of the others didn't like her either, but Mr. Drummond was the bold motherfucker that let her know just how unwanted she was among them. He's lucky that Ms. Quinn was a good principal and got him out of there before my dad had a chance to beat the shit out of him.

This, though, where the person in charge is the one doing the dirt? Nah, he's going to have his day," Saniya assured. "I hate to say it like this, but it's a good thing that the motherfucker also had a history with a few of the other teachers and even some of their younger assistants too. It will give her case a hell of a lot more leverage. Mom didn't mess around; she went right to the school board itself knowing that the superintendent would probably try to cover it up to save face. She gave the other women the chance to speak up that they didn't have before when they were afraid that his word would supersede theirs and he'd ruin their careers. Well, we've got him cornered, and my mom's attorney told her that if even a few of the women followed through with their promise to testify against him, we'd have a good chance of winning."

Earl nodded, hoping that his former principal would get what he deserved. If there was one thing that Earl hated, it was liars and people who took advantage of others for their own benefit.

"Yeah, dudes can be pretty disgusting," Earl remarked, trying and succeeding to ease the tension that his question had created. "Not all of them, obviously. I think I found one of the better ones," Saniya said with a smile before turning the television to one of the music-centric channels. Suddenly, the room was filled with the dulcet sounds of a tenor saxophone as Saniya looked at Earl lustfully. "I don't think we've ever fucked with music playing before. I know that I'd kill the mood if I played Kronin with your musical elitism," Saniya joked, getting up and sauntering over to her boyfriend.

Earl was silent as Saniya kissed him passionately. As their lips remained locked together, Earl's nerves began to settle. He wanted to impress her by picking her up and carrying her over to the bed, but at the risk of potentially throwing her to the ground, he opted instead to just maneuver her so that her back was against the foot of the bed.

Saniya took a brief moment to break their intense, sensual battle for dominance to take her shirt off, revealing a lace bra. Then, she removed Earl's shirt and undershirt, exposing his slender upper body. Earl was self-conscious of how skinny he was, but knew that Saniya desired him no matter what he looked like. "We're finally free, from school, and from any distractions," Saniya said, her voice wispy and ravenous.

"Fuck me like you're never going to get a chance to touch me again," Saniya demanded, and Earl threw her onto the bed, an answer that satisfied the grinning girl beneath him immensely. The next hour was unlike anything the two of them had ever physically felt before. They made the period of their ephemeral freedom count as their lustful war spilled into other rooms, onto the couch across from the television, even as far as the counter of the kitchen island that the extravagant room lauded. Having finally fulfilled their cravings for one another, they collapsed onto the bed.

Sweating, panting heavily, they took a minute to gather themselves, too tired to retrieve their clothes that were scattered all around them.

"That... was... amazing," Saniya rasped out, getting a laugh from Earl. Earl was so worn out that he couldn't speak as Saniya eventually scooted next to her exhausted lover and nestled herself into his body. They spent the next fifteen minutes cuddling, a silent contemplation hovering between them. "I've been thinking about some options for college," Saniya stated, breaking the quiet atmosphere. "I think I want to go for a fine arts degree, then get an MFA degree and see how much I can better myself. I always want to push myself forward, no matter how good people think that I am. There's never a plateau for improvement."

Earl smiled, almost sadly. Saniya spoke so ardently about her future, knowing exactly what she wanted to do with her life. Earl was the exact opposite, fresh out of high school with no ambitions or goals. As he looked over at Saniya, who had allowed herself to drift thinking about her aspirations, he almost envied her. "What about you, E?" Saniya inquired, which Earl dreaded. "...I don't know yet. Charlotte's been asking me that lately, and I'm not sure. I know that I don't want to just go on to college without having any clue of what I'd want to do, that would be a waste of money that Charlotte already has a hard time managing." "She does want you to go though," Saniya said, using one arm to prop herself up and look at Earl while she played with the little tuft of hair on Earl's chest. "I think it's worth talking about, especially since we have the whole summer before needing to register for any classes to decide." Earl regarded her by raising his eyebrows, uncertain of how to answer Saniya's concerns.

"Clearly we both have the capacity for creativity. You speak very well, E, and I remember you telling me that you always loved English class. Why don't you consider writing?" Earl had to stop himself from scoffing, not wanting to seem dismissive. "It feels like everything's been written already. You know, every story," Earl said. "I'm no Epsen Knight, I don't know what I would write about. I also have a tendency to not finish the things that I start. I feel like I get bored too quickly." "Or you're afraid of failure," Saniya chimed in. "All I'm saying is that maybe you could take up a writing class or something at the community college." Earl's face contorted into a visage of disgust, having his own thoughts and opinions about community college.

"You really should've taken the SAT, E. You could've gotten yourself some good scholarships that wouldn't have cost Ms. Charlotte a dime."

But you'd rather feel sorry for yourself.

Earl stuffed the voice into the back of his head, almost having the whole day pass without it making itself known. "First and foremost, I need a break from school. I want time to myself to figure out what I want to do before I just up and go to college or something." "But we have three months, baby. That's not enough time for you?"

Why don't you man up and tell her that you have no intentions on going to college?

"I need to figure things out before I dive into that kind of thing. So many people go to college and waste their time, deciding that they don't want the degree that they spent two or three years trying to get. There's also the group of hopefuls who get the degree that they want, and then when it's time for them to get a job befitting of their efforts from college, suddenly, employers demand that you have experience instead. I have a cousin that went to college for marine biology, and do you know what she's doing now? Social security! I could do that, you don't even need a goddamn degree for that! Now she's indebted to her college, and for what? What does she have to show for all her hard work? A job that any jackass with a clean record and a decent suit can get."

Saniya contemplated Earl's stance with a sense of underlined melancholy, her eyes searching the room for an answer to his cynicism.

You always do this to her, hurt her feelings. All the support she gives you and like everything else in your life, you somehow manage to fuck it up.

"Sans, I'm sorry," Earl said, pulling her closer to him and holding her head to his chest. "...I just want you to be happy, E," Saniya said, quietly enough that Earl almost missed it. "I don't want you to be lost anymore. I want to watch you succeed and accomplish your dreams. I want us to grow together. I know we're just two young people who will go through so many changes in our lives, but I want us to go on that journey together. I can't stand it when you're hurting and it feels like there's nothing that I can do about it."

It broke Earl's heart to hear Saniya speak like that, and if that wasn't enough, he noticed her eyes. She appeared to be a few seconds away from bursting into tears. It was one of the things that Earl loved about her the most, that she wore her emotions on her sleeve, something that he was unable to do. "Sans, baby, look at me," Earl said as he gently lifted her head to look him directly in the eyes.

"You are the best thing that's ever happened to me. Do you remember when we first met in 11th grade when you moved to Washington? Ms. Cameron made us sit next to each other in art, a course I didn't want to take, but I needed an elective course to pad out my credits." Saniya giggled as she remembered the start of their friendship. "Yeah. The first thing she had us do was make masks, and we had to use each other as models for the clay molds. I remember that you sneezed and messed up my hard work, but I improvised and made a… decent mask. You did kind of ruin my vision though," Saniya joked, causing Earl to lightly pinch her exposed nipple in protest.

"I was a wreck when I met you. I didn't have anyone else to talk to, and we'd always finish our projects so fast that all we had was free time to chat. I'm sorry for pushing you away during that first month. I guess I couldn't handle the idea of having a friend that meant as much to me as you did, and I was so deeply entrenched in self-destruction and misery that I almost lost you completely. You saved me, Sans, from myself. You saw something in me that nobody else did: *Potential*."

Saniya's eyes gleamed with joy as she listened to Earl speak so lovingly about her. She held him tighter, wanting to be nowhere else but in his arms.

"I remember how I used to be before I came here when my classmates made fun of me because of my mom getting Mr. Drummond fired. My friends started bullying me, and there were always assholes who would throw food at me whenever it was time for lunch. Ms. Quinn did the best that she could to make things easier, but no matter what happened, I was always targeted. Eventually, my mom got sick of it and moved us here, where my uncles lived. I stuck with you, no matter how hard you pushed me away, because I knew. I learned the difference between unapologetic, mean-spirited people, and people who were just in pain. I knew you were hurting, and I know that it may not have been the sanest hunch to operate on, but I knew that if I showed you enough compassion that I'd at least make a good friend. Now... here we are, a year and a half later, just having fucked each other's brains out. Their laughter filled the room as they held each other with no intention of letting go.

"It's true that I was in pain and lost, for a long time. I still am, in a sense. I spent so much of my childhood pissed off at my parents, my classmates or myself that I didn't even know who I was. I couldn't tell you the last time I was happy before I met you. I was so obsessed with dreaming of a better life that I'd given up on my own. Then, I met you, and your spirit gave mine the jolt it needed. Even through my façade of being a cold, apathetic robot, you gave me warmth and tenderness. I love Charlotte, I do. She picked me up when my parents wanted nothing to do with me.

But she grew up in a different time, forced to deal with external threats like racism, prejudice and all of that while not understanding the idea of something being wrong with the self. I think that sometimes, she just isn't sure what to do with me. She loves me, but in terms of understanding me, she doesn't know what to do. She did her best to give me everything I wanted, every toy, every game system, everything I needed to be content. But there was still this... fog. I was stuck in it, and then you came and gave the darkness of my mind the light it so desperately needed."

Saniya giggled as she tapped Earl's nose, kissing it lightly in the process. "You should definitely become a poet or something, E. You have such a way with words," Saniya said as she kissed Earl.

"I won't ever leave you behind, baby. I love you, and I'll help you get to where you need to be. As much as I've done for you, you've reciprocated that for me. You helped me adjust to a new place, and you are easily the most loving boyfriend I've ever had. We've done so much, and we have so much more to do and experience together."

Earl beamed at her, thinking about how strange it had been at first since Saniya had not only been his first real girlfriend, but the one who took his virginity. He hadn't been with anyone else, and he had no desire on needing to be with anyone but her.

"Thank you for being you, Sans," Earl said as he wrapped his arms around her and pulled her into another deep kiss. They had to forcefully break their entanglement after a loud crashing sound thumped against the wall of their bed.

"...Must be Ben," Earl muttered, remembering that a good chunk of his now-former classmates also booked a graduation celebration at the hotel. Saniya rolled her eyes, regarding the mere mention of Earl's friend distastefully. "The pig. I tried to warn Peyton, but I guess he sunk his hooks into her too," Saniya remarked, knowing Ben's track record with the girls of their graduating class, and even some from their school's junior and sophomore grades. "No freshman girls though!" Ben's golden rule flashed swiftly through Earl's mind, but he knew better than to snicker at the thought now.

"How you two coexist, I have no idea. You're so sweet and kind, and Ben is loud and sticks his dick into whatever smiles at him." "...Let's just focus on us, baby." Earl's attempt at drawing her attention away from Ben succeeded, and she smiled at him warmly. "Anyway, I love you more than you could ever know, Sans. I'm grateful for every day that you chose me out of everyone that you could've had. I love your dedication to your dreams, I love your hopeful outlook on life, and I love your freckles," Earl cooed, kissing his giggling girlfriend's face.

"You're more than I ever deserved, and I promise to always cherish you and never take your love for granted. Don't worry about me and college, we'll figure that out together, I promise. I'll always be yours, you'll always mine, and I'll stand by you no matter what." All of Saniya's dimples glossed onto her elated face, adoring Earl now more than she ever had before. She wiped a tear away from her eye, almost overloaded from Earl's affection.

"...I don't know what to say, baby. All I know is that there's no man in this world that can compare to you, your heart, your soul, and your love. You never have to worry about any time where I won't be as in love with you as I am, right now. In fact, there's only one thing that's as good as your heart and your mind…" In one swift motion, Saniya rose from her snuggled position next to Earl and got on top of him, grinding her pelvis against his groin. Earl groaned blissfully, wondering how Saniya could've possibly already recovered from their previous session. Regardless, he knew that she had yet to be fully sated, and he was up to the challenge that loomed above him. "Ready for round two, E? You better be because the night is still young, and I'm not *nearly* finished with you yet."

Chapter 6

Two and a half years of your life, wasted. You should've done what you were told back then and expressed more of an interest in doing something, anything that wasn't this. You'll be doing this shit for as long as you live. Your authorial dreams will die, and then all you'll have to look forward to is working your way up to manager in this sorry excuse for a "job." "Alright, man," a voice uttered, snapping Earl back into reality. The young, bearded man took his hat off and held it over his heart facetiously, unable to hide his elation."It's been an honor working with you, captain. But, I'm afraid that it's time for me to ride off into the sunset." Earl returned the flippant gesture and gave their surroundings a quick scan, making sure that none of their managers were around to see the comical display they were putting on before Charlie's big sendoff. "Wherever you go, never forget us smaller folks. We kept this ship running smoothly for a long time, and now, we've lost a crucial part of the SS machine." Earl and Charlie laughed as Charlie looked at the unfortunate abbreviation boldly emblazoned onto the front of his hat.

"Yes, I'm sure the führer will be pleased that one of his incompetent cronies will be heading off to the great braunschweiger in the sky!"

The two amicable employees chuckled again, Earl making sure that no customers were nearby to witness their comedy that was dangerously close to being offensive. Earl liked Charlie a lot more than his other co-workers. Whereas most of his fellow employees would slack off in the back, Charlie was always right there in the trenches with him, serving customers and happily getting on each other's nerves. Charlie managed to break through Earl's barriers of disliking people from the second he met them, and the pair somehow managed to get along from the start of their year-and-a-half association.

Now he gets to go on to a better job, and you're still stuck here slicing lunch meat and making sandwiches.

"Sieg Heil, Bruder!" Charlie said quietly, teasing a very unpleasant hand gesture, but deciding to give the panicking Earl a traditional soldier's salute instead. "You should see the look on your face!" Charlie said, snickering at Earl's priceless reaction. "We're still on-camera, man! They'll fire me for glorifying racism, or whatever silly-ass reason they'd try to get me fired for! You already know that Jane doesn't like me!" "Ah, fuck Sub Shack!" Charlie proclaimed, making sure that nobody in his immediate vicinity other than Earl heard him.

"I can't wait to burn this hat and apron when I get home! Are you sure you want me to leave now? I can rock these last thirty minutes with you and we can show these lazy fucks what the dream team can do one last time!" Earl's lip curled upwards in appreciation, but despite the fact that he hated seeing Charlie leave for good, he knew that Sub Shack had wasted enough of his time.

"Nah, you go ahead. It looks like it's going to be slow as hell in here anyway until 3, so I can cope for at least thirty more minutes by myself!" "…Do they have anyone else scheduled with you?" Charlie inquired. "Nope, it's just me until Jaiquan and Isaiah come in at 3. I can hold down the fort until then, you know me," Earl assured, causing Charlie to nod respectfully. "Alright then, E-Squared. Don't forget that we have to take some time to hang out soon! Just because it's the end of the dream team here doesn't mean we can't do something down the road!"

"Of course, man," Earl concluded as he and Charlie did their strange signature handshake for the last time. Earl followed Charlie's gait until he was out of the door, pumping his fist as he exited the building as an employee for the last time. *The jokes, the stupid observations, the camaraderie, all gone. The worst part is that you know that you're never going to text him, and since you recently deleted all of your social media accounts, you have no way to stay in contact with him. Sad.* That just left Earl to wander around since nobody had approached the counter, wanting to submit their order. He stood in front of the meat display where they were required to retrieve meat of a customer's liking, use their slicers to cut it to the customer's specifications, and then move over to the sandwich station where they had to finally assemble sandwiches for the Sub Shack's voracious patrons with the vast assortment of condiments, toppings and bread types.

As Earl stared at the familiar meats: turkey, chicken, all manners of beef, specialty meats, bologna, almost every lunchmeat that one could imagine, he couldn't help but shake his head.

The store was usually so busy that even regulars of Sub Shack were unrecognizable to Earl. After a while, they'd all blend in as one mass that demanded service, and Earl saw himself as a robot who only did what he was told. He stared into the glass of the display case, beholding the reflection of himself in his orange and green uniform, the standard for Sub Shack employees.

A crystal ball painfully reminding you of your mistakes and foretelling your future. At least Charlie made this shitty job somewhat fun. What now? You don't like anyone else here, not your co-workers, not the customers, not the management, nobody. How does it feel to be the best and have nothing to show for it? How does it feel knowing that people like Charlie get to move on while you're stuck in this hell, being forced to serve people complacent in their ordinary lives who you believe you're so much better than? Then again, if you never realize your potential, I suppose you're no better than they are after all, huh?

Earl closed his eyes and took a second to focus his energy on ignoring the intruder. His mind began to shift to his humble beginnings at Sub Shack that had seemed like it had been an eternity ago. He'd been stuck at home following high school for an entire year, unwilling to do anything with himself and stubborn to humor the concerns of his loved ones. Charlotte begged Earl to at least find a job if he didn't want to go to college, but her pleas fell on deaf ears. That is, until he could feel himself slipping further away from his sensibilities as his mental state deteriorated and his relationship with Saniya began to suffer greatly, starting with unresolved, meager disagreements that spiraled into loud, tearful screaming matches. That's when Earl told Charlotte that he didn't think he could take it anymore, and Charlotte forced him to see his doctor, who prescribed him his anti-depressants as a solution.

Desperately, Charlotte had finally convinced him to fill out job applications, and Sub Shack, which had just opened a location down the street from where they'd lived, swiftly accepted his resume. Ron, the store manager, had promised him and a few other Sub Shack "originals" that used to work alongside Earl that they were a part of something substantial. They were given the illusion of rewards and advancement based on work ethic, which suited Earl just fine as he earnestly believed Ron's heartfelt sentiments.

You fell for the old first-job finesse. Got your

occupational cherry popped, and you served them with the loyalty of an obedient household pet. "You can make this a career if you're willing to put in the effort!" Working hard has yet to yield any significant results for you. The original crew moved on, leaving you shackled here as the earth rotated without a care for your workplace tenacity.

Suddenly, he felt the need to hear Saniya's voice. He walked off to the side, out of the line of sight from any potential customers or nosy co-workers. Crouched behind an old display nearing the refrigerator unit where they kept all their back-up meats, he took out his phone. Figuring that everyone else was apparently allowed to do what they wanted while they were on the clock, he could too, and he found Saniya's number and called her up. Two rings later, she responded.

"Hey, E!" Saniya chirped.

"Hey, Sans," Earl said, a genuine smile plastered on his face. "Aren't you supposed to be working? What are you doing calling me?" Saniya asked, a hint of jest in her inflection.

"I think all of the managers are in a meeting, and everyone else is off slacking in the back because there's nothing to do," Earl answered, poking his head out to see if anyone had approached the counter. "Oh! What's wrong, are you that intent on hearing my voice?" Saniya joked. "…Yeah."

"Awww, that's so sweet, E!" Saniya cooed. "I'm so sorry about Saturday, but I've been hit with a lot of work lately." "Well, can I see you later? I've been feeling a little bad, and I really want to see you. Charlie's last day was today, you know. He got that teacher's aide job he wanted."

"…That sucks, E. I know how much you liked him. You're going to stay in contact with him, right?"

"…Sure!" Earl said, but even he thought his apprehension was obvious. "Baby, you have to put yourself out there. Don't limit your time outside of work to me, you know as well as I do that you don't want to be stuck in your room all day," Saniya reasoned. "Plus, I'd like for you to have a wider circle than just me and… Ben." "We'll see. I'll make an effort to stay in touch with Charlie, I promise," Earl said, already primed to defuse any animosity that was sure to spark from the mention of Ben. "Good! As for us hanging out later, I don't know if I can make time for it, baby. I was actually going to knock out some more schoolwork, and then go to bed early so that I could be ready for an exam tomorrow. If you're not feeling that great though, then maybe I could—"
"No, no," Earl insisted, trying to mask his displeasure. "It's okay, you're trying to set yourself up for better things. I—"

"Excuse me, is anyone here?!" The commanding screech broke through Earl's conversation, causing Earl to swing his head around. "I'll call you back later, Sans, okay? I love you!" Earl said quickly. "I love you too, E. Bye!" Earl hung up the phone and walked out of the corner, trying his best to look like he hadn't been doing something he wasn't supposed to. When he caught sight of the customer, he'd wanted to do nothing but go back into his corner and hide. "It's about damn time. I've been standing here for over a minute!"

Not this fat motherfucker.

One of Sub Shack's more vocal, picky customers, the man fumed at Earl from behind his thick, bottle-cap glasses. Rolls of flab covered his neck, burst from the sleeves of his small shirt, and his face was almost crimson-red with indignation.

Phil.

It was one of the few customers that Earl had known by their name and face, having a reputation for being one of the more difficult patrons of the store. It was bad enough that Phil didn't seem to care for Earl's admitted lack of saccharine, fawning customer service in their past interactions, but now he'd angered the overweight man by not being available as soon as he walked up to the counter. *Of all fucking days. Don't bend over backwards for someone who probably can't even bend over. You're not in the mood for this today.*
"Hello, Mr. Ph—"

"Honey ham, Farmridge brand of swiss cheese," the man croaked out, breathing heavily as he did.

"Both, thick-sliced. And try not to fuck it up this time," Phil ordered. It took everything Earl had in him not to follow Charlie's example and leave right then and there, but he did as requested and took out the ham and cheese from the case, bringing them both over to the slicer. Earl started with the ham, and rather than slice it as thick as the slicer could get it, he suppressed his impulse of ignorance and cut one sample slice to show Phil.

"Too thin. Again."

After three more attempts, Earl showed Phil a piece that he snatched out of Earl's gloved hand and ate, a nonverbal sign of acceptance. Earl sliced about four pieces and then worked on the cheese, which was met with further clear-cut, distinctive directions from Phil. Once that was finished, Earl took the ingredients over to the sandwich station in order to prepare Phil's sandwich. "What kind of roll would—"

"Plain white, and change your gloves before you touch the bread. You should know this by now, this isn't your first fucking day."

Earl's thoughts were too frenzied to coherently isolate as his hands started to shake angrily. He took his gloves off, threw them away and then grabbed a fresh pair, doing his best to not let his repressed rage show in his actions. Just then, Earl's least favorite manager, Jane, appeared from the back. She shot Earl a dirty glance and then flashed Phil an almost inhuman smile when she recognized him. "Hey, Mr. Clarkson!" Jane said happily, her two big front teeth threatening to blind Earl with their whiteness. *The bitch probably enjoys seeing you suffering like this.* "Is everything to your liking?" Jane asked cloyingly. "No. I can already tell from his attitude that he's going to fuck up my sandwich, so could you please make it for me, Ms. Jane?" *Now the fat fuck wants to be civil.*

"Of course!" Jane said, putting on a pair of gloves as Earl stepped out of the way. "You can actually clock out and go home," Jane said to Earl, not even looking near his direction as she said it. Her intonation was placid, but the affability of the statement made Earl's blood boil because he knew how she meant to say it. Phil and Jane proceeded to have an amiable conversation, very much antithetical to the interaction between Phil and Earl, as Earl threw his new gloves in the trash and walked away to clock out of his shift. On his way out, he could see Phil sneering and pointing at him, no doubt complaining about what he perceived to be awful customer service. Jane made sure to give Earl one last look of utter disapproval as he walked out the door and to his car.

Fat fucking fuck, and that gap-toothed cunt with her thick caterpillar eyebrows.

For a few minutes, Earl stood in the parking lot, composing himself before he got into his car and slammed the door, uncaring that he might inadvertently break it. He didn't want to disturb

Saniya, so he did the next best thing and decided to go to the one other person who could deal with him when he was as erratic as he'd become.

Chapter 7

Earl's fist thumped against Ben's door continuously, his irritation being so great that he neglected to use the doorbell. After pausing to wait for Ben, Earl looked down, noticing that he still had his Sub Shack uniform on. "…Fuck," Earl muttered, reprimanding himself for not going home to change first before showing up at Ben's.

Earl rolled his eyes and tapped his foot impatiently, wondering what was taking so long.

As he raised his fist to bang on the door for the third time, it opened. "Listen, Ben, I—"

Holy. Shit.

The person that revealed themselves wasn't Ben whatsoever, and for a second, Earl wanted to double-check to make sure he'd knocked at the right door. Instead of Ben, what Earl got was the most beautiful, wonderful sight that he'd personally laid eyes upon. The long, straight, jet-black hair; her defusing, hazel eyes; her hourglass shape that accentuated all the right places, she was physically unlike anything that Earl had known to be real, even in his wildest day-dreaming instances or most decadent fantasies.

"Hi!" the attractive girl stated cheerily as she stood in front of Earl, her midriff exposed and her smile as perfect and radiant as any Earl could readily recall.

If the cashier from the other day was an eight, whoever this is easily breaks the rating system. She's beyond beautiful.

"You must be Earl!" she said, prompting a dazed nod of affirmation from the mesmerized young man. "Ye-yeah," Earl gulped. "I am." "Ben told me that he was expecting you at some point during the week! I'm Imani!" she said, stepping aside and gesturing for Earl to enter the house, which he did timidly. After closing and locking the door, Imani spun around to address Earl. His eyes swiftly darted away from her, not wanting to get caught checking out her prominent haunches.

*Thick thighs; robust, supple ass; full lips; the most delectable pair of tits. You wouldn't know what to do with a woman like this. There's no way that Ben met her at a bar, this has to be some kind of joke. Ben's nice and all, but he's with **this**?*

Earl felt pangs of guilt stab at his chest, the image of Saniya briefly popping into his head. "I'm sorry about not coming to the door straight away, by the way," Imani said, apologizing. "Ben was in the shower, and I was listening to music and heard you as a song was changing." "No problem." Earl cleared his throat,

95

which had become remarkably dry in the last few minutes. "Did you come here straight from work?" Imani asked, looking Earl over. "Yeah," Earl squeaked out, his embarrassment over forgetting to change now threatening to crush him. "I've never actually been to a Sub Shack before. Not even on a cheat day," Imani remarked. "I try not to indulge myself too much. I don't know if Ben spoke about me at all, but I do a lot of yoga and jogging, so I have to be careful when it comes to calories!"

It shows. I bet you're getting hard, aren't you? Thinking about how amazing it would feel to—

"I can't imagine being that disciplined! I've always been a little scrawny, so I guess I've never needed to worry about what calories I intake or not!" Earl said, trying to redirect the blood back to his brain. He'd never been more thankful that his apron was covering his crotch. _"Intake" is really the word you went for? Can you at least try to speak like you didn't come from Vaudeville?_

"Well, I'm a social media model, so I need to stay in shape so that I can keep those likes up! The more traffic I generate, the more money I get, and that hustle is always one of the most important aspects of my day-to-day! Besides, being fit isn't just about making a bunch of dudes horny and a bunch of girls jealous," Imani said while dramatically running her hands down her body.

Maybe God made some people faster than others, but this one, he must've really taken his time with to meticulously craft every last detail.

"It's also about keeping my mind clear so that I can stay focused on my goals. I'm into the belief that feeling good physically can lead to positive mental and emotional health. I like the idea of having a good aura, you know?" "Yeah, I get you," Earl said as Miles made his appearance, coming down the steps to stare at the pair. With a mewl, almost as if to greet Earl, he chose the corner containing his small bed and lazily sprawled himself across it. "Ben told me about your book!" Imani exclaimed, causing Earl's heart to drop into his stomach. "I think that's so cool! When is it going to be published?"

That's a question you ask yourself every other day. It's always nice to get reminded of your shortcomings, isn't it?

"Honestly, with the feedback I've gotten from potential agents, it's not looking like I'm going to be published traditionally," Earl said, knowing that he'd already exhausted all his options concerning the conventional publishing route. "I could self-publish it, but I don't have the money to hire a good editor to make sure that my product is good enough to sustain itself in that market," Earl continued, slipping into his pessimism. "Besides, when you do that, you're literally going against thousands of other small-time, unrefined writers, and your work gets lost in the mix. For every one author that somehow successfully breaks out of the self-publishing mold and gets popular, there are tens of thousands of writers who never see that dream come to fruition. I don't want to be just 'another one.' I want my work to mean something, to be enjoyed on a grander scale. I'll find a way to get my book out there though," Earl said, surprising himself with the inkling of hope that made itself known in his words. Imani rose her eyebrows and nodded, impressed with the vision that Earl outlined to her. "I think that's good! If you want something badly enough, you'll eventually get it. At least, that's what I've always believed."

We'll see about that.

"Looks like I missed a hell of a party!" Imani and Earl looked to the stairs and saw Ben trot down the steps towards them, a silly grin decorating his face.
"Hey, baby," Imani cooed as she gave Ben a prolonged kiss. Earl's eyes drifted away from the doting demonstration, feeling a sharp knot forming inside the pit of his abdomen. "Why the uniform? Did you come here to make us sandwiches?"

Earl's eyes narrowed as he gave Ben the sharpest, most biting glare that he possibly could've, his disposition now normalizing after Ben's emergence. There was something about Ben's regular demeanor, today, that Earl wasn't in the mood for. "I forgot to change, you smug asshole." Every word cascaded from Earl's mouth with venomous overtones. Ben, noting his friend's genuine anger, rose his hands defensively and looked downwards to the ground. "I'm sorry, dude. I can tell that you're not exactly in the best mindset right now." *Always so eager to please. Sycophantic, philandering, stupid—*

"Do you want to go down to the basement to talk about it?" Typically, if Earl were particularly cross with Ben, they'd go to the living room and put on the television as background noise so that Earl could vent. Ben would be his usual, affable self and defuse Earl's issues. This time, however, Ben wanted to bask in the glory of his new recording studio."…Sure. I'm sorry to bother you, by the way. You told me you were going to have her over," Earl remarked, automatically nodding his head in Imani's direction, "but I didn't know I'd be disrupting anything." It wasn't until after he'd done it that Earl mentally castigated himself for addressing

Imani in the blasé manner that he would Ben's other girlfriends whenever he met them. The nod was an unspoken cue of his, denoting that he had no intentions on interacting much with Ben's latest distraction, knowing how most of them ended up anyway. Imani simply giggled as she observed the two, occasionally glancing down at her phone to check her WeLink page to make sure that everything had been running smoothly. Specifically, she sought out the popularity and approval of her most recent photos to ensure that they were doing as well as she'd liked, smirking when she saw the positive results she'd been hoping for. "No problem, Big E!" Ben chirped, "actually, Imani and I finished playing an amazing game of Twister about an hour ago! I'm sure that you and Saniya have brought that out from time to time!"

Earl brought a hand to his forehead, then pinched the bridge of his nose while shaking his head, mortified that Ben had the temerity to bust out one of his indecent euphemisms while in Imani's company. Imani, initially confused, slowly understood the lewd undertones based on Earl's reaction, and then lightly smacked Ben's arm. Unlike everyone else in the room, Ben had been having the time of his life as he descended into a fit of hysterics, rousing Miles out of his short-lived slumber. "Priceless. Oh, I wish I had recorded that moment," Ben said as he wiped a tear from his eye.
"You know how I feel about being recorded for your silly-ass videos." Earl scolded Ben, the both of them knowing how it usually went on the rare occasion where Earl did something that Ben found worthy of potentially posting on the internet. Earl would demand that the video be deleted, and Ben would eventually acquiesce to the request.

"You can call them silly if you want, but I make my money in being 'silly' for my fans!"

"...Half of your videos are you covering popular songs, and the other half feature you just fucking

100

around," Earl dryly declared, which got a laugh from Imani. Ben regarded his friend's statement with the most exaggerated gesture of being offended that he possibly could've mustered up.

"For your information, I *also* talk about cool shows that I like and try to help my fellow guys keep themselves looking and feeling their best!" "Yeah, what original, thought-provoking content. I'm sure everyone is waiting with bated breath for your next big hypothesis on how a symbol that you see when you pause a show at a certain point is a sign of some big, governmental conspiracy. Ooh, or how about the benefits of exfoliating?! I'm sure that hasn't been done before!"

Imani laughed even harder at Earl's abusive comments about Ben's livelihood, doubling over as Ben frowned. She became silent when Ben raised his hand and sent it flying with a set destination, her prominent posterior. "Ben!" Imani shouted as she flinched and glanced over at Earl, who also gave Ben a protestive look. "He's not funny, baby," Ben said sternly, pointing a finger at Earl. "He's hilarious! In fact, you two should have your own show or something because you guys have me in tears over here!" With a groan, Ben gave up, deciding to end his trading of barbs with Earl for the time being.

"Alright, kids. Comedy hour is over," Ben announced as Imani smirked, amused with Ben's implicit surrender. "Let's go down to the studio, E! Are you coming with us, baby?" Ben inquired, turning to Imani. "I'm kind of tired, actually," Imani said, yawning. "I didn't exactly have time to rest after 'Twister', so I'm going to go up and take a nap," Imani said, making sure to use air quotes when she got to Ben's terminology. "Fair enough!" Ben puffed out his chest and put his hands on his hips proudly, pleased not only with his "Twister" performance, but with the repeated usage of the expression. Imani rolled her eyes and then turned to address Earl, who'd been stealthily admiring her, but she didn't seem to notice. "It was nice to meet you, Earl!" Imani extended her hand to him, which Earl readily met with his own.

Her hands are so soft, like silk.

"If I don't wake up before you leave, I hope that you randomly drop by Ben's more often! I'll try to be around more so that I can have a front-row seat to the show!" With that, Imani made her ways up the stairs, and Earl had to actively avert his gaze as to not make his appreciative inspection of her anatomical assets too flagrant. When she disappeared, Ben gave Earl a wink, his admiration markedly less inconspicuous.

"Girl is sexy, isn't she?" Ben put a hand on the table next to him and crossed one leg with the other so that his stance was only slightly prideful of his new girlfriend. *"Sexy" is an insult to her. You should be ashamed, Earl. Saniya definitely would be.* "She's

102

cool." Earl shrugged while maintaining a blank expression, causing Ben's eyes to narrow with incredulity. "It's okay to admit that I got a good one, E! I know that you've been faithful to your one and only, but come on! You don't think she's cute?"

Yes.

"I think that you should focus on something other than women for five minutes." The deflection appeared to do its part as Ben threw his hands up in defeat. "Fine, fine, you win. I'll be good. Let's take this conversation down to the basement!"

With Ben leading the charge, the two quickly found themselves back into the technological den that was Ben's recording studio. Ben took his seat in the chrome swivel chair in front of the large console, spinning around happily as Earl sat in the other, less ornate chair next to him. "So, Big E, what's up? I'm all ears!" Ben began to toy with some dials on the large console as Earl took a deep breath, ready to recount the "highlights" of his work day. "Well, one of the employees I actually liked left the job today, so that wasn't too great."

Ben looked over at Earl with an earnest look of commiseration as if he were playing the role of his therapist. "Then, at the end of my shift, one of the customers I absolutely detest comes in and asks for a sandwich because that's how great my luck is. I cut the meat and cheese for him, which he makes sure is exactly how he wants it, and then when I go to make the goddamn sandwich, he starts complaining about me needing to change my gloves!" Ben wasn't quite the encouraging listener that Saniya would've been as he turned in his chair in contemplation, hearing Earl's recitation of his work-related woes.

"Soooo... I'm not trying to be an asshole, but isn't that part of your job? You make sandwiches for people, I don't see the issue." *Son of a bitch.*

"It was the way he approached the counter and his general attitude," Earl hissed, his teeth almost gritting together. "He was impatient and disrespectful. To top it off, one of my managers came out, and suddenly, he's happy! She took over, told me to go home, and then I was so annoyed that I forgot to go home and change before coming here." Earl sighed, noting that Ben didn't seem to react as he'd been expected to.

"I'm sorry to put this on you, Ben. I'd have went over to Saniya's and told her about it, but she's busy trying to catch up on schoolwork, so... yeah."
Earl scratched his arm and looked away, now acutely aware of how much he'd been whining. After hearing himself articulate it out loud, he realized that worse things could be happening than being a little upset over his job. "No problem, man! You know I'm always here for you when you need it, even if it's just to vent! Do you mind if I ask you something though?"
"Sure." "I get that sometimes a job can get on your nerves—"

How the fuck would you know? You haven't had a real job since you quit that retail place a few months after we graduated to become an…
"internet personality."

"—but if it's such a pain in the ass, why not quit?"

Earl tilted his head at Ben's question as if it were simultaneously bewildering and utterly stupid.

"…It pays much better than most entry-level jobs. Plus, at two and a half years, I've at least gotten a few raises to validate myself staying there."   "Yeah, but you're miserable." *Accurate. Also, not entirely work-exclusive.* "It's the only way I can support myself. Without that job, I can't pay Charlotte her rent, and I can't pay my car insurance. I'll be financially crippled."

When Earl finally made eye contact with Ben, he saw something that he'd seen very often from Saniya, from his fellow support group members, even from Charlotte on occasion. *Pity. Story of your life. An assemblage of shattered glass that occasionally tricks itself into thinking it'll ever become whole again.* After the silence that followed, Earl's eyes shifted to the live room that they were sitting in front of. He observed the instruments, saw the microphone directly at the center of the area and his gaze lingered, remembering that he felt *something* when Ben had him record a few lines for fun the other day. It wasn't the usual lineup of adverse emotions that involved suppressed anger, embitterment or put him into a deep, depressive funk either; it was something new, something that he'd only recognized at one other time in recent memory.

When you first started writing.

It was silly, almost insane, but as Earl tried to dismiss the thought, a familiar voice rang throughout his mind. *Just do something to keep yourself occupied. Inspiration can come from the most unlikely of places.* Earl smirked as he recalled Dr. Tommen's sagacious advice, and he turned his head to Ben, who'd been watching Earl curiously.

"…I can't believe that I'm going to say this, but you were kind of right when you said that the studio has a cathartic effect." "Did I say that?" "Not word-for-word, but you know what I mean," Earl said as he stood up, his eyes focused on the microphone. "I think I want to record something. Not for exposure, obviously, but you know… just to get the creativity flowing since I haven't written anything since I've been querying." Ben's eyes lit up, astounded by Earl's request. His head excitedly went from Earl, to the live room, and then back to Earl. "Are you serious?!"

"Alright, don't make me reconsider it," Earl stated, causing Ben to wave a hand over his face to match Earl's seriousness. "Gotcha. Do you want a beat or anything, or do you want to go in there and freestyle a little like last time?" Earl's eyes scanned the machines in Ben's control room, ruminating on his choices. "Ah, fuck it, may as well put a beat on it. It might help me come up with something to say." Ben's enjoyment was palpable as he let out an enthusiastic hoot, much to Earl's dismay. "Now, this doesn't mean that I want to be a rapper or whatever it is that you think you can try to convince me to do. This is just for the hell of it."

Earl pointed an accusatory finger at Ben, who relayed that he understood with a thumbs-up.

"Speaking of, do you still have that recording from the other day? You didn't go behind my back and upload it anywhere, right?" "All I did was use it to see how much I could do with the sound-mixing, I promise. Nobody else has heard it."

"Not even Imani?" Earl asked.

"Nope, I'm a man of my word!" Ben insisted, crossing his index and middle finger together to symbolize his sincerity. "Would you like to hear some of the samples that I came up with out of that recording?" "No! I don't want to hear my own voice. Just put on a simple beat and let me have a minute to think in there." "You got it, dude!"

Earl walked into the live room and stood at the microphone, adjusting the pop filter as he recalled Ben's instructions from their previous session. "What kind of beat do you want?" Ben said, his voice crackling over the speaker system. "Something aggressive, I guess." Earl gave Ben an indecisive shrug, and Ben reached for his console, already apparently having something in mind. "Put on the headphones that are on the hook next to the microphone so that you can hear it."

Earl did as instructed, and a few moments later, the beat kicked in unexpectedly. It was loud, but not enough to deafen, and it reminded Earl of the days where he'd listen to old-school rap, back when he believed it had a purpose and clear message. He unknowingly began to bob his head to the beat, and as his mind cycled through potential rhymes, he looked up to see Ben's grinning face. Without needing Earl's verbal reprimand again, Ben saw Earl's narrowed eyes and grim expression, immediately spinning his chair around to allow his friend the privacy he'd needed.

Earl closed his eyes and channeled all the helpless frustration he'd felt at work. When he reopened them after mumbling through some practice rhymes, his face was alight with steely determination, and he could feel an electric surge unlike any he'd ever felt coursing throughout his body –
♪ Fat motherfucker wanting ham and swiss…

I'll be shocked if you can see your dick when you take a piss. My backs against the wall, it's time to heed the call – Of the words that flow from my maw because I'm gunning for it all. Forget what you thought you knew, discern the truth from the lies, watch a man be deified, my time is nigh, right before your eyes. ♪

Suddenly, a loud crash rang throughout the room, causing Earl to nearly jump out of his skin in shock. **"Oh, shit!"**

All Earl could see as he fell to the ground was a shadow dart out the cracked door of the live room. Confused, he looked around and saw the cymbals that had fallen from their stand, impacting the floor with an emphatic bang. Ben's hysterical cackling echoed throughout the live room for about two full minutes before he settled down enough to explain what had happened. "We forgot to close the basement door! Miles ran into the live room, but before I had a chance to do anything about it, he'd jumped onto the cymbals and scared the shit out of you! That was great! Oh, if only I had my phone ready!" Ben wiped a tear from one of his eyes as he looked back into the live room, and he could feel the heat of Earl's glare through the glass window separating the live room from Ben's control room. "Okay, okay. Let's just keep going, alright? You had a good flow, so finish it up."

To Ben's surprise, Earl didn't give him any backtalk or angrily storm out of the room. Earl got back up to his feet, readjusted his headphones and continued on as if nothing had happened.

Nobody's ever going to laugh at you again.

♪ I'm tired of lunchmeat, I'm tired of chump change, That 9 to 5 diligence, yet still broke, now ain't that strange? I just try and do the best I can to fucking maintain, but it's hard being trapped between my demons and my disjointed brain. Ambitions just out of my reach, but save your pity, please don't preach. Can't dissuade me, I'm fighting back, no slack, ahead of the claque, call it a knack. No more silent pain, no more moving in vain, it's all there for me to attain. This isn't a Shakespearean allegory; this is the dawn of a young king's story. ♪

Earl stood there, riding a high that he'd never imagined feeling. He could feel his heart beating in his chest, his breathing echoing in his ears, and he felt lighter than ever before. The world disappeared around him for a moment, but this time, it wasn't darkness that enveloped Earl. Even his unwanted intruder was glaringly silent. He hadn't realized that he'd walked out of the live room until the raucous applause made itself known. "That was amazing! No bullshit, dude, that was legitimately fucking fire!" Earl blinked absently at Ben before he fully returned to reality, and he immediately felt self-conscious, almost forgetting that Ben was there in the first place. "Thanks, I guess."

"Are you embarrassed?! You shouldn't be! Dude, do you know what I could do with that?! We—"

110

"No."

The powerful word reverberated throughout the entire basement as Earl made himself abundantly clear to Ben. "You can play with it to your heart's content, but don't you dare do anything reckless. I know you, and you need to be stopped now before you get any crazy ideas." Ben looked as though he was prepared to fight Earl back on his stance, but not wanting to push his luck, he decided to let it go.

"I'll respect your decision, sir. That being said, you still killed it in there." "It was just so I could relieve some stress, Ben. No more, no less."

Earl took out his phone, which had been muted for work earlier, and two things leapt out at him. The first was the starting sentence of another rejection from a literary agent, and the second was the amount of missed calls from Charlotte. Groaning, not bothering to call her back, Earl slid his phone back into his pocket and began to make his way up the stairs. Ben stated the obvious, though he knew from Earl's crestfallen disposition what had happened. "…Ms. Charlotte?" "Yeah."

A short-lived freedom. Reality strikes again.

Chapter 8

"I needed you, and you didn't come straight home after work. Whatever you were doing isn't more important than tending to what's here, where you lay your head." Earl hadn't gotten a full sentence out before Charlotte interrupted him, as she usually did. Charlotte glanced up at him for a quick second before going back to stuffing clothes in the washing machine. "I was with Ben for a little while, Charlotte. We were just talking." "Well, you can '*just talk*' to Randy. He's out in the backyard cutting the grass, he wanted to see you about something."

What does the druggie possibly want now?

Earl ignored Charlotte's snark, instead biting his tongue and choosing to walk to the patio, preparing himself to make the interaction with Randall as short as possible. He slid open the patio door and was hit with the smell of freshly-cut grass, inwardly hoping that the allergies he was susceptible to wouldn't occur. He took a few steps into the yard, with its old, leaning fence that had long-since needed to be replaced, the discolored toolshed at the back of the yard that Randall used every once in a while, and the dining area of Earl's youth that hadn't been occupied in ages.

You've always lived in a bubble, isolated from the world. You haven't explored half of the places in a twenty-five-mile radius of this house. You're under grandma's thumb, always have been, and now you have to take orders from a heroin addict who can't even keep a steady job for longer than a year. You shouldn't resent anyone but yourself. You're the useless one, you're the one that's a prisoner of your own routine.

"Hey, boy, over here!"

Randall turned the lawnmower off and gestured for Earl to come over to him. Suppressing a sigh, Earl strode over slowly, unmotivated to indulge Randall's urgent gesticulations. "So, look, boy, I need some more money. You think you can get me a twenty?" "I just gave you ten the other day. You have a full-time job, why do you need *my* money?"

Randall ran his tongue across the gaps in his mouth where a few of his teeth used to be. He chuckled to himself, almost in jest of Earl's question. "How about you just do what I ask and get me the money?" Earl could feel his fingernails digging into the palms of his hands as he balled his fists, keeping the ire he had for Randall contained.

You old, condescending piece of shit. No wonder Charlotte didn't want to marry you all those years ago. You're an irresponsible, disgusting waste of space, and the fact that Charlotte continues to allow you to stay here to spend our money and speak to me any way that you please makes no fucking sense. Some kind of father figure you turned out to be. I'd rather have either of my parents emerge from out of nowhere to take credit for raising me than have to look at that gold tooth, or your receding hairline, or smell the cigarette smoke on you ever again.

"Okay. I'll head over to the ATM machine because I don't have any cash on me." "Good. Hurry up now, I need that money in the next hour or so."

Probably for drugs.

Defeated, Earl turned his back to Randall, preparing to make the journey over to the nearest ATM, which was less than a ten-minute drive from the house. "I don't know what you're so pissy about, boy. It's not like that book of yours is going to be worth shit anyway. You've been out of school for how long and ain't even interested in college? Yeah, you may as well get used to that uniform because you're going to be serving up sandwiches for a long time."

Fuck you, fuck you, fuck you, fuckyou,fuckyoufuckyouFUCKYOUFUCKYOU— Earl slammed the patio door shut behind him as he snatched his keys from his pocket and tried to put the key in the keyhole to the front door, his hands shaking furiously. Charlotte looked away from her gossip show long enough to give Earl one final directive. "By the way, Earl, I need you to go to the supermarket. I want a few things for dinner.

Call me after you get finished, I should know what I want by then." "…Yes, ma'am." He swallowed the bile that threatened to rise from the bottom of his throat, wishing that he had the motivation to permanently leave the house it seemed like he'd never be able to separate himself from. He loved her, but Charlotte exhausted him to no end. If it wasn't the countless trivial errands, it was the fact that she was unwilling to listen to him or truly stand behind his dreams. They'd just had each other for the longest time, as the majority of the Veares family had turned their backs on both Charlotte and Earl years ago in the aftermath of the death of Charlotte's mother and the splitting of her estate. Despite being as fair as possible, Charlotte's brother and sister demanded more from her, which ended up hurting Charlotte immeasurably on top of the loss she'd suffered.

Earl was attuned to her fears despite her edge, knowing that Charlotte had lived a life where she had no choice but to be a little caustic and opinionated. She'd been hurt and betrayed by people who she was supposed to depend on the most. Earl heard stories about how Charlotte, out of her and her siblings, was the least liked by their mother. Earl also remembered how dementia gripped his great-grandmother during the latter stages of her life, and how taxing it was on both him and Charlotte before she ultimately passed, peacefully, in the company of her children.

Regardless of Charlotte single-handedly caring for her mother while her siblings jeered and spoke ill of her behind her back, they still ran her down for not doing enough. It was never enough. That, combined with Charlotte's abusive ex-husband and the racism she'd had to deal with growing up caused Earl to never wonder why Charlotte was the way she was. It also explained why she settled for Randall, a druggie who was, at the very least, a comparatively safer option, and handy around the house whenever something broke. Maybe Randall had been different at the beginning of their thirty-year relationship. Regardless, Earl found himself zoning out while he was driving, considering his options as it pertained to the unlikely possibility of him branching out on his own.

You're trapped. She needs you, and you need her. That bond in itself is wringing you for whatever dormant glimpses of hope you have left. You can't leave her with that drug-addled asshole, the guilt would eat you alive. However, staying there with her stresses you out and drives you closer to the precipice of your mental limits. Life is a cruel, hedonistic bitch that feeds off your misery and anguish, isn't she? The best thing about your mind is, ironically, the worst thing about it. Its awareness. Your arms are too short to grasp your aspirations, and the world will go on, indifferent to your agony. You weren't given a dream to obtain it, it's just another way for the powers that be to punish you until you decide to—

"Shut the fuck up."

Earl was getting fed up with his intruder, refusing to acknowledge him any longer. He desperately wished he'd taken his anti-depressants before he left the house, but it was too late now. His forced his mind to travel to his fantasies; his unobtainable, but happy reveries. He thought back to his dream, where he'd met his literary idol and was the creatively free, happy author that he was so certain he'd be. Instead of Saniya by his side, this time, it was Imani.

Imani.

In his latest daydream, he lived on a hill, raised above everyone else in his gated community, living in an extravagant manor befitting that of an accomplished A-list celebrity. He wakes up with a monogrammed robe on a hook next to his side of the lavish bed, and he looks over at Imani, who greets Earl with a seductive smirk. Before he gets to enjoy his morning proper, though, he throws on his robe and walks out to his balcony to smell the fresh air. He looks down on all his neighbors and waves at them, to which they reciprocate his bountiful, positive aura tenfold. There's no intruder, no pills, no struggling, none of the things that Earl had grown to detest. Earl could breathe. He could look forward to the day rather than wish he'd never have to see another one. He was free. And as he admired the view from his balcony, he heard Imani call to him, wanting him. He turns around and sees her, strategically covering herself with their bedsheet. She didn't show enough to entice Earl fully, but just enough to make his mouth water, to make him crave her.

He walks over to her, the sound of his expensive slippers clopping against their spotless marble floor, and he stops before his goddess. She puts a hand on his chest, having other ideas in mind for them. Grabbing him by his hand, she leads him to the room next to their bedroom. As they walk into what appears to be the shower room, beautifully patterned with the regalest walk-in shower, Imani turns the faucet, allowing the water to flow from the showerhead. Making sure to tie the thin bedsheet in a knot so that it doesn't fall before she's ready, she claps twice, which encourages the introduction of soft classical music. Earl's favorite. Whether it be Rossini, Mozart, Beethoven, any of the greats, it didn't matter to him. All he was transfixed on was her, how her body moved with the sway of the sheets, greatly complementing the curvatures of her physical form. She was almost like a present dying to be unwrapped, but he'd dare not ruin the sensual ritual his goddess created…

just for him.

She placed a hand in the water, making sure that it was to her liking. When she was satisfied with the temperature, she suddenly snatched off the bedsheet in one fast motion. Before Earl had known it, she'd hopped into the shower and beckoned him over, nonverbally requesting his presence. Earl, entranced, pulled at his bathrobe and allowed it to fall to the floor as Imani studied him, pleased with the view. This was the moment he'd wanted, just the two of them. He walked into the cascading water and beheld his goddess, hardened by her bare, alluring physique. There were no more secrets between the two as Imani walked through the water and wrapped her arms around Earl's neck. "Take me. Shroud me with nothing but your desire."

Earl could do nothing but nod as she held her body against his, feeling the fullness of his girth. She closed her eyes and leaned forward, wanting their lips to meet in wanton fervor. Earl followed suit, closing his eyes, wanting to be lost in her touch. Her breath caressed his ear as her body challenged his for carnal dominance. The loud blaring of a car horn caused his eyes to snap open and the realization that he'd drifted into oncoming traffic made him turn his steering wheel as hard as he could away from the car that was only inches away from colliding with him. With a loud screech, Earl skidded away from certain death at the last possible millisecond, but crashed head-on into a tree, causing the airbag in the old sedan to deploy and cushion Earl's head from bouncing off the steering wheel. Earl was shell-shocked, and his world went into slow motion as his nerves reached their peak of hysteria. Shaking, and with the broken horn blaring as loudly as possible, he fell out of the driver's seat and reached for his phone. Too shaken to assess the damage of his vehicle, he dialed a number and raised the phone to his ear, almost dropping it from how much he was quivering.

"Hi, E! How are you?"

He tried to speak in a calm, even tone, but eventually, the horror of what had transpired got the best of him and he began sobbing, uncontrollably. The world split into two, then three, and his ears began ringing, unable to hear his girlfriend's panicked concern. His head thumped, almost to the point where it felt like his brain wanted to leap out of his skull, and it took a few minutes before he was able to speak a coherent sentence to Saniya. "…Saniya, I need you. I just crashed my car. I think I totaled it. I need you to come as soon as possible, please."

--

As morning broke through the blinds of Saniya's apartment, Earl opened his eyes slowly. Cognizance returned to him after a dreamless night, and he'd wanted nothing more than to slink into the floor, to disappear. He mentally replayed yesterday's tragedy continuously knowing that he'd be required to go home and explain to Charlotte how he'd crashed his car. He peered over at Saniya next to him, who snored only slightly as she remained tethered to her dreams.

Charlotte's going to give you an earful, you already know that, right? Rather than whiplash and a few bruises, I know that you regret your little vehicular incident not being fatal because look at what you have to deal with now. No car, so now, you need to make sure those shoes are comfortable because you're going to be walking to work for the foreseeable future. But hey, what's a half-hour walk? Earl crawled out of Saniya's bed carefully, not wanting to wake her, and walked to the dresser on the left of the nightstand next to his side of the bed. He opened it, reaching into the drawer containing a few of his own clothes that he'd kept there in case he spent a few days with Saniya.

Grabbing a pair of underwear, a tank-top, pants and a shirt, he snuck to the bathroom, deciding that a shower may ease the anxiety that his car accident gave him. *What do you tell Dr. Tommen and friends next month? "Oh, I nearly died because I was fantasizing about a fictional life with my best friend's new girlfriend!" I'm sure you'll make his day when he tries to analyze that! Or, will you lie?*

Maybe never acknowledge it?

Staring blankly into the bathtub, Earl changed his

121

mind, desiring to take a bath for a change in lieu of a shower. *Why don't you just give in? You're a fuck-up. You weren't even worth the label of "has- been," you're a "never-was." Never-was a creative genius. Never-was a good grandson. Never- was a good friend. Never-was a good anything. It was better back when you had nothing going for you, at least you didn't fail horribly. You had the gall to pretend that you were someone worthwhile, an "artist." Now, your little heart is broken because you're another husk that's going to coast through life, unsatisfactorily. Enjoy your 9-5 and your "What Ifs" because that's all you have to look forward to.*

Earl plugged the drain of the tub and turned the faucet, letting the water begin its steady ascent. He rested the clothes he brought in with him on the left side of the sink, and he took his phone out and cycled through his apps, searching for his musical playlist. *Trying to drown me out? That always works. Go on, put on something nice. Play something jazzy, or maybe you're feeling the classical route? Operatic, maybe? Anything to convince yourself, I suppose.*

Earl looked through his playlist until he came across the particular song he'd wanted, Chopin's Nocturne in E-flat major, Op. 9, No. 2. Earl allowed himself to smirk sadly at the title of one of his favorite classical pieces, which had given him as much peace as anything could these days. He tapped the arrow next to the title, which caused the soothing opening notes of the piano-centric melody to play through the speaker of his phone. He turned the volume of his phone up as loud as he could, or as much as the admittedly cheap device would yield. Anything to dampen the discouraging noise inside of his head.

Earl set the phone down on the right side of the sink and began to disrobe, wincing occasionally as his chest had still been sore from the accident. When he was fully undressed and the water had rose to its desired level, he turned the faucet again, curtailing the continual stream of rushing water. He ran a hand against the surface of the water, which had almost been ice-cold to the touch. Earl needed something, anything, to compensate for the discernible emptiness of the fog that draped itself around him.

After drawing his hand back, he put one leg into the water, shivering as he waited for his body to adjust to the drop-in temperature, then the other leg followed behind it. He lowered himself into the water as his body gradually acclimated to the frigid conditions. The water stopped mid-way at his neck, and he leaned back, struggling to allow the music to whisk him away to anywhere that wasn't in the reality he'd found himself buried in.

You have a unique opportunity now.
Earl could feel the water bitterly nipping at his body, threatening to make it completely numb. He closed his eyes and began to wave his arms to Chopin's sweet harmonies as if he himself were the conductor directing a grand orchestra. As he pantomimed

holding a conductor's baton in his left hand, pressing his index and middle finger to his thumb, the first tear unexpectedly hit the water with a small plop. Earl took a shuddering breath as a second tear droplet emerged from his right eye, making a thin, watery trail down the side of his face. He choked back a sob as he did his best to ignore the past, to stop his mind from flashing back to the life that he felt as though he'd wasted. Despite his best efforts, managing to somehow dig

himself out of abject apathy and isolation for most of his childhood, he'd ended up feeling worse now than he ever had before. He wondered what trying to find a purpose achieved if all it meant was that instead of accepting his underachievement, he'd instead endeavored to feel as though he'd come so close to being fulfilled only to have it taken away from him.

You have the power, for once, to control something in your life. Don't be afraid. Welcome and embrace the darkness, the nothingness. Just try.

Earl let his body slide forward as he submerged the rest of his neck and head under the water, his vision capturing the undulating waves as the water rippled from his actions. The music he'd put on became distorted and muffled, almost otherworldly. Earl closed his eyes and let his tense body relax, initially overwhelmed with the prickly, brisk sensations that assaulted his face.

Breathe. Let yourself fade.

Earl opened his mouth, accepting the intruder's request. As he felt the water hit the back of his throat, an immediate, loud banging sound caused his body to shoot up from the water, startled by the noise. "E, I gotta use the bathroom!" Saniya yelled from the other side of the door as Earl began hacking, coughing up the water that had begun to choke him. "Are you okay in there?"

"Yeah," Earl assured in-between his almost violent coughing fit. "You surprised me, that's all!"

"Well, get out of there! I really have to go!"

Earl stood, got out of the tub and snatched out the plug at the bottom, causing the water to slowly funnel into the drain. He dried off with a towel on the rack across from the sink and put his new clothes on. Fully-dressed, he reached for his phone to turn his music off, but the vibrations of an incoming call sent the precariously placed phone tumbling over the edge of the sink and to the tiled floor of the bathroom. Cursing to himself, he picked his phone up, seeing a long crack from the top of his screen to the bottom. The crack nearly split the word "home" that shone in big letters on the screen into two, and Earl decided not to receive Charlotte, who he knew was the one behind the call. Saniya had called her once to inform her about the initial accident while Earl was getting evaluated by a doctor, then called again afterwards to tell Charlotte that he hadn't been severely injured when he had begged Saniya to let him stay at her place for the night. Regardless, he wasn't ready to have that conversation with Charlotte yet.

He opened the bathroom door, seeing the early-risen, but pleasant face of Saniya. "Good morning, E! How are you feeling?" "Fine. I'm a little sore, but I think that I'm still good for work."

"Actually, I just called your job up and told them that you weren't going to be there today because of the accident. You seemed… rattled last night, and I wanted you to have time to get yourself together." Earl did his best to maintain his composure upon hearing Saniya's news. He'd needed every cent that he could scrape together. Knowing that the Sub Shack wouldn't let him make the hours back up, he knew he was going to be in trouble, financially. He felt the urge to scream, aware that he was getting hit with a chain of inauspicious circumstances in such a short period of time. "I was going to let you be surprised later, but considering everything that's happened, you deserve to know that you have something nice coming up later today!" Saniya gushed, wearing a large smile.

"I've had this planned for a while, and today is the only day that it's going on! This evening, we're going

126

out, and I think you're really going to enjoy yourself! So, take the next few hours to just chill, and I promise you, it'll be worth it!" With that, Saniya sped past Earl and into the bathroom, closing the door behind her. Earl sighed deeply and held an exasperated hand against his forehead, more concerned about his personal well-being than with whatever Saniya had planned for him.

Chapter 9

Saniya's car weaved effortlessly throughout traffic as she gave her wary boyfriend the occasional animated glance, eager to reach their destination. Earl forced a smile every time she looked his way, otherwise, he'd direct his attention towards the passenger-side window, ruminating to himself.

What model is this again, 2017? To think, all it took for her to get set up like this was for her mother to get smacked on the ass by a pervert. "Do well in school and you can have whatever you want!" Pampered. Meanwhile, you have to depend on her to take you places. You're an albatross for the poor girl, dead weight. She's trying to do something to cheer you up, and here you are, moping and pouting. Let's not mention the reason why you crashed your car like an idiot in the first place. "Where are we going, Sans?" Earl asked, feeling guilty over his ingratitude towards Saniya's efforts. "We're almost there, baby! We're about five minutes away!"

Earl didn't recognize the path that Saniya was taking to get to wherever she was going, so he couldn't even begin to have guessed where they were headed. I'm sorry about the past few months, E. I know that I've been extremely busy, but I hope that this will make

128

up for it a little! Don't worry, the semester is going to
end soon, and then we'll have most of the summer to
hang out and... enjoy each other." Saniya winked at
Earl and then redirected her attention back to the
road, stopping at a red light.

She was always so adorable.

*Maybe it's the freckles that cinch it, but she's always
been cute, smart and driven. She's all the things that
you wish you were, or if you are, it's not enough to
make a difference.*

Earl watched her drive, analyzing her face. It wasn't
the sex, it wasn't how cute she was, it was the small
things that others forget to admire about their
significant others that he loved about Saniya the most.
The looks of agitation that would last for a fraction of
a second when someone would cut her off, the small
huffs of frustration when someone didn't use their
turn signals, Saniya was always about order and
cleanliness. "Feng shui is underrated. I think people
are so awful sometimes because their living spaces
are in such a state of misalignment," Earl recalled her
saying to him once. He remembered when she first
moved into her apartment; she'd spent hours
rearranging things and refused his help whenever he
asked or tried to assist. "If you start messing with
things, you'll throw the energies off. It has to be me.
All he could do was laugh and let Saniya do what she
wanted. Those were the types of memories that Earl

had cherished above all others. He may have had his own host of issues to deal with, but Saniya was the purest thing that he had going for him, and he knew it. Part of the reason that Saniya working all the time frustrated him so much was because he wanted nothing more than to be with her, and her ambitions stood in direct conflict with that wish.

Selfish fuck.

"Are you alright, E? You look like a fat kid that just spotted a bakery." "It's nothing. I was thinking about you, that's all." Saniya let out an exaggerated "Aww" while smirking at Earl, who rolled his eyes sarcastically in response. "What, was I face-down and ass-up while you were over there daydreaming?" Earl recoiled, verifiably stunned by Saniya's assessment of his captivation for her. "Do you think I'm that disgusting and depraved?!" The brief expression that Saniya directed at him, puckered lips and raised eyebrows, told Earl all that he needed to know.

"No!" he maintained. "I was thinking about the time when you first moved into your apartment. Remember your obsession with 'optimizing energies'?" "First of all, that book helped me decorate the apartment," Saniya declared, pointing an accusing finger at Earl while he chortled. "Secondly, you know I need to change it up every couple of months, or else the auras in the apartment are thrown off! Plus, it helps to put me in the mood to paint!" Earl quickly redirected the conversation, an image of his disheveled mess of a bedroom suddenly entering his mind. "Have you been working on anything lately?"

"Ah, just some sketches. I haven't gotten back to the canvas in a while because I'm learning some new techniques, but trust me, when I get that brush back in my hand, I'll be ready to go! Speaking of, I still need to design a few book covers for you! You think a publisher would force you to use one of their illustrators? If not, we can be a legit force to be reckoned with! I catch their attention, and you keep their eyes glued from page-to-page with your beautiful story!"

Earl's smile faded as he contemplated the state of his literary endeavors. The well had went bone-dry in terms of sending out any more queries. Some agencies responded faster than others, but Earl's confidence in his work had all but depleted. Saniya sensed Earl's discomfort and spoke, trying to clarify her stance. "E, it's going to be alright, I promise you. Do you know how long it took some of the most popular authors to finally get their work recognized? I know that you worked hard on it. I believe, as unbiased an opinion as I can have, that you have a story that needs to be told. But, look, even if an agent won't go for it, I know that you mentioned self-publishing a few times. Why not look into that? It isn't ideal, but it might be the best course of action."

She doesn't get it. Doing that guarantees that you'll be lost in the shuffle, and you've explained that before. Earl ignored the intruder, knowing that Saniya meant no harm in bringing up his book.

"We'll see."

Saniya made a left turn, and her eyes lit up. Earl followed her gaze, seeing nothing but balloons and displays in front of a store. As they got closer, Earl saw the name on one of the displays as they pulled into a parking spot: Axlam Suleman.

"Surprise, baby!" Saniya exclaimed, spreading her arms triumphantly as far as the space in her car allowed. "I've been paying attention when you've talked about how amazing her writing is and how much she's inspired you! The initial plan was just to buy you a copy of 'The Desperate Sails of Somalia,' but as luck would have it, homegirl's in town for a book signing! I saw it about a month ago and knew that I had to capitalize on it!" Earl's jaw dropped as he stared at the bookstore, which he now recognized as Books 'N Bunches, a place he hadn't been to in quite some time. He turned his head to Saniya, who nodded enthusiastically, then turned back to the store. Without a word, he unbuckled his seatbelt and got out of the car to scrutinize further. As he walked up to one of the displays, he saw one of the most beautiful covers to any book he'd ever seen.

The illustration portrayed dusk, which gave the sky a crisp, organic gradient of yellow and purple. The title, "The Desperate Sails of Somalia," was adorned in a way that it didn't eclipse the aesthetic of the sky, simultaneously touting a font that gripped Earl the second he saw it. Right below the title was a big, ominous ship that was mostly black, but had a muddy ring of maroon etched within it. The large sea vessel was heading straight for a smaller, less imposing ship that had obviously been constructed by a group of people who weren't exactly adept in shipbuilding.

At the helm of the small ship was a man with his back at the strong gust of wind whipping against him. He stood tall, undaunted, as his comparatively lesser ship threatened to face off against the behemoth eclipsing it. The sea below the two ships carried unpredictable, dangerous waves that were subtly tinted with dark purple to go with the color scheme of the novel. Earl stared longingly at the depiction before him, mesmerized.

It's... beautiful. The font, the usage of purple and yellow together, everything about this just... pops. Your wildest dreams couldn't come up with something this elegant, and you claim to be some literary prodigy.

"As an aspiring artist, I have to admit, whoever illustrated this book knew what they were doing. Purple and yellow make great complements to one another, and I know that you love purple, so it must be especially attractive to you." Saniya had joined Earl, standing next to him as his eyes studied every minute detail, which were far from scarce.

"Let's go in before more people show up! I didn't realize how popular Axlam was!"

Earl noticed the amount of people chattering just outside of the shop, all there for Axlam. Looking over at the other set of doors leading into the building was the official meet-and-greet poster for Axlam with her face front-and-center. Before Earl could fully ponder the moment, Saniya grabbed his arm and led him into Book 'N Bunches.

The seven-figure book deal, the immediate selling of movie rights, and two more books in the trilogy?

The girl has it all.

Once inside, Saniya directed Earl to the front desk where racks of Axlam's magnum opus stood behind the pleasant cashier. Earl tuned the ensuing interaction out as Saniya bought him a copy of the book. *Oh, sweet irony. I bet this must sting for you, the entire event. Don't feel too bad; she went to school specifically to ply a trade in writing. Meanwhile, you snatched an idea from watching a show late one night, and you thought that because you're good at being a smart-ass that somehow, it'd translate into being a good novelist. She was bred for a career in literature, and you were bred to finance her natural talents over your own supposed ones.* "—unboxing video?" "…What?" Earl blurted out with an absent blink, finally acknowledging Saniya.

"Do you remember the time I caught you crying when you watched Axlam's unboxing video? That'll be you one day!" Saniya iterated, using her middle finger to pluck Earl at the center of his forehead. "Don't go off in that daze you like retreating to. I just got you a cool book!"

That was the first time that Earl had heard of Axlam Suleman. It was a month before the official release of her book and the universal acclaim that accompanied it. Earl saw the video of Axlam opening a package and seeing the first complete, final version of her book. The second that her mind caught up with what she held in her hands, she burst into tears. Earl couldn't help himself, bawling his eyes out alongside her. Having sent out his first round of queries, something about Axlam's raw emotion had moved him. Optimistic then, he'd hoped that he would join her in becoming one of the pioneers of a new wave of young, black authors who defied the general perception of their ethnicity with their stories of hardship and pain, but ultimately, success and fulfillment.

Instead, Axlam stood at the top of the mountain alone, and Earl was less than a blip on the radar.

A feeling of claustrophobia overcame Earl as he looked around and realized that he and Saniya were packed into a big, expansive room with a bunch of other people, all holding copies of "The Desperate Sails of Somalia." He hadn't noticed his own copy in his hand until he felt his fingers digging into it.

He felt it, the volcanic anticipation that was about to unleash itself amongst the crowd. His eyes fell to the front of the room which featured a bigger version of Axlam's book cover hanging above the yellow-and-purple themed table, almost reminiscent to a leader of a country preparing to address their people. Either side of the table featured more merchandise than Earl could identify from his position. There were lockets, watches, clothes, necklaces, everything had been painstakingly arranged for Axlam. "I didn't think I'd be as into this as I am, but I'm having an amazing time, baby!" Saniya hooked one of her arms with Earl's and rested her head on his shoulder, swept up in the buzz of the event.

Earl, on the other hand, remained trapped in a mixture of disbelief and amazement. Even the audience contained an eclectic potpourri of fans: Young, old, black, white, all ethnicities and ages in-between. "I remember when one of the agents that rejected me about two months ago sent me a list of recommendations to encourage me to improve the beginning of my book. You can probably guess what one of the titles were. I don't think I ever told you about that."

Saniya looked at Earl with slight confusion, letting what he said bounce around in her head before responding. "...The first actual sentence you've spoken since we got here, and you want to focus on your past rejections? I thought you'd be happy to attend Axlam's signing; this was supposed to motivate you and reignite that passion to pursue your dreams of becoming an author!"

"I'm grateful! I'm just... overwhelmed. It's kind of like an out-of-body experience for me, Sans. Like I'm living in someone else's dreams."

And coveting them.

"I understand. It is unlike anything I've personally attended before too, honestly." As if a dam had suddenly broke, the applause and cheering of the antsy crowd erupted as everyone seated rose to their feet. Axlam emerged from behind one of the bookshelves at the back of the room and froze at the fervor of the people in attendance. Earl had admittedly become star-struck himself at the appearance of the young author; her hazelnut complexion, slightly darker than his, her regal hairstyle that had started as braids and then cascaded into a waterfall of raven locks that favored the right side of her head. Her dress had been unlike anything Earl had remotely been familiar with, being long and thin with a silk-like texture. Going with the color scheme of the event, the dress was mostly purple with yellow floral patterns running down its left side. Axlam had somehow mastered a combination of oozing understated sex appeal and overt nobility, making herself stand-out amongst anyone else.

Axlam dropped to her knees and took off her thick, yellow-rimmed glasses while rubbing her eyes. Trying and failing to keep it together, Axlam succumbed to tears, covering her face as much as possible. *Theatrical.*

Earl couldn't help himself, recalling the unboxing video Axlam had posted online, and a few silent tears broke through his veneer of awestruck astonishment. After a few moments, Axlam rose to her feet, straightened out her dress and someone from the front of the crowd held out a tissue, which she walked over and accepted. She wiped her eyes and blew her nose gingerly before discarding the tissue into a wastebasket next to her table. She positioned herself at the head of her table and took a few deep breaths as the crowd began to calm down and stabilize. Her hand reached for the microphone that one of the event organizers handed over to her, and they shared a few, inaudible words before the nondescript employee walked away, making sure that Axlam was alright.

"Okay, I know that nobody here paid to see a writer cry in front of them, and if you did, then clearly, you have some really specific... interests that I don't think

I can help you with." The audience laughed as Axlam blinked a few times, making sure that she'd gotten everything out of her system and wasn't susceptible to another deluge of emotion. "It's weird because even though this is my fourth time doing this, it still doesn't get any less incredible. Introductions first, my name is Axlam Suleman, and I'm the author of 'The Desperate Sails of Somalia.'"

You can't hope to beat that kind of response. Everyone loves her, including Saniya. She just has that intangibility that comes only a few times in a generation. "Seriously, you guys are the best fans that a girl could ask for. But, let me explain myself in case some of you out there are wondering why I'm dressed like this." Axlam gestured to herself, going as far as to playfully wriggle her glasses.

"It ties into the book, so let me set the stage a little before I get into it. So, 'The Desperate Sails of Somalia' is based on actual Somali customs and culture. My parents, who are natives to Somalia, eventually immigrated to America where they lived in Rhode Island, where I was born! During the tail-end of college while I was getting my degree in English, my parents decided that I needed to become more attuned to my cultural roots. We spent a summer in Somalia, and it changed my life. I got to learn so many cool things about the different tribes and groups, the cultural diversity of the region, it was a humbling experience.

Coming back here, I realized that people have certain biases about Somalia and its people that rubbed me the wrong way, so I had the idea of a story where I'd not only open people's eyes, but take them on a fun journey in the process! No, they aren't all poor, illiterate pirates. The Somali have a lot of amazing contributions that you wouldn't begin to believe. Take my dress, for example!"

Axlam spun around, showing off the elegance of the unique dress that she wore. "The dress I'm wearing is called a 'dirac', which is what most of the young Somali women wear. It typically comes in cotton or polyester, but there are also a bunch of other cool accoutrements and styles to it. Honestly, it's mostly worn at weddings or religious celebrations, but it's also worn casually with certain variants. It helps that it's extremely stylish too!" *She has a natural charisma that doesn't need to be forced, whereas the best you have is your sarcasm, which I'm sure would be welcome and not tiring after a while.*

"I had the idea of dressing up as a pirate, but I didn't want anyone to think that I was out here representing Mr. Edward Teach and his gang of misfits. I definitely don't want people to assume I've sided with the enemy." Axlam began to lean against the table while she spoke, indicating that she'd become more and more comfortable. Earl, however, nervously scratched the back of his neck and his leg twitched as he kept shifting in his seat.

"So, now, we can get into the book properly! Basically, my story is about Troy Givens, who starts out as this cocky, conceited guy who only cares about himself and frequently uses his friends and family to get by. His college professor, Alexander Langdon, who teaches classes based on the many different idiosyncrasies of the African-American culture, gets tired of the complacency and indifference of his students. He feels as though they don't truly appreciate their history, and offers to take them to Somalia for a month over the summer as an academic study of sorts.

Well, Troy acts up, taking the culture lightly and making fun of their customs. That's when he comes across a member of the Yibir, a division of the Somali who were alleged practitioners of magic. It turns out that Troy barks up the wrong tree when trying to be condescending and dismissive of the Yibir's capabilities, and he's put into a coma that sends him back in time to Somalia at the end of the 17th century. In a dream that he has while trying to navigate and survive amongst the foreign, treacherous landscape, the Yibir informs Troy that he has to somehow defeat one of the world's most dangerous pirates if he wants to ever come back to his world, and that, of course, is Blackbeard."

"...E, is this secretly one of the best books ever? That sounds so cool!" Saniya whispered to Earl, who smiled in response, but as soon as Saniya focused on

Axlam again, Earl's smile transformed into something resembling contempt. "Troy, after some difficult situations, finally comes across a sympathetic group that's willing to take him in, and he learns that Africa is going through multiple political changes. Unfortunately, this means that most regions, especially Somalia, have descended into a state of anarchy with many of the tribes, big and small, having different ideas of leadership. Meanwhile, America and Europe, having a tentative alliance, wants to drain Africa of its people, its identity and its resources.

Somalia, as it turns out, ends up having a lot of rare, precious resources due to its placement at the Horn of Africa. The Europeans find out about it and assemble a naval fleet, with Edward Teach at the forefront, to go over to Somalia and bring back as many slaves and resources as possible. Edward Teach, now young and ambitious, sees the opportunity as a chance to establish himself amongst the myriad of pirates terrorizing the waters. You get to see the dichotomy of Teach's transformation into Blackbeard, essentially, and Troy's journey of humbling himself and helping to unite Somalia, and in a larger sense, Africa, before it's too late."

Applause broke out again amongst the crowd as Axlam beamed, proud of her accomplishments.

It should've been you.

Axlam continued, talking about the vision and scope of her trilogy, the audience doting on her every word. The longer she spoke, the more Earl seethed in silence, fidgeting in his seat until finally, it was time for Axlam to start signing copies of her book. As they'd been in the middle of the crowd, it took a while for Saniya and Earl to make their way to the front of the queue. Then, Earl found himself face-to-face with Axlam. "Hi!" Saniya greeted Axlam as Earl stood there with his best stone-faced expression. "My boyfriend Earl and I loved hearing you speak! I came here wanting to surprise him, but honestly, I think I'll need to get a copy for myself!" "No problem, here you go!" Axlam said, taking a hardcover copy from the stack at the end of her table and opening it to the inside cover.

"Usually, they don't like it when I just hand books over, but it can be a secret between girls! You didn't even tell me your name!" Saniya was caught off-guard by Axlam's generosity and took a second to regain her poise. "I'm Saniya, that's S-A-N—"

You're up next. Bite the bullet and do what you have to do. Axlam finished jotting down her signature as she turned to Earl, who handed over his copy of the book for her to sign.

"You'll have to forgive my boyfriend, he's a bit of an admirer of yours. He's trying to break into the

143

novelist game too!" "Oh!" Axlam exclaimed, pleased to hear about another potential up-and-comer. "How's that been going?" "It's finished, but I haven't heard anything back from any agents yet." Earl's lack of enthusiasm was prominent in his voice as Axlam looked up after signing Earl's copy, sympathy lining her face.

"Trust me, I've been where you're at now. I actually had a manuscript written up before 'The Desperate Sails of Somalia' that agents unanimously agreed was nowhere near ready for publication. I shelved it, wondering if I was ready to be an author or if the field itself was for me or not. It was during that time of self-doubt where I'd spent my years in college trying to perfect the art of storytelling and creative writing, yet coming up short, that I went to Somalia and everything just… clicked for me.

I hate to sound like a self-help book or motivational speaker, but honestly, you have to stick with it and be willing to take the criticism that you're going to get to improve yourself and your work. Never take it personally as an attempt to dissuade or demoralize your efforts. Keep at it, Earl, and if your heart is into it, it'll pay off."

Axlam handed Earl's book back to him with a sincere smile, and all Earl could do was mimic the expression back to her.

"Thanks. I'll keep that in mind."

Saniya and Earl left the event shortly afterwards, and on the way back to the car, Earl checked his phone, still sporting the long crack in the screen from when it fell earlier. It indicated five more missed calls from Charlotte and one message from Ben. Ignoring Charlotte, Earl tapped on the message from Ben, opening it up for him to read.

"You're invited down to my parents' for dinner later at around 6! They haven't seen you in a while, so it would be cool if you could swing through! I also have some insanely good news, dude!"

Earl realized that the message had been sent over two hours ago, and he checked the time to see that it was currently 6:15. He opened the passenger-side door of Saniya's car and got in, then Saniya plopped down in the driver's seat and sighed. She revved up the engine, backed out of the parking space and began the drive back to her apartment, refusing to make eye contact with Earl until he directly addressed her.

"What's wrong?"

"I don't understand why you had to act like that in there, E," Saniya said after a minute of silence, clearly expelling a build-up of frustration. "I thought after totaling your car yesterday that now, more than ever, you needed something to go right, and I feel like you didn't appreciate any of it. You embarrassed me in front of Axlam by being standoffish when all she tried to do was give you sound advice." *Let her know how you really feel, don't be a coward.*

"I'm sorry, Sans. I guess that after everything that happened with my car, I wasn't in the mood for anything like today. It wasn't you, baby, I love you and appreciate everything that you did for me. I'm just... disoriented lately, that's all."

Pussy.

"Okay, E. I get it. I think we just need to make some time for us. The schoolwork is letting up a little, so we should be able to spend more time together starting at the end of the week." "That's good, baby," Earl remarked, happy to have defused the situation. "Oh, do you mind dropping me off at Ben's parents' house? He invited me over for dinner, and apparently, he has something important to tell me." Earl didn't bother to look at Saniya, already sensing the eyeroll. After a few seconds of silence, Saniya acquiesced, but not without shaking her head in disapproval first.

"Fine. Do you need me to pick you up afterwards?" "Could you, please? I really don't want him to try and rope me into something ridiculous tonight."

"You don't have to go along with what he says, E, assert yourself. Should've told him to fuck off years ago." Earl didn't say another word, knowing that

146

Saniya was one sentence away from exploding. On the rare instances when Saniya got angry, it was a miserable time for whomever was caught in her maelstrom of rage. They rode in silence for the remainder of the way, and Earl promised himself that he'd not only make it up to her somehow, but he'd be a better boyfriend, easing her stress instead of adding to it.

Chapter 10

Saniya peeled away into the dusk of the evening, too agitated to bid her lover any semblance of farewell. Earl had turned around to apologize, wanting to make amends, but it was clear that Saniya needed some space. He sighed as he allowed himself a moment of serenity, staring up into the sky as the light purples mixed with the bold oranges of an encroaching twilight. "Dude, what are you standing out there for?!" a familiar voice yelled out as Earl closed his eyes and drew out an exhale, unable to enjoy the view hovering above him. "I've been waiting for half an hour! You're lucky that my parents just set the table or else you wouldn't have eaten!"

Earl turned to see his friend wearing shorts and a white t-shirt, the standard fare for Ben. Somehow, this stayed consistent even throughout the colder seasons, with Ben citing that he was immune to nature's frigidity. "Alright, alright! I'm here, Ben. So, what's this alleged good news that's gotten you so excited?" "After dinner, Big E! Right now, let's get something to eat! My dad made macaroni salad, baked chicken, spinach and the garlic mashed potatoes that he knows how to hook up!"

Ben practically snatched Earl into the house as Earl stepped within his arm's reach, closing the door gently behind them. "Earl? Come on in, let us see you! It's been too long!"

Earl followed the wonderful smell, his stomach howling as soon as the savory aroma hit his nose. Mr. Wiggins, Ben's father, was an accomplished chef who Earl had known to be unparalleled when it came to home-cooking. He'd been reminded of the first time that he was invited over to Ben's house while they were still in high school together, and Earl admitted that he was apprehensive over eating food that wasn't from home, despite the fact that Charlotte cooked maybe twice out of the year consistently. Ben, however, made sure that Earl's ignorance was summarily corrected.

Earl wandered into the dining room, which was more lavish than he'd remembered since his last visit. A chandelier gracefully hung above the dinner table, and two new, sleek oil paintings welcomed fresh faces at either end of the room. It was no wonder that Ben's townhouse had a similar, but not as refined, mien of affluence to it, even before he became a prominent internet persona. "Hey, Earl! How have you been?" Before he'd had a chance to respond, Ben's mother already had her arms wrapped around him, her golden hair almost getting into Earl's open mouth. "You look so good! We haven't seen you in months!"

"Yeah, I'm really sorry about that." Earl apologized to the slightly shorter woman with the light-blue eyes and the smile that hadn't lost a beat in its vigor. "I've been working on… a few things." "That's wonderful! Keeping yourself busy is one of the surefire ways to make sure that you keep your mind healthy and sharp! Oh, how's Charlotte?" Earl hesitated, feeling a surge of guilt over not contacting Charlotte and letting her know that he was okay.

"She's alright. Same old, same old. She does what she can to keep everything in check."

You're a great conversationalist.
Keep it short, sweet and vague.

"Earl! About time you poked your head from out of the brush!" A hand clapped Earl on his shoulder from behind, causing him to jump. Once he spun around, he was only a few inches away from the urbane visage of Ben's father. Or, he would've been, if Mr. Wiggins wasn't so statuesque. "Sit down, please, I'm about to bring out the food! There will be plenty of time for everyone to chat and catch up over a piping-hot delicious meal! I'll go call Maddie down, and then everyone will be accounted for!"
Mr. Wiggins walked out of the room, and a few seconds later, his voice rang throughout the house. *"Maddie! Come on down, dinner's ready! Stop hiding*

150

out in that room, we've got guests!"

Earl's eyebrows furrowed in confusion as he sat down at the table with Ben seated diagonally from him. Ben's mother sat at one of the two ends of the table, facing the spot designated for the head of the household, the placement of which Earl assumed would soon be filled by Mr. Wiggins.

"Guests?"

He'd meant it to be an internal musing, but the word flew from his lips without warning. "Of course! Ben didn't tell you I was coming?"

Fuck.

The clip-clopping of heels to the smooth hardwood of the Wiggins' dining room denoted the entrance of Imani, who emerged from the hallway directly behind Ben. She had been quite a few feet away from Earl, but he could still somehow smell the sweet scent of whatever perfume that she had on. "I just wish that Ben had told me not to dress up for this because I feel as though I *definitely* overdid it. I can be a bit of a try-hard, especially when it comes to first impressions." Earl desperately tried to deter his eyesight away from Imani, who'd worn a short-sleeved dress that left almost nothing to the imagination. The midnight-blue dress came up past her knees and ended at the middle of her thighs. It had a deep neckline that proudly showed off the top of her breasts and hugged her waist tightly, teasing the immaculate figure beneath. *There are a lot of eyes in here. Are you sure that now is the time to salivate over that olive-toned goddess?* He'd have told his intruder off if he wasn't so sure that he would be labeled as insane in the eyes of everyone at the table.

"How have you been, Earl?" Earl decided to focus on Imani's eyes and nothing else as he gulped quietly before answering her question. "I've been fine. Nothing too substantial has happened over the last few days."

Disregarding the car accident that you didn't bother to tell Ben about, the fight with your girlfriend and the fact that you tried to kill yourself, yeah, everything's been fantastic!

"How about yourself?"

"The usual; moderating my social media pages, trying to get my modeling stuff around. The good thing about Ben is that he has a little more of a following than I do, so I've been using him to bring up my numbers a little!" Ben gave her a mischievous glance but realized his mother was sitting on his right, so he decided against "disciplining" Imani as she took the seat to his left, directly opposite of Earl. "Really funny. Earl is bad enough with his dry sense of humor, but I don't need you being a smart-ass too."

152

"Ben! Not at the dinner table!"

"…Sorry," Ben mumbled at his disapproving mother, causing Imani to give Earl a sly wink, as if the two were in collusion. Earl offered her a small nod of acknowledgement before looking downwards at the empty plate in front of him. He fidgeted with the utensils at either side of the plate while Imani and Ben continued to playfully annoy one another, almost wishing that he hadn't shown up. "The wait is over, and dinner is served!" Ben's father began to bring out trays full of food while everyone made sounds of

gratitude at the presentation and aroma of Mr. Wiggins' cooking. When he brought out the final piece of the feast, saving the baked chicken for last, a pale, young woman with short, black hair came sprinting into the dining room, breathing heavily as she entered. "Of course, Madison shows up at the last second to eat and then creep back to her room," Ben stated nonchalantly, causing the skinny girl with very angular facial features to roll her eyes. "Fuck you, Ben," Madison hissed, causing a horrific gasp to escape from their mother. "Madison! What is with you two tonight? Can't you see we have company?" Madison shot Imani an uninterested glance, but when her eyes shifted over to Earl, her grouchy disposition changed immediately.

"…Hi, Earl. It's been awhile," Madison whispered,

barely able to maintain eye contact with the object of her unrequited, unnoticed and inhibited affections. "Hey, Maddie. How are you?" "I'm cool. You?" "Eh, I can't complain."

Madison slunk over to the only available seat left at the table, directly next to Earl, as Ben's father went about portioning food over to everyone, amused by the antics at the table.

"Hi, I'm Imani!"

Madison regained herself long enough to tersely answer Imani's overly-enthusiastic tone. "Yeah, I'm sure you'll be around long. To your credit though, not a lot of you make it this far, so congratulations." If Earl hadn't liked Ben, he'd have guffawed right then and there. Earl poked fun at Ben's long list of girlfriends from time to time, but he always did it in good humor. Madison, despite her young age, reminded Earl of himself, but without a filter to whatever was on her mind. *"Madison!"*

Everyone's head whipped to the front of the table where Mr. Wiggins stared his daughter down with eyes promising pure fury. "You will *never* speak to a guest that way under my roof. I tend to let you slide with more leniency than I should, but you won't get away with that, you understand me?" Madison did nothing but nod, her scathing tongue swiftly cooling off and losing its bluster. "You apologize to Imani. Now." "No, no, it's alright," Imani assured, raising her hands to indicate that she took no personal affront by what was said.

"I'm the new chick, but trust me, I plan on staying around for a while. I don't blame you for being skeptical. Ben told me about his... background." Imani shot Ben a knowing smirk, and for a moment, Earl thought that Ben was blushing, something he'd rarely seen. "I promise you; I'm not offended. I knew plenty of guys that changed girlfriends like clothes, but the difference there is that Ben has a lot of heart and good intentions. Ben doesn't go around taking women as trophies. He treats me so nicely, and I can see the two of us going very far together."

Madison kept her eyes down as to prevent herself from doing anything that might've sent her father over the edge again, already knowing that she'd pushed her luck enough for the night. "Still," Ben's father responded, "an apology is still in order. Madison?" "...I'm sorry, Imani." Content with her apology, Mr. Wiggins encouraged everyone to dig into the meal, which they did readily. The remainder of the dinner went by without incident. Ben and Imani gave each other subtle glances and teased one another, Mr. and Mrs. Wiggins told stories about their youth and the beginnings of their own relationship, and Madison and Earl, minus the occasional statement or observation, stayed mostly silent. At one point, Madison's leg brushed against Earl's, and she blushed before looking away sheepishly. The two would continue having similar awkward collisions, and every time, Madison seemed gradually more flustered as the night progressed. Earl knew that Madison had a thing for him, she always did. Ever since Earl had met Ben's family in the initial stages of their friendship, he could practically feel Madison's infatuation. Due to her being five years his junior, turning eighteen at the beginning of the year and graduating from high school next month, he promptly ignored her strange behaviors.

At the end of the meal, Ben excused himself from the table, inviting Earl to the back of the house so that he could unveil the news he'd promised to disclose. After kissing Imani, which gave Earl a slight sense of nausea, Ben and Earl made their way to the sliding glass door at the back of the house, which led to a luxurious veranda much more ornate than Earl's plain patio. Ben sat down in one of the lounge chairs with a contented sigh, and Earl followed, plopping down into the chair with the sensation of what he imagined falling into a cloud to be like. The duo listened to the sounds of crickets for a minute or two as darkness trespassed all around them. The dimmed outdoor lights, however, kept the young men bathed in a soothing, reddish hue.

"Madison, man," Ben finally said, staring off into the shadows of the night. "Why did she have to disrespect Imani like that? I get that I can be a pain in the ass sometimes, but I love Maddie. Sometimes, it feels like she has this… secret hate for me." Earl felt the need to snicker at the term "secret hate," but opted

156

against it. He could tell from Ben's face that he had been serious, which was rare amidst his natural mellowed state.

"I think that maybe you're taking it too personally. Madison has always been a little sharp-tongued, as far as I know." "It was the way she said it, Earl. I don't know, I guess I just feel that Imani is different than anyone else I've ever dated. She has a certain way about her that isn't like all the other girls. With some of them, they wanted to date me because I was popular on the internet. Other times, they looked at me and just saw a distraction for a little while. A few really liked me, I think, but there was always a catch. Like, they had hang-ups over exes, or they'd never take me seriously because I'm so 'fun' and they wouldn't want to talk to me. I mean, *really* talk to me, like asking about my family or the things I want to do with my life." Earl was shocked to hear Ben's sentiments regarding the cycle of women he'd gone through. Back in their high school years, Earl knew that Ben liked the thrill of sex. He'd made a game out of it, going as far as rating the girls he'd been with, which Earl subconsciously did to random women he saw sometimes. Ben had matured, sure, but this level of introspection from him was something that Earl was unaccustomed to.

His whoring ways have come back to bite him on the ass. Earl shook his head lightly as he forced himself to allow Ben's words to tune his own brain out. "The life of bouncing from chick to chick just... wasn't fun

157

anymore. Honestly, I stopped doing that about two years ago. I've been looking for something like you have for a long time, E, and now it feels like I have a chance at it. Imani is great in so many ways. Yeah, it helps that she's sexy as hell, but there's so much more to her than that. She talks to me, she listens, and I like the cute laugh that she does. I want this to work out, you know?"

Earl couldn't help but give his friend a genuine smile, proud of the journey that he's been on. Between the jokes and the haphazard chaos, he'd create, Ben was much more than meets the eye.

"I hope it goes the way you're hoping for, Ben. It is weird that you brought her over for dinner though; that's a rare honor for anyone you've been with. How many have you let your parents actually meet?"
"...Whoever I took to the senior prom, but that was more me not being able to hide her from my parents. I can't remember her name though." *Veronica.*

"There was also that chick that I was breaking bread with, and my dad walked in on us. ...Tabitha? I think it was Tabitha. Got lectured for half an hour over it too."

And there it is, he's back to normal.

Earl threw the throw pillow that rested against his lower back at Ben, who caught it, expecting retaliation. "Nice try!"

The two friends shared a laugh, and then Ben's face contorted to one of concern, which made Earl tense. *He's about to lay some bullshit on you.* "Alright, Earl, I need to let you in on something, but I need you to promise me that you'll keep an open mind. At least let me finish talking before you say anything. Deal?" Earl sighed, dreading whatever plan Ben had concocted, but nodded slowly while staring at him. "No promises, but go ahead." "I don't know if you've ever been to it or not, but there's this website called 'Tonally' where people can post mixtapes, songs, albums, anything that's musical. They have a subscription service where if you pay twelve dollars a month, you can upload whatever original music that you want. It's set up so that if you make a song over two-and-a-half minutes long, you can post it for people to buy. If the song doesn't meet that limit though, you can't profit from it."

Oh no.

"You could post songs for free, but we aren't doing that. When you upload a song, it'll track how many people have listened to it, and they can like it and comment. You can set-up a thirty-second sample, but to listen to the whole thing, people have to buy it. They have three payment options: One dollar, which Tonally takes ten-percent of, two dollars, where they get a twenty-percent cut, and three dollars, where they get thirty. Albums work differently, but whatever. When you post a track and have it available for people to buy, Tonally sends you a check a full month later, after taking their share. A lot of underground rappers use Tonally."

"…What did you do?" Earl replied in exasperation. Ben reached into his pocket and pulled out his phone, quickly moving his thumbs across the screen until he got to where he needed to be. He smirked, tapped his phone once, and then held it in his hand, waiting.

"Ohhhh shiiiiiiiiiiit"

Ben chuckled to himself as Earl's voice, autotuned, blasted from the phone. Earl stared ahead, refusing to look at Ben as he recognized that Ben used the soundbite from when Miles had startled him by knocking over the cymbals. Suddenly, the crisp tones of a violin fused with the booming bass of the instrumental that followed shortly afterwards, and even Earl had to raise his head once he heard how well the two somehow sounded when meshed together. "I went in and recorded a couple of violin samples after you left that day. I liked this one the most," Ben exclaimed, shaking his head to the beat.
A few seconds later, Earl's voice reemerged, synced perfectly to the flow of the song.

♪ Kicked while I was down, call it misstep,

160

A failing chef without the sous, no chance, no prep. My back's against the wall, it's time to heed the call. Of the words that flow from my maw because I'm gunning for it all. Forget what you thought you knew, discern the truth from the lies, watch a man be deified, my time is nigh, right before your eyes. I just try and do the best I can to fucking maintain. But it's hard being trapped between my demons and my disjointed brain. Ambitions just out of my reach, but save your pity, please don't preach. Can't dissuade me, I'm fighting back, no slack, ahead of the claque, call it a knack. No more silent pain, no more moving in vain, it's all there for me to attain. This isn't a Shakespearean allegory; this is the dawn of a young king's story. ♪

The music began to fade, bookended with the beat taking a backseat to the violin as it played off the triumphant, upbeat ending to the song. When silence met the veranda again, Ben put his phone away and looked at Earl carefully, trying to gauge his reaction. "…You promised me that nobody would hear that, Ben." "I know, I know, but did you hear it?! I had to cut some lines out because they didn't really fit, but you have to admit that the final edit sounds amazing! Do you know how many people have heard it? 100,000. Do you know how many people liked it? Over ninety percent of them! Then again, it helped that I went to every last social media account that I had and encouraged people to listen to it, but the feedback has been incredible, and it's only been up for about a day or two!"

"A day or two?! And you didn't think to tell me?!" Earl exclaimed. "No, because I knew you'd shut it down!"

You could've caught him had you kept any of your accounts, but you decided to delete every social media outlet that you had, like the asocial recluse that you are.

"Ben, I'm not a songwriter!"

"Okay, hear me out. Can we get real for a second?" "Yes, Ben, tell me about realism; tell me how you're so entrenched into this idea of what is realistic or not." Ignoring Earl's cynicism, Ben continued. "There's a strike that's going on in the music industry right now over people pirating the songs of the big-name artists. They aren't making as much money as they should, so they all got together and agreed to not make any more music until every single torrent site or anywhere else where music can be illegally downloaded is gone. Tonally has gotten huge over the last month because it's given so many people the chance to get their music heard. We have a unique opportunity here, Earl, there's never been a better time to follow this up."

"…Ben, I'm trying to get my book pub—"

"Come on, E! How long have you been at that and been disappointed every time you get a rejection? You're wasting your talents by sitting around and choosing to let something you can't control make you miserable. You can use that experience to make some good music! You have a flat, but different voice that stands out because you're so real, raw, and plus, you can say things that I can't say anyway." "...Like 'nigga'?"

"I mean, yeah!"

Earl's lack of amusement meant that Ben's plan to loosen him up hadn't worked as well as he'd hoped. "I'm just saying. I have my fanbase, and that gives us a damn good start when it comes to exposure. This is what I've always wanted, and in a way, this is what *you* want too! Didn't recording for that little while make you feel good? There's no limit to how far we could take this! Think about it this way: Your face and name being out there also means that you could use our platform to sell your book yourself! Don't let that artist die out, Big E, show those big-name artists that you can do it better because I know you hate how modern music sounds, and you could challenge that! If all that isn't enough to convince you, then how about this? We'd be swimming in money. Like, the big bucks, and we can split it right down the middle!"

As Ben feared, Earl got up after giving him a prolonged, disgruntled look, refusing to acknowledge anything that Ben had tried to sell him on. "Take me home. Saniya is a little pissed off with me, so I don't want to bother her for the night." "…Oh yeah, she did drop you off. What happened to your car?"

"Got into an accident yesterday. I'm fine, but I totaled the car, so for the time being, I need a little help getting around." "Yeah, yeah, I got you," Ben stated, taken aback by Earl's casual mention of crashing his car.

"Could you at least think about what I said?"

Ben opened the sliding door for Earl, who glared at him in response and went back into the house without another word. When they rejoined Ben's family and Imani, they saw that Madison was gone, and that Imani was getting along quite well with Ben's parents. "Baby, I'm going to take Earl home and be right back, okay?"

"Okay! I'm having a good time getting to know your parents anyway, so take your time!"

Earl said his goodbyes to Ben's parents and Imani waved at him, causing him to return the gesture and sneak in one more longing glance as he and Ben disappeared into the hallway leading to the front door.

People presume to know what the fuck you want. They don't, they didn't put in the time or effort that you did to craft a worthwhile narrative. To abandon that would be stupid, and plus, Ben's idea is ridiculous. You told him it was just for fun, and he didn't listen, as usual. As Earl stepped into Ben's car, another fleeting thought popped into his head and disappeared almost as quickly as it came.

Although...
maybe the whole thing isn't as terrible as it sounds.

Chapter 11

The following week was mundane, and Earl had never been more dissatisfied with the quality of his existence than he was now. He'd ignored Ben, made up with Saniya and apologized profusely to Charlotte, who screamed at him the morning after Ben dropped him off. Between work, lazing around at home and running errands for Charlotte, Earl had considered taking a bus as far away from everything he'd been accustomed to and living out a new life. His fantasies of emancipation, however, wouldn't come to fruition.

Randall was sound asleep in his and Charlotte's room, and Earl and Charlotte were eating a pre-seasoned piece of corned beef that Charlotte had bought from the store with sides of mixed vegetables and rice, the only homemade thing being the rice. Earl's fork scrapped against the plate listlessly, a far cry from Mr. Wiggins' cooking, as Charlotte chewed on a piece of beef.

"What's wrong with you, boy?" Charlotte asked between bites. "Nothing. I'm just thinking some things over." "What's there to think about? You got a decent job, a good girlfriend and you're in good health. If you wanted more out of life, your black ass should've gone to college."

Earl stifled an abject sigh, knowing that Charlotte was

never going to let him abide by his decision to disregard college.

"You could've been the first Veares to go to college, Earl. Your father was smart, but he chose the wrong path in his life, and there's nothing that I could do about that. I'm sorry that God gave you the parents that you got, but you have to make the best out of it." Earl cringed, not desiring to think about either of his parents. Earl Sr. had been in jail for as long as he could remember, only vaguely recalling seeing him a handful of times at certain points of his childhood, but no more. Earl had resented him, especially for passing his name onto him, but he didn't hate Earl Sr. as much as he hated his mother. "And that mother of yours… I hope she stays gone because if she ever comes back, I'm going to have some shit to say to her. How a woman could just walk away from a baby is disgusting. But, you're my sanity, Earl, so I think raising you was God's way of telling me that it was meant to be."

Earl smiled sadly as he reflected on Charlotte's words. He hadn't seen his mother before, not even having the slightest idea of what she looked like. In fact, most of everything that he'd come to know about his parents were through the accounts of Charlotte and his uncle, back when they had an amicable channel of communication.

"I told your father not to fool around with her because she was lazy and irresponsible. But, it's all for the best. I give you a hard time, but only because I had been too lenient while raising your father and Porkchop. They were bad-ass little boys growing up." Porkchop was the name that everyone called Randall's son, who Charlotte took in and raised alongside Earl Sr. "I'd be at the principal's office every other day, it seemed like. Fighting, cussing, vandalizing, they didn't care. Your father and Porkchop would compete to see who could get the most pussy, and the girls would come in and out so much that I would just buy boxes of condoms for those boys. 'Don't bring in any mouths you can't feed,' I told them." Charlotte smirked as she recalled the memories she had of her sons. Earl chomped at a piece of broccoli, dreading, knowing that he was going to be brought up at some point.

"Then, you came along. Your mother dropped you off at the door and said, 'I don't want this bastard anymore,' and then drove into the night. Your father had been in jail for selling dope at that point, and I guess that she wasn't strong enough to be a mother. I never did like her, even from the moment Earl introduced us. She was fat and sloth like. But she did give me one
important thing, and that was you."

Fuck the both of them.

Earl's fork tapped against his plate impatiently, having heard the story multiple times throughout his life. He wasn't sure whether or not Charlotte had

168

nothing but her past to look forward to, or if early-onset dementia was setting in. Regardless, he knew that he had to grin and bear it.

"You were quiet, even as a child. Never had a lot of friends, and if you did have some, you stuck out like a sore thumb. I didn't know how to raise someone like you, but I knew that you were destined to be something great one day. I just didn't know what. I don't want you to be like your father, Earl. He was someone who sat on his talents and brains until he'd wasted them completely. It hurt me to see my son go down that path, but I'm not going to let my grandson follow him down the drain. I *want* your book to succeed, but I just want you to do it the right way." "Actually," Earl said, finally seizing an opportunity to add his input into Charlotte's speech. "I've been writing again."

"Oh? That's good! What's your new book about?" "...It isn't a book." Charlotte immediately stopped chewing and stared straight at Earl, pondering the meaning of his statement.

"...What the hell is it then?" "Well, Ben had a recording studio built into his basement. I've been spending the week trying to write a song because—" "Write a song? A song about what? What the hell kind of song could you have written? With the white boy? Lord, tell me my baby hasn't lost his fucking mind yet."

Earl waited for Charlotte to get the displeasure out of her system before explaining himself. "Look, it's nothing drastic, I'm doing it to pass the time." *You mean you want your time in the spotlight, but you can't tell this old bitch that. Her generation was founded on liquor and repression, she wouldn't understand.*

"Earl, no offense, baby, but that's the stupidest fucking thing I've heard you say in a while. What about your book? Have you given up on it?" The rejections had peaked early in the week where Earl knew that he had officially bled his options for representation for his book dry. Still, he had to tell Charlotte something, anything, to quell her rising indignation. "No, I'm just doing something on the side to keep myself writing while I wait for an idea for my next book to come to me." "You artistic types, I'll never understand. I hear about what happens to musicians these days, you know, and the industry ain't always kind to them." "Yeah, but I wanted to do something different, you know?"

"No, I don't know. I don't know what the hell makes you think that you can just up and decide to make music. At least writing a book made sense because you know you're smart, and you like to show off by using those big-ass words you like so much." Loud cackling filled the kitchen as Randall walked in, not bothering to change his sweat- stained shirt from the previous day.

"Did I just hear that shit right?!"

Earl didn't have to look at him for his blood to start boiling, and his shaking hands caused him to drop his fork onto his plate. "What, are you planning on starting a boy band?!" "Randy, leave him alone," Charlotte warned. "Boy, I'm going to give you the best piece of wisdom you're ever going to get. Charlotte's too afraid to say it, but I ain't! God makes two kinds of people: People who make something of themselves, and people like you, who live to give hose successful people a reminder of how low they should never allow themselves to sink. You're always going to be a nobody, just like your daddy, and it's okay to admit that. The limelight ain't for some folks. What, you want to be a failed music-maker *and* a failed book-writer? Quit while you're ahead and master the art of sandwich-making." "Fuck this," Earl said, unable to bite his tongue as he pushed past Randall and stormed off to his room. "That's right, run! That's what you usually do!"

Earl slammed the door as hard as he could, almost knocking one of his framed pictures off the wall. He paced erratically, wanting desperately to punch something, but deciding against it. He reached for his bottle of anti-depressants and choked down two, deciding to curtail his negative thoughts before they arose from whatever dark part of his mind, they dwelled in. A minute of deep breathing later, Earl could hear Charlotte and Randall engage each other in a screaming match over him, and he decided that he wasn't going to stick around much longer to deal with that. He opened one of his dresser drawers, pulled out a folded-up piece of paper, shoved it into his pocket, and took out his phone in search of Ben. When he found the number on his short list of contacts, he sent out a concise, clear message.

"Come get me. I'm considering what you said."

--

"Hey, Earl!" Imani stated cheerily as she saw the pair saunter into Ben's house. Miles mewed in Imani's lap as they watched television in the living room, and Ben strode over and gave Imani a quick kiss. "No 'hi' for me?" Ben teased with a goofy smirk. "You live here, sir. Earl, on the other hand, is your guest!" "So are you, baby! Don't act like you live here now!"

"True, but lately, I'm here more than I am at my apartment anyway, so I should be considered something above 'guest' status!" Earl watched the two banter from the archway leading into the living room, a distant smile on his face. *Remember when that used to be you and Saniya? Everything was so fun and exciting back then. Now...* "Oh, Earl! I'm so sorry about your car! Ben told me what had happened, are you alright?" "Yeah, I'm taking it a day at a time. I've been so used to driving around

172

everywhere that not having a car is weird, but I'm adjusting."

"Adjusting" is a nice way of putting it. Charlotte already reamed you enough over it, and now without your own transportation, you're at your lowest. At least you didn't hit anyone or mess up any private property, so you have that going for you. "That's good to hear! I hope that your luck changes soon, Earl. I can only imagine that the past few weeks have been hard on you, but you'll persevere!" "Hell, yeah he will, especially since he agreed to record some songs with me!"

Ben's enthusiasm could hardly be contained as Imani's mouth dropped in amazement. "You're actually going to record something?! Ben let me hear what he uploaded on Tonally, and I gotta say, you guys have some talent!" "I told him I'd consider it," Earl said flatly, shooting Ben a hot glare over letting Imani listen to the sample that he'd created. "Yeah, let me get him down there before he changes his mind. Are you alright up here, baby?" "Yep! Miles is keeping me company, and plus, I have some shows to catch up on, so ya'll do what you gotta do!"

Ben hugged Imani and gave Miles a quick pat on the head before walking out of the room with Earl in tow. Once they were down in the basement, they took their usual seats, Ben flopping down on his swivel chair, and Earl sitting at the chair next to Ben. "Alright, so

173

where do we start?" Earl asked apprehensively.

"Well, did you actually write something, or do you want to just freestyle it?" Earl dug into his pocket, retrieving the folded-up piece of paper hidden within it. He unfolded it, gave it a quick, cursory glance to make sure that everything worked, then handed the paper over to Ben.

What if he doesn't like it? Maybe this whole thing was idiotic after all.

Ben found himself bobbing his head to a rhythm that only existed within his own head as he muttered through Earl's song. When he was finished, he looked up at Earl, then at the paper, then back at Earl. "Yeah, dude! I think we can definitely do something with this! I have to ask though, what are you thinking in terms of the beat? I'm going to follow your lead! Whatever fits the vision that you have for the song, I'm down for it!" A small gasp came from Earl, who was shocked to have so much control over the direction of his song. His eyes darted around the room as his brain worked to articulate what it was exactly that he had in mind.

"So... I kind of have this idea of a slow, sullen sort of thing. Like, depending on how good you are with the piano, maybe we could do something with that? I don't want to direct you too much, but I definitely want the song to be more... deliberate." "Luckily, I'm

174

getting more and more comfortable with the piano. I'm glad that my mom made me play the violin and piano growing up; I remember hating it back then. But, we're about to make bank from it, so I'm glad that she did!" Ben looked over Earl's lyrics again, making sure that he had an idea of what Earl wanted. "Just so I'm clear, you want it to sound… sad?" "Not 'sad,' per se, just… serious, I guess." "Gotcha," Ben said as his eyes unfocused, obviously thinking about how to arrange the beat of the song.

"Alright, so give me about an hour or two to come up with something. When I'm done, you can come down and spit some of those hot bars! In the meantime, why don't you keep Imani company? I'm sure she'd like to have someone to speak with!" "Oh," Earl murmured, his heart racing at the prospect of being alone with Imani. Ben, noticing Earl's wariness, made a 'pfft' sound and waved his hand dismissively.

"Dude, it's you, you're my best friend. You aren't some scumbag I don't know or trust. Go on up and be social!"

Earl got up slowly, egged on by Ben, and trotted up the stairs towards the living room where he knew Imani was situated. As he walked towards the room, Imani turned her head to see who'd entered, smiling as Earl stood awkwardly at the archway. "Sit down! I'd appreciate the company anyway; Miles has abandoned me, as you can see." Imani pointed to the corner to Earl's right, the furthest away from the television. Surely enough, Miles was sprawled out on his back, lying comfortably. Imani patted the open spot next to her on the couch, and as Earl inched closer, he could smell the almost sugary scent that seemed to be exclusive to her.

"I bet she tastes as good as she smells. She's tall enough to lay across the couch and—

"So, what's going on down there?" Imani said, letting the television become background noise.

"Ben's doing his thing, making a beat before I go down there and hopefully do something halfway decent with it." Imani smirked and moved a lock of hair away from her face. She didn't say anything for a minute, and when she looked back at Earl, her face was glowing with sympathy. "…I don't mean to steer this conversation off a cliff, but now that we have a chance to actually talk, I want to tell you something."

I want you too.

"Ben talks about you, more than you'd think. He's told me so much about you, your relationship with your girlfriend, your grandmother, and I want you to know that I felt some of what you've been through too. Maybe not all of it, but a good amount." Imani adjusted her position on the couch to face Earl, sitting with her legs crossed as she spoke. Earl was entranced, eager to latch onto her every word.

"My father wasn't in my life, and if he was, he'd just use my mother for a convenient night if he happened to be in town and then leave without anyone knowing the next morning. My mom would always welcome him back too, hoping that the next time they had sex, he'd do it because he loved her. She wanted their marriage back, but he would show up to prove that he still had power over her. That made her bitter, and I think she indirectly took that out on me.

Growing up, I was ugly, and there was no other way around it. My front teeth were crooked, I had horrible acne, and I was flatter than a pancake. However, my mom was one of those 'beauty is in the eye of the beholder' kind of mothers, so when I started middle school, she'd always enroll me in these silly-ass beauty pageants. Well, you can imagine how that went for me." Imani scoffed mirthlessly as she looked past Earl for a second, remembering the issues of her youth. Earl was about to say something, but Imani focused on him again, chuckling.

"I'm sorry. Sometimes, my mind wanders. Anyway, after being pranked or humiliated by the other girls, I would run to my mother crying because I didn't want to do it after the first time, but of course, I had to deal with it two more times. By the time high school had rolled around, I'd finally grown into my body, my

177

teeth had straightened out thanks to braces, and due to some timely beauty products, my skin cleared up! By this time, my mom had realized that maybe my father wasn't going to reciprocate her 'love' for him, and she started her anti-men crusade. Sometime before my junior prom, my mom told me that I should never trust any man, ever. All men are immoral, they always put themselves before you, they are all destined to cheat, the whole nine yards. She embarrassed me in front of my junior prom date by saying to me, right in front of him, that I had to be smarter than him, to not let him 'use me up then discard me like trash.' I don't know, she got reckless, and when I found the opportunity, I moved out a year after my senior year. To this day, when I call her to keep her informed of what I'm doing, she'll tell me not to be as stupid as she was. Ugh, you should've heard her when I told her that Ben was white, she flipped the fuck out."

Imani and Earl laughed as the end credits to the sci-fi show that was on the television ended, leaving a temporary blackness on the screen. "Yeah, that is pretty crazy. Honestly, I couldn't tell you much about my parents other than what Char—" Earl hesitated, realizing that Imani hadn't been accustomed to him calling his grandmother by her first name, so he forced himself to refer to her by her familial status.

"—my grandmother told me about them. My father chose the streets over being a dad, and my mother decided that she wanted nothing to do with me and gave me over to my grandmother when I was a baby. I saw my father a grand total of three times, the last time being… eighth grade, I think. He showed up randomly at our doorstep and he told me about all of the mistakes he made, how sorry he was that he hadn't stepped up, and he promised me that everything would be better. Of course, he ended up right back in jail a month later, and nothing had changed. I've never seen my mother, not even a picture of her, and who knows if I ever will."

"I'm sorry to hear that, Earl," Imani lamented. "It sucks when we have to carry the burdens of our parents, but I genuinely feel like those experiences make us better people in the end. It shows you what *not* to do so that you'll be better equipped to deal with anything that arises." "I guess that's one way to look at it." Earl matched Imani's hopeful countenance, and then Imani turned towards the television. "But, enough bringing up the past, let's live in the present! Wanna watch some mindless reality TV? Don't ask me why, but I love the scripted drama of it so much!" *Anything to be near you.*

"Sure!"

For the next hour and a half, Earl and Imani chortled at and made fun of "Life and Times of a Repentant Husband" which featured men of the church "straying" away from their wives and their journey to become one with the Lord, and their wives, once more. During the middle of the second episode, Ben walked into the room, his arms proudly outstretched. "I've done it! Now, come on down and let's make some sweet magic, Big E!" Earl winced at Ben, whose face shifted to shock, then horror, quickly understanding Earl's reaction. "…That's not what I meant! I mean—I just—we…"

Imani descended into a fit of laughter as Ben's face became a veil of crimson. Earl had to laugh himself, seeing one of Ben's usual shticks backfiring on him in such a spectacular fashion.

"Come on, Earl. You and these goddamn dry-ass jokes." "Hey, you said it!" Earl retorted as he rose from the couch to follow Ben to the basement. "Kill it, Earl!" he heard Imani say, accompanied by a wink. He bowed his head quickly in acknowledgement before disappearing behind a corner with Ben. They did the usual set-up with Ben at the helm of the console and Earl preparing himself in the live room. "Let me know what you think of the beat, Earl!" Earl nodded at Ben's request and waited with his headphones on. Soon afterwards, the piano made its arrival, carrying its soft notes through the canals of Earl's ears, beautifully and crisply. After a ten-second, soulful piano prelude, the soft thumping of the bass came in, and Earl knew that Ben had mastered his task.

Earl gave Ben a silent thumbs-up, and Ben fist-pumped happily. Earl took a second to close his eyes, making sure that he'd had every line perfectly memorized, then when he was ready, his words flowed elegantly with Ben's beat...

♪ The screech breaches the air; the scenery loses its magic. A boy coddled by inertia, no interest in being nomadic. The night descends, no more time to make amends. Debris all around him, mangled bodies, limp limbs. He sees himself, a broken, lifeless husk.

Overseer to his end, unexpected, swift and brusque. He reaches out to return, concerned, can't even discern that in the blink of an eye, his life's been tragically spurned. Do you believe God is real or not?

♪ If he can hear you, can he answer your prayers or not? Have you truly been blessed, or maybe you've been forgot. Perhaps you've been in Hell all along, and only control how fast you rot. His mother cries, father blames it on the Lord. "How could you do this to us?" but remains ignored.
He can hear and see his family, but they can't reciprocate. He screams and howls, but can't accept his fate. The seasons pass, parents full of hate, they can't abate or acclimate; for his family, it's just too late....

♪ From one end to another, and he weeps all the same. Feels as though it was his fault, so he shoulders the blame. Do you believe God is real or not? If he can hear you, can he answer your prayers or not?

Have you truly been blessed, or maybe you've been forgot? Perhaps you've been in Hell all along, and only control how fast you rot. The years trudge on, eventually, times takes its toll. One's buried by squalor, the other, closed-casket, riddled with holes.

♪ He prepares to give himself to the wraith of grief. But they emerge right before him, much to his relief. Dad smiles, and mom is filled with joy, both reunited with their long-lost boy. They depart, a family, finally interlinked. You then wonder if God's as deaf as some seem to think.

♪ Maybe God works without us knowing. Always delivering, not telling, but showing. Give him a chance; don't fret, you'll see. Sometimes you must suffer to view Heaven for what it's supposed to be.

Chapter 12

A football flew through the beautiful, crisp afternoon, and summer was in full effect. Earl watched for a while as the father and son duo played catch in an open field, seemingly not having a care between them. *The moment of truth is coming up. We're going to find out if Ben was trying to sell us some bullshit or not.* Conceding to the intruder's observation, Earl felt his heart race at the thought. What if he'd been just as unsuccessful in writing music as he'd been in writing his book? What if Randall was right, that he was destined to exist as a cautionary tale for others? *Fuck Randall. You, at your core, are a pure artist. Maybe your storytelling skills were being channeled through the wrong medium.*

"I'm back!"

Earl shifted his body from the bench he'd been sitting at in Saniya's direction, who was dressed appropriately for the nice weather. Her skirt blew in the breeze as she sauntered over with the snowballs that she'd had a craving for. Knowing that Earl's meeting had changed to being in the afternoon this time, Saniya saw an opportunity for them to have a nice date before he had to depart. She handed Earl his cup of shaved ice, which took on a vibrant green color as a sea of dark green made the mountain of ice seem almost ominous in its presentation. Saniya gave Earl a plastic spoon, and he relished the first taste of his favorite snowball flavor on the rare occasion that he and Saniya got to go to one of their old dating haunts. As he shoveled the treat into his mouth, his lips puckered with the delectable, bitter tang of the sour apple flavoring.

"Just how you like it!"

Earl smacked his lips in satisfaction, knowing that Saniya knew that he liked to request the employees of the snowball stand to make his extra sour, which they always obliged. "Thanks, baby! What flavor did you get this time?" "They have this new 'adult' menu that allows you to add liquor, sooooo I got a pina colada snowball. It's delicious, E. I'd let you try some, but I know you'll hit me with 'You know I don't drink,' so that means there will be more for me!"

Earl looked at his girlfriend with disbelief and let his body language match the exaggerated tone of his expression. "Sans, you're the designated driver, and it's barely even 11 o'clock yet!" "Oh, you act like I'm going to get super drunk. I'm responsible, I know my limits! At least I know how to switch it up, Mr. Sour Apple! That huge menu, and that's the only thing that you ever get from here!" "Listen, I like what I like! You know how I feel about risks; I don't want to waste my money on things I might not like!" "Yeah, but I'm treating you! Are you sure you don't want

184

some of my snowball? Maybe it'll calm you down heading into your meeting!" She held the snowball inches away from Earl's nose, who gagged as the mixture of rum, coconut and pineapple assaulted his nostrils. "You can be so boring sometimes, E!" Saniya said, pouting.

"If I did drink, I wouldn't want to show up drunk to a meeting featuring people suffering from depression and anxiety. I don't think that's the vote of self-motivation that Dr. Tommen would approve of." Saniya shrugged, acknowledging Earl's point, but being too proud to verbally admit its truthfulness. For a few minutes, the pair enjoyed their respective treats as the cool breeze gave the slight humidity a good, level temperature for hanging outdoors. Kids played, and adults happily chattered about their lives amongst one another. There was an unspoken tranquility to the snowball stand and its serene surrounding area, supporting picnics and other leisurely summer events, that was unmatched anywhere else. "Can you believe that in five more months, it'll be our six-year anniversary?"

Saniya broke the placid silence between them as Earl nodded, gleefully ruminating over the timeless memories they'd shared. "It's unreal, isn't it? We've been through a lot together, Sans." "Yeah. I'm sorry, E."

Earl sat his snowball down next to him, hoping that it wouldn't topple over as a result of the light, morning breezes. He craned his neck towards Saniya, seeing nothing but sadness.

Is she about to break-up with you? What is this?

"...I know it's been a rough few months for us. We've barely gotten to see each other, and when we do, it feels like there's this tension between us. I don't want you to think that I don't love you or don't care anymore because I do. The semester is over now, which gives us nothing but time to do whatever we want. In fact, if you want to stay over tonight, you're more than welcome to!" _It has been a while since you've done anything with her privately. Maybe some alone time and space to reconnect will do you some good._ "That's great, Sans! I'll have to take you up on that. Drop me off at the house after the meeting, let me get a few things, and then we can head on back to your place!"

"Cool!" Saniya chirped, glad to be spending time with Earl in a meaningful way. "What have you been up to lately, by the way? You haven't mentioned your book in a while."

Shit. What do you say? Do you want to risk mentioning Ben and the fact that you're less than a week out from getting your first check from the song you guys did? Damned if you do, damned if you don't, but you should probably tell her now or else she'll be pissed if she discovers it on her own. "Earl?"

He'd zoned out, and Saniya was in the process of waving her hand in front of his face to bring him back to earth. "Yeah, I've been doing some stuff." "Like?" Earl picked his snowball back up and ingested another spoonful, stalling to find the courage he needed to be honest with her.

"So, Ben and I have a project going on."

Saniya's arm stopped midway through scooping up more of her snowball, and she lowered the spoon back into the cup. She closed her eyes, inhaling and exhaling slowly with her head facing away from Earl. When she turned back, her face had been utterly blank, unyielding to any emotion. "What's the project?" Saniya said flatly. "So, three weeks ago, Ben and I recorded a song, and—" "Whoa, whoa, whoa."

Saniya used her free hand to signal for Earl to stop speaking, and she put the cup that she had in her other hand down next to her on the bench.

"Recorded a song? Meaning, what, you want to be one of those people who lurk outside of liquor stores trying to sell their mixtapes?" *Here we fucking go. The complaining. No wonder you let her do what she wants.* No, it's nothing like that. Ben has a *legit* recording studio in his basement, and he had this idea for me to channel my creativity into lyricism while I

187

was working on trying to get my book out there."
"And when the hell did this start?" "About two
months ago. That's around the time he had the
recording studio installed. Nothing is official yet, but
the song is floating around online."

"…I don't mind you doing something to keep
yourself occupied, but you know how I feel about
Ben. Honestly, I don't know what to think about the
whole thing." *It doesn't matter "what you think," it's
going to happen regardless.*

"It's something to do, Sans. I doubt it'll go anywhere
significant anyway, and then Ben will move on to the
next fad." Saniya considered Earl's comments, her
fingers drumming against the wood of the table. Earl
did his best to maintain his understanding veneer, but
he was angry. Saniya had grown more argumentative
over the years, and it was wearing on him. "Yeah, we
know how Ben likes to keep things short-term,"
Saniya commented, relenting her full scorn.
"Speaking of, what poor girl is his victim of the
month this time?" It was as if a lever had been flipped
inside of Earl because he could slowly feel his
tensions ease at the mere implication of Imani. He
shifted in his seat so that Saniya couldn't see any
abnormal growths protruding from the crotch of his
jeans.

"Her name is Imani. She's cool." "Is she black?" Earl
nodded. "Ugh, girl's doing us proud."

188

She's more supportive than you've been lately.

Saniya rolled her eyes and continued working on her snowball, ending that portion of the conversation. Earl felt as though he should say something to cheer her up, so after thinking about it, he settled on mentioning her art. "Are you planning on painting this summer?" "Hopefully! I have a lot of cool things planned!" Saniya perked up when Earl broached the topic of her artistic intentions over the next few months. *But of course, the bitch turns her nose up at anything you want to do, then expects you to fully back her when she wants something.*

"I want to play with oils and acrylics this summer to improve my shadowing. Mediums, dry-brushing, and something we learned called 'sgraffito" to manipulate the very fine details. I want to see how elaborate I can get to make my paintings *really* pop! Who knows, I may be confident enough to try and sell something by the end of the summer!" Earl smiled, but Saniya had known him well enough to recognize the difference between a genuine smile, and a forced one. She sighed, realizing that she'd been hard on him with Ben and his new side-hobby.

"Earl, I didn't mean to hurt your feelings. It's just that sometimes, you can be a little..." Earl's eyebrows furrowed, and he did his best not to appear standoffish or combative.

The last thing he wanted to be was the person that he was when they first met. He'd found himself offended by Saniya's pause as she scanned him, deciding whether or not to say what she was thinking. "I can be a little what?" he said with a little more hostility than he'd intended. "All I'm trying to say is that you tend to let Ben dictate what the two of you do. In fact, you have a tendency to bottle things up and enable people to do or say what they want to you sometimes." "…So, what are you trying to say? That I'm weak? That I'm easily influenced?"

Saniya saw Earl become more agitated by the second, and realizing that they were surrounded by other people, she didn't want to make a scene in front of everyone. "…Forget that I said anything. I want to have a nice summer with you, Earl. Can we drop this? Please? I really don't want this conversation to bother you." Earl got up from the bench with the remainder of his snowball and threw it into the trash, slamming it down with emphasis. "Let's go. It's almost time for my meeting anyway."

He didn't give Saniya another glance as he walked towards her car, ignoring the apology that she'd tried giving him, but he refused to turn around. *Fuck her.*

--

Usually, Earl would take the time to scrutinize his damaged compatriots, but today, he had his eye on something new, something with big, substantial hips. She rushed in during the middle of Carly's recounting of her latest public outburst and apologized profusely, but stood toe-to-toe with Carly when she shot up from her seat and got in the new girl's face about interrupting her story. Carly hated that. Dr. Tommen defused the situation, as he was expertly accustomed to, and introduced the group to Kim, who sat to Earl's right. Kim explained that she had ran late because she had a difficult time finding a babysitter for her one-year-old. She also had a slight accent, sounding as though it had origins from South America, but Earl paid that little attention. Kim had, to put it delicately, some meat on her bones. She was far from what many would consider "fat," but she certainly was a lot more woman than most that Earl had encountered, thick in all the right places. Earl considered Kim's hips her greatest asset as the chattering of the circle became like distant white noise as he let his mind go to its most decadent places.

Eventually, Earl found himself, again, with all eyes on him as Dr. Tommen's voice graduated from a muffled mumble to crisp, audible words. "It's your turn, Earl. Is there anything you'd like to say? Did you follow through on my advice the last time we convened?" "Uhhh... yeah."

191

Earl cracked his neck and prepared to speak, uncharacteristically happy to present his newest endeavors. He'd had a point to prove, that he wasn't as fragile and malleable as Saniya had implied, he was. "I did as you told me, Dr. Tommen. A friend and I started something that stokes that fire inside of me that I hadn't felt since I first started writing. We're trying our hand in music!" Earl analyzed the nods of approval from the circle, who'd known about Earl's rollercoaster of moods and emotions since he'd joined them. "I don't really care about success or anything that extreme—"

Liar.

"—but it's renewed my essence, if that makes any sense. I've had to deal with a lot of self-doubt throughout the years, and even the people closest to me treat me like I'm going to burst into tears or lash out if they try to reason with me. It's like I don't have a voice unless I'm here, with you guys. It feels good. I don't have to internalize everything; I can speak freely with little judgment. You're all like another family to me, and I do need to dedicate myself to reaching out to some of you sometimes. I guess it feels as though I've been dealing with so much by myself for so long that I don't know how to let people in, so I promise to do better with that going forward. Other than spending my time jotting down lyrics and seeing what works and what doesn't, that's it! I don't have any long, depressing diatribes in me this time. I wanted to let you all know how well things have been going lately after digging myself out of my rut. I hope that everyone here has an equal measure of peace in the time between meetings too."

Dr. Tommen couldn't have looked happier as he led the circle in a round of applause for Earl and his latest update. Earl looked over at Kim for a moment, seeing her eyes sparkle with inspiration. *You don't give a fuck about any of them, that was all a show to impress the new girl.*

Kim was the last to speak, being the newest person in the program. Earl only heard select tidbits of her sad, but admittedly plain, life.

Father of the child skipped out on her, she thought it was love, blah blah blah. If people weren't so stupid and willing to fall for the duplicity of our generation, maybe they'd avoid
getting hurt. But, not everyone can play it as safe as you do. Zero risks, only gambles when it's one-hundred percent guaranteed.
When the meeting concluded and everyone had said their goodbyes, Earl walked out to the outside of the building and prepared to text Saniya that he was ready to be picked up. Just then, a tap on the shoulder caused him to turn around, and sure enough, Kim was standing before him. *Manipulative.*

"Hi. Um, I just wanted to say that what you said

really resonated with me. After Roy, I felt like everything had been taken from me, and so much of what I did depended on him that I didn't know what to do." "Well, you're braver than I am. I don't know how you do it, taking care of a child by yourself. With problems like the cost of living being too high and hourly earnings being too low, I commend you for being able to keep up. I don't think I'm built for something like that."

You aren't.

"You're sweet, but it's something that you get used to after a while. Christian is a blessing and makes me that much more motivated to work on myself so that I can be strong enough for him one day." Kim laughed and straightened out her short hair, obviously having something else on her mind. "This is going to sound weird, but I'm a little intimidated by this whole 'support group' thing. I get weird around people I've just met. Don't get me wrong, I'm a social butterfly, but it takes a minute for me to warm up to people." "Well, Dr. Tommen encourages us to stay in contact with each other, but obviously, not everyone reaches that level of comfort amongst one another. If you'd like, I can help you ease your way into the group! Honestly, I don't have a lot of their numbers either, and if I do, we never talk. But I always like having new people to talk to, so would you like to exchange numbers?"

Saniya would kill you.

"Sure, I'd like that!"

Kim gave Earl a flirtatious, playful vibe that he hadn't known personally since Saniya and him first got together. As they exchanged numbers, Earl could feel a rush of dopamine course through his veins, conforming with the thrill of getting a girl's number after being with Saniya and only Saniya for so long. *You don't have to text or even call her. Nobody has to know, really. It's not like you don't have some of the other's numbers too, so maybe this is innocent.*

"Alright, so, I'm going to head home so that I can relieve my babysitter, but I'll see you around some time?" "Definitely!" With one last lingering look, Kim turned away from Earl and sauntered to her car, swaying her hips so that Earl got a bit of a show. Earl didn't take his eyes off her for a second until she got into her car, winked slyly and then drove out of the parking lot. As Earl took out his phone and began to call Saniya, one thought made itself known out of the many swimming through his head.

Or maybe that exchange of numbers wasn't so innocent after all.

Chapter 13

Here we are, riding around in your girlfriend's car, and you can hear a pin drop in a bed of feathers. Don't apologize; it's her fault.

The car ride to Charlotte's house signaled the most silence that had ever existed between Earl and Saniya in their entire relationship. As Saniya focused on the road, her unspoken discontent being shown through her erratic, impatient driving as opposed to the usual calmness that she displayed while cruising through the streets, Earl's eyes were fixed to his side of the car. His mind wandered, considering his options between following through with his request to stay over at Saniya's or staying home. But, the more he thought about it, the more he couldn't stand the idea of pointlessly dawdling within his room.

Over the last couple of years, Earl had wanted to detach himself from his former sanctuary, feeling as though he couldn't breathe within the four walls he'd stayed enclosed in since his childhood. Getting closer to Charlotte's house, Earl began to feel physically colder as the familiarity of the area caused him slight distress.

Same shit. Same trees, same houses, same people walking the same dogs. The only thing that isn't part of the routine that you've been plagued by is sitting down and writing songs.

Earl wanted to grant his inner dialogue a compliant nod, but caught himself before he could actualize the motion. These days, the intruder either tended to take a step back from the myriad thoughts that Earl dealt with, or he and the intruder found themselves aligned in ideology rather than being a detriment that Earl had to actively ignore. The intruder would be actively antagonistic on occasion, but for the most part, he'd been the synergic voice that Earl refused to articulate. Where he was judged or condescended to previously, the intruder became Earl's place to fall when it felt as though everyone else hadn't understood him.

Earl caught a glimpse of a tree with the faint imprint of a forceful impact. He winced, knowing that they'd just passed the site of his automotive accident. "I don't know why you always have to make me out to be the bad guy when all I want to do is help you. I want to support you, but you close yourself off when you get overwhelmed, and that can make it difficult for me to interact with you sometimes."

Earl turned to Saniya with an initial blank stare, but the internal reminder that he had no intentions on staying at the house with Randall and Charlotte made him amenable to the conversation. "Yeah, I've been a little stressed lately." Earl wanted to placate Saniya, so to get back in her good graces, he'd decided to shoulder the blame for their falling out at the snowball stand. "I've been trying to get myself back into a good mindset so that I can write another song or two, but every time I think I've cracked my writer's block, I end up reading the lyrics back to myself and erasing or throwing away the draft. It's not you, Sans, I'm more frustrated with myself as of late than anyone else. It's been hard attempting to shift my creative outlet from outlining and writing books to writing songs, but I've been trying to stay optimistic." "So, this whole music thing…"

Saniya took a minute to formulate the proper answer knowing that Earl would be likely to escape within himself if she misspoke.

"I think it's cool, I just don't want you to psyche yourself out or be disappointed if things don't match up to your expectations." Saniya looked over at Earl with a small, hopeful smile, and Earl simply mimicked it. "I don't want to make it seem like I'm trying to censor you or be this nagging figure that discourages you from following your dreams. If you want to pursue music on the side or even if you want to shift from being an author to becoming a musician going forward, I want you to know that I have your back completely. I know that you wouldn't be one of those… what do you call them?"

"Mediocre, Marble-Mouthed Misogynists." Earl corrected. "You never have to worry about the Quad-M Effect with me, Sans. How people like that get hot is beyond me, but as they say, there's no accounting for good taste! Isn't that right, Ms. Grande? I know you like that dumpster-fire noise. Everyone is either a 'Lil', a 'Young', or has a bunch of random numbers or letters in their alias. Which one would you be?"

"I'd have to choose 'shut the hell up' as an option," Saniya rebutted, punching Earl in the arm they rounded a corner, now less than five minutes away from Charlotte's as Saniya expertly avoided a pothole in the road. "Also… I promise that I'll be better about Ben. I know that he's your friend, and even though he used to treat girls like livestock, maybe he's changed."

"I genuinely believe that he has. He recently told me that he got tired of his former womanizing ways and he seems to care about the one that he's with now. I have to say; it does seem like he's changed a lot since then." *But really, haven't we all?* Saniya bobbed her head with her lips pursed as she tried to wrap her mind around the idea of Ben changing for the better. "…To be fair, we were all in high school. There wasn't a better time to get a little loose, other than college, so I can see where I may have harbored too harsh of a grudge against him." It was baffling, Saniya's sudden acceptance of Ben. In fact, Saniya had shown such self-awareness that Earl was almost afraid she had ulterior motives, trying to lure Earl into a false sense of security. *She must either really love you, or she's planning on slipping poison into a drink of yours later.*

Saniya laughed her musical laugh as she behold the

surprised, dumbfounded expression next to her. "Don't get me wrong, I'm still with my ladies when it comes to predatory men, but do you remember the friend I told you about, Aimee? The one with the boyfriend who was one of the nude models that we had to 'draw inspiration' from in my first year?"

Earl knew too well, Aimee being the only standout friend of Saniya's that he knew about due to his outrage over the nude model in the first place.

"…Yeah, why?"

"She's kind of inadvertently shown me that the modern-day woman can be just as trifling as any dude roaming the earth. I realized that I'd had my blinders on to it until Aimee… 'enlightened' me." Saniya honked her horn at a car in front of her that was driving in accordance to the speed limit. After receiving no response or indication that she'd been heard, she merged into the next lane and overpassed the car, giving them the middle finger as she did. "Lately, she's been playing the field because she claims they've been together too long, even though it's only been two years. Well, to save you the long list of vivid debauchery that have been her exploits in the past few months, she's attending an orgy next week without Lee knowing about it. She tried to invite me, telling me that a walk on 'the wild side' may do me some good. I think she's a little bi-curious because that's not the first time she's tried to proposition me, but I guess she figures that the orgy may be the gateway to bedding yours truly!" Earl ignored Saniya's flippant, exaggerated smile and instead focused on the news that she'd been invited to cheat on him.

"What did you say?!"

"Honestly, we've been together for a *long* time, E. I mean, what would be the harm in a one-time, sensual extravaganza?" Earl rolled his eyes and shook his head as Saniya cackled. "I'm almost offended that you have to ask me, E! I said 'Hell no,' of course! Many things wrong with that scenario: One, there are *way* too many people.

"But, yeah." Saniya continued, going back to the original topic. "I'm not with that kind of activity. Besides, you know how I feel about
cheating, especially considering what I went through with Dominic. Never again."

Earl immediately felt bad about his salacious thoughts regarding Imani, even Kim, as Saniya brought up Dominic. He'd been one out of the three of her exes, and arguably the worst. Earl recalled the story vividly... Dominic and Saniya were together when her mother had gotten one of the most-beloved teachers fired for racial bigotry. Dominic, seeing the ire that had descended upon Saniya by the predominantly-decided to side with the other students rather than with his girlfriend. Dominic not only insulted Saniya behind her back, but he cheated on her with three of the cheerleaders of the school's football team. That fact was shouted at Saniya during one of their last conversations, accompanied by pictures and videos of his misdeeds. She'd tearfully asked Dominic why he'd do that to her, and Dominic told her that she "wasn't the kind of girl that he wanted to be with for longer than a year." Since then, Saniya had a zero-tolerance rule for philandering and promiscuity. Earl also suspected that she'd held a certain unfavorable bias towards white people in some regards, but he'd never been bold enough to broach that possibility into a conversation. "Fuck him, Sans. You have me. You've had me for almost six years, and the two of us will continue on for years to come!"

"Yeah, you're right. You've been my peace, my heart, and I don't know what I'd do without you, E. I promise, this summer, there won't be any bullshit or arguing. I want to relax, have fun, and if you play your cards right, we can do some other things too." Saniya winked at Earl, biting her lip in the process, which immediately made Earl's pants tighten. If there was one thing that she knew instantly got him ready for the bedroom, it was her signature lip-bite. With a final turn, Saniya and Earl finally arrived at Charlotte's, pulling into the driveway without any other car present.

Good. That motherfucker is at work today.

202

"I haven't had a chance to see Ms. Charlotte in a while!" Saniya said excitedly as she exited the car. "Speaking of, my mom's been asking about you, so at some point we'll have to pay her a visit too." "Of course! Your mom adores me!" Earl exclaimed as he fiddled around with his keychain, isolating the house key he'd been searching for. "True! The other day, she brought up the first time you met my dad, and I was crying with how hard I laughed. I know you remember that, don't you?"

"I remember being charmed by him when he threatened to tie cinder blocks to my feet and throw me at the bottom of a lake if I ever hurt you." "Yeah! He'd just seen that movie about the witches too, which makes that moment so much better, I swear!" Earl shook his head as Saniya walked over and hugged him warmly. She remained nestled in his arms for a few seconds before she freed him to open the door and enter the house. Earl looked to his immediate left into the kitchen, then to his immediate right to the living room, both of which were unoccupied. Before Earl had a chance to reach the conclusion that Charlotte was most likely asleep in her room, she trotted out Her eyes lit up with joy as she noticed Saniya walking in behind Earl, and she hastened her wobbly gait towards them. "There's my future granddaughter-in-law!" Charlotte proudly stated as she flung her arms open to embrace Saniya, who returned the enthusiastic gesture. "Hi, Ms.

203

Charlotte! Long time, no see!" "Well, you know I don't go anywhere, girl. This old lady doesn't do shit but watch television and drink wine coolers! And what are the two of you up to anyway? Working on those great-grandchildren, Earl?"

"...No." Earl replied flatly. "I'm going to grab some clothes and stay at Saniya's for a day or two." "That's fine, grab the overnight bag in my closet to pack some things in, baby. Saniya and I are going to catch up!" "Yeah, we'll be out here when you're done!" Saniya said as her and Charlotte sat on one of the leather couches in the living room and chatted, leaving Saniya to bring Charlotte up to speed on the latest round of gossip at her university. Earl huffed and went to Charlotte's room to retrieve the overnight bag she suggested he take, which he found buried deep inside of the closet. After checking to make sure that there wasn't anything in it, he walked back out to the hallway and glared at Charlotte before going into his room and closing the door behind him.

Charlotte can be so embarrassing. She acts like she's still in college herself sometimes, and she can't shut the hell up for twenty minutes. I know you love her, but you have to admit, it can be a bit much, especially when she starts up the coddling in front of other people.

None of this even matters. You have to elevate yourself to where you know you need to be. Even if Ben sold you a pipe dream when he pitched the potential of starting a musical gig with him, you're going to bounce back. You won't just survive; you'll finally be able to live.

Earl smirked to himself and prepared to leave his unkempt room behind, but stopped dead in his tracks as he recalled something that he'd have been remiss to forget. He strode over to one of the two chairs and moved a pair of pajama bottoms to reveal a black notebook, his book of potential songs. He opened the book to his latest entry, which he'd spent the week trying to perfect, but simply couldn't get right.

Later. Now, let's get out of here. We don't know what Charlotte could be saying to Saniya.

He stuffed the notebook into his bag and hoisted the strap slung over his right shoulder. He finally walked back into the hallway, ready, and he closed his bedroom door behind him. Before he could turn around, he could already feel two pairs of eyes homed in on the back of his head.
"We were just talking about you, boy! Come on in and sit down, music man!"

Charlotte's voice scratched against the walls of his mind like nails on a chalkboard, and Earl had found himself more and more irritated by the second. Not wanting to cause any unnecessary drama, however, he walked over to the couch adjacent to the one Saniya and Charlotte were seated at, forming an L shape in front of a cocktail table lined with scented candles. He sat, already annoyed by Charlotte knowing the state that she was in. When he'd initially walked into the house, he'd smelled the faint scent of marijuana, a daily tradition of Charlotte's. He'd also seen the three wine coolers on the kitchen table, two of which were empty, and one which had about a gulp's worth of liquid left.

"Saniya was asking me about what you were like as a kid. I told her about the time you somehow got that big, apple-shaped head stuck in the stair bannister at our old apartment. You don't remember that?" "No," Earl said tersely.

Tipsy and high? Like that Thanksgiving back in middle school where she made fun of you in front of everyone that came over!

"He cried for about half an hour, and Randy had to use a hacksaw to get him out. Fucked the staircase up. Back then, he looked like a stick bug trying to balance an orange with how big his goddamn head was, and that hasn't really changed since then." Earl could feel his fingers gripping the seat of the couch tighter as Charlotte continued on. There was a slight slur in her intonation, and her eyes had a glassy, reddish film coating them. "Really? I never knew that you were a crybaby back in the day!" Saniya commented with a devilish grin. "Oh, not just that. Did he ever tell you about Trey?"

206

No. Fucking don't.

"Trey was one of the boys who picked on him in middle school. He told my baby to get back into his spaceship, and Earl wasn't having any of that." Saniya hung on to Charlotte's every word, eager to hear more about Earl's undignified childhood. "Charlotte, can we no—" "Hush up, I'm telling a story."

Charlotte's eyes were bleary, yet forceful, ending Earl's protest. She went on with the tale despite the rage building inside of her grandson. "Anyway, Earl found some courage that day and told Trey to meet him outside after school. He was ashamed that Trey had insulted him in front of his friends, and he wanted to save face. Girl, when I tell you that Earl got the ass-whippin' of a lifetime, words can't describe how badly Trey fucked that boy up!" Charlotte cackled, leaning over on the couch while Saniya cracked up as well, fully entertained by Charlotte's tale. "I mean, I had to give the boy's hindquarters a good lashing here and there when he was growing up, but I got the call to pick him up from the school since he'd missed his bus back home, and when I got up there, I saw him with a black eye, a bloody nose and a busted lip! He burst into tears on the ride home, and it took me hours to get him to finally calm down. I had to give the boy a bag of frozen peas to stop his eye from swelling up to the size of a golf ball. After that, he never really got into any more fights, and I bet you that he never got in Trey's way again! Hell, the school didn't even bother to suspend Early, though he'd technically initiated the tussle. I guess they figured he'd suffered enough!" Tears of laughter streamed down her face and she could barely breathe from her fit of hysteria. Earl had had enough, and he rose from the couch with absolute rancor lining his dark expression.

"That's enough!"

The exclamation reverberated off the walls of the living room as Earl screamed, breathing heavily as he stared down Charlotte. "What the fuck is wrong with you, boy?" "Saniya, we're leaving."
Earl didn't acknowledge Charlotte's question, instead making his way towards the front door. Saniya got up, brushed herself off and attempted to follow Earl, but Charlotte had other plans.

"Earl, get your ass back here! I need you to run to the store for me and grab a few things!" Earl stormed back into the living room and the volcano of anger that had been dormant, residing within Earl for an untold amount of years, had finally erupted. "Run to the store? How am I supposed to manage that? I don't have a fucking car! I'm not about to waste Saniya's gas to go get you some bullshit from the market! Get that drug addict to do it when he comes in!"

"You watch your fucking attitude, Earl!"

Charlotte nearly toppled over trying to stand up, but she managed to prop herself up on her own two feet. Saniya stood between Earl and Charlotte, unsure of how to defuse the implosive situation. "No, I'm sick of you and this bullshit! I've spent my entire goddamn life appeasing you, supporting you, doing whatever asinine shit you wanted me to do! You aren't going to sit there and make me look stupid in front of Saniya and then laugh about it to my face like I'm not
there!" "Earl, baby, it's okay... She didn't mean—"

"No, I know what she meant! She doesn't know what to say out of her mouth, and she doesn't realize the toll that living here has had on me. I'm trapped! If it's not being guilted by her 'throw me in a nursing home and live your life' bullshit, which she knows makes me feel bad, it's the fact that I can't do shit with the money that I slave over because I need to pay 'rent.' I have to give Randall money when he spends his paycheck up buying heroin, and then what do I have to show for any of it? Fucking nothing! She's always been overprotective and overbearing, she always talks down to me and the things that I want to do, and then she lets that asshole go unchecked to leech off of us? Fuck that." "You better find some goddamn sense. I'm warning you, Earl," Charlotte threatened, pointing a swaying finger at Earl. "Or what, you'll get the belt? Sorry, I'm too old for that shit now, it's not going to work.

I'm not a fifteen-year-old anymore, and I'm tired of you fucking treating me like I am." "You see this, Saniya?" Charlotte directed to the girl between them, gesturing to Earl. "Try to teach a boy to be a man, and he doesn't want to do it. Your problem, Earl, is that you expect the world to give you whatever the fuck you want without having to work for it or prove yourself. I don't make you pay rent to spite you, I do it to prepare you for the real world, which you clearly aren't ready for. That's what's wrong with your sorry-ass, entitled generation now! Of course, you're going to fail, but because you can't learn from your mistakes and handle them the right way doesn't mean you should take it out on me. You should be grateful to have a roof over your head, food to eat and a grandmother who provides for and loves you. Yeah, I ask you to do for me, but what's the harm in that? What are you trying to say, huh? What's the point of all this yelling and carrying-on? What are you going to do, move? If that's the case, then why don't you get the fuck out if you're so miserable here?!"

What followed was a foreboding silence that let Charlotte's heavy question linger, making the room feel heavier than it was. Earl tried to hide the hot tear that fell from his eye, but it dropped straight out and onto the floor as he started nodding after contemplating his answer. "You know what? I just might. I'm sick of being punished for wanting better. I'm tired of feeling like I'm tethered to you and can't free myself. I'm not this fragile, naïve bitch that everyone seems to think I am. I don't care if you end up in a fucking home or not, but I'll tell you what, you can figure that shit out for yourself because I'm gone." Charlotte let out a dismal, shuddering breath as Earl took his bag and walked out of the living room and through the front door of the house, refusing to look back once. Saniya trailed behind him, trying to speak to Earl, but to no avail. Charlotte collapsed onto the couch, putting her head into her hands as she began to wail. Despite the losses she'd suffered, the pain she'd been through and the lessons she'd had to learn the hard way, nothing had ever stung like Earl's unmistakable, caustic proclamation.

Chapter 14

♪ If I told you I grew up poor as hell, abandoned, fending for myself, my grandmother praying for some wealth, stayed worried about my mental health. Would you believe me?

♪ If I told you that I was never accepted, humanity tested, intents intercepted. Ridiculed, played for a fool, with the game constantly changing the rules. Would you believe me?

♪ Couldn't relate to those around me, thoughts and feelings tried to drown me, tried to make it "us," they made it "them," tried to use me at their whim. Then I met a girl, she changed my world, gave me endless love, my heart unfurled, At last, someone can relate to me, but I had no direction, craved a dream.

♪ Friction at work, had me going berserk, tried to yield to the ingratitude. Got tired enough, stopped giving a fuck, wanted more in life than servitude. Bore my soul on the page, that wasn't appreciated, legacy fading, not even abbreviated.

♪ Accidentally found my stride, yet I'm vilified by some who are blind to the vision that I've created.

They told me I'm soft, I'm calling their bluff. They aren't up to snuff when compared to a diamond in the rough, and that's tough.

♪ I understand the huff and puff, but all of its guff, now please ask yourself: "Is it really him that I should rebuff?" Put away the cameras, no more humoring fluff.

Disproved the hypothesis that there's a chance I'm not real enough. ♪

The beat settled, and Earl took off the headphones. He took a deep breath, having released all the tension of the last few days. The argument with Charlotte snowballed into yet another argument with Saniya about Charlotte's intent behind her words. Earl, having lost his patience for verbal disagreements, spent the bulk of his time hanging out at Ben's place to unwind. His frustrations came to a head when Ben let him scroll through the comments on his Tonally page so that Earl could see the generally positive feedback that their first song had received. Rather than the good, however, Earl focused on the few random, negative critiques that popped up occasionally. "This is wack! Homeboy sounds soft as shit!" "I hope the strike ends soon so that people don't flock to garbage like this." "Is this what people like these days? Dude sounds like a bitch." Earl's first song, which he had affectionately come around to calling 'Light From Darkness' was loosely based off the plot of his own book, and the fact that it wasn't unanimously appreciated sent him over the edge. In just a day, as he sat on the couch in Saniya's apartment he'd finally crafted 'Not Real Enough' after a dearth of creativity.

He exited the live room to applause, Ben nodding crazily in approval of Earl's newest song. All Earl had directed Ben to do when Ben went to pick him up was give him a commanding, fast-paced beat, and he'd do the rest. "E, that was great! I knew that you had it in you!" "Yeah, that was awesome!" Earl whipped his head around to the voice at the stairs and saw Imani, who'd been hiding just out of Earl's line of sight while he was recording in the live room.

"Ben said that you get a little nervous when you're being watched, so he told me that I could chill over here and just listen! You got something legit there, Earl!" Earl's mouth flapped mechanically, yet no words came out. Ben snickered. "See, dude? You've got it! I'll get to work on that recording soon, but I wanted to mention that today might be our big day!" Earl gulped, knowing that Ben meant that today was the day that they were slated to get their first check from Tonally. Ben had explained to Earl that there was no way for him to check and see how much they were going to get until they'd actually had the check in their hands. "Yeah. I guess we're going to find out if we're cracked up for this or not." Ben nodded at Earl's assessment of the situation but gave his friend a sincere look of pride. "Not a lot of people get to this point though, dude. If it turns out that we just made like, one-hundred dollars or something, I'll be happy to have accomplished that.

"I have a good feeling about it though, guys. Positivity goes a long way in being able to see things through to the end! Plus, I let my followers know about the song too! Between Ben's 600,000 and my 350,000, that's almost a million listeners! That's not including people outside of the two of us that listened to it because it was featured on Tonally's top tracks of the month." Earl did his best not to look in Imani's direction too much, or he'd be unable to look away. Imani wore a tank-top with some tight, thin sweatpants that outlined every inch of her body. Simply her presence in the basement with them and being able to pinpoint her distinctive scent was enough to get his heart pumping, but he did his best to keep to himself.

Earl saw the car accident as a reason to force a stop to his daydreaming habits. So far, he'd only done it in private where he could reflect in peace.

Because he'd been so occupied, either with music or otherwise, the intruder had become more infrequent.

After all these years, Earl genuinely felt as though he had the advantage in the war with not only his dips and dives in mood, but with his mind as a whole.

"Oh, E, I realized that you didn't have any social media accounts anywhere anymore! What happened?" Earl wanted to be snarky, but considering all that Ben had put into their musical endeavor, he couldn't help but have a renewed admiration for his long-time friend. "I didn't see a point in it. The only people I had as friends were people I hadn't seen since." Ben gave Earl an eyebrow wiggle and a mischievous grin, and Earl immediately knew that Ben had a scheme brewing. "That's going to have to change, Big E! You have to give yourself leverage because if nobody can find you, then they won't care about what you're doing! In fact, I've got something to show you that I think will grow on you!" Ben took out his phone, tapping and swiping until he found what he was searching for. He handed the phone over to Earl, whose eyes widened as he saw the familiar WeLink format with his and Ben's name together on the web page.

"What the hell is this?!"

"Imani created a new account on WeLink for us! Since we hadn't discussed a name yet, I thought of 'B&E' until we got together to brainstorm another name. Unless, of course, you have a cool name that you want to give yourself!" Earl wanted to question Ben, but the longer he stared at their new joint social media account, the more it made sense, despite his natural apprehension towards the idea. "Yeah, it's something that I made really quick to help you guys out!"

Imani swung her legs proudly from her seated position at the third stair from the bottom.

"Thanks, Imani. It's nice."

"Oh, baby, can you check and see if the mail's here yet?" Ben asked with a cheeky wink. "Sure! I can go check on Miles while I'm up there. I've been sitting too long anyway; I need to go stretch my legs." *Or wrap them around my head.*

Earl shook his head as Imani trotted up the steps, and he coerced his mind to focus on Ben.

"If it turns out that we don't get much from this and we aren't as musically-inclined as we thought, then I just want to say… thank you, Ben." Ben's eyes widened, and he covered his mouth as if Earl had said the most startling thing he'd ever heard. "Did… did you just thank me?"

Ben asked incredulously.

"Is there a secret camera crew upstairs ready to run down here and tell me that I've been got? Are you sick? Is this some Earl clone that I'm talking to?" "No, you idiot," Earl growled, eliciting a delighted chuckle from Ben. "I want you to know that I understand that I haven't been... the easiest person to befriend. I've cussed you out, I've ignored you, and yet somehow, we're still as cool as we were years ago. I appreciate that, man." Ben's smile went from ear to ear as he got up and wrapped his arms tightly around Earl. After the first few seconds of paralysis from confusion, Earl stiffly smacked Ben on the back a few times, somewhat reciprocating Ben's rush of sentimentality.

"You aren't as hard to be around as you think, Earl. Out of all my friends, you're definitely the one that's always there when I need you. We crack a lot of jokes, but I'm glad that we decided to do this. It's been the most fun I've ever had, dude. Getting the chance to come together, chill and create music has been incredible. I couldn't think of anyone else I'd have picked for this over you... "Oh, God."

Ben's amusement could be heard over the hum of the machines situated in the control room as Earl's face scrunched up in disgust. "Never change, Ben. The world absolutely needs more of your disgusting innuendos." "I'd never, E!"
"Guys, come up here! I think this is it!"

Imani's excited shouting prompted Earl and Ben to zoom up the stairs, following Imani's voice to the living room. As they approached her, she held up an ornate, midnight-blue envelope and held it out for one of them to grab. Earl and Ben looked at each other, afraid to take the envelope.

"Come on! You guys deserve this!"

Finally, Ben reached out for the envelope and made his way to the couch. His eyes scanned the back of the envelope, seeing Tonally's logo, a pair of headphones, as the seal of the envelope. "Is it time?" Ben asked, looking up at Earl to confirm. All Earl could do is nod as Ben carefully peeled away the seal down next to him. Imani and Earl stood side-by-side, watching Ben's face to assess any emotion that'd give away the good or bad outcome of their endeavor.

This is it. You've been thrown in the deep end. From here, you'll do one of two things: You'll float, or you'll drown. You can't afford to tread water anymore.

Earl could feel small beads of sweat forming at his forehead. He kept smacking his lips to keep his mouth from drying out and he could hear his heart pound against his chest as if trying to escape. After what felt like an eternity, Ben closed his eyes, lowered his head, and his shoulders fell gracelessly. Earl could feel his heart drop into the bowels of his stomach, and the shock was enough to keep his body from crumbling into a heap.

"Well, E, at least we had a good time."

Ben smiled sadly, and Earl had to fight back the tears he could feel stinging at the back of his eyes. *Again, and again, you come up short. You're a miserable piece of shit that will die with nothing. Nobody will remember your name, Earl. You'll be just as forgotten and irrelevant as you are now. Randall was right.*

"You're my partner in this, E. It'll be alright; we'll go back to the drawing board and do it better next time. Right?" "…Yeah."

With a reserved nod, Ben got up and walked over to Earl, handing him the papers so that he could witness the news firsthand. Earl caught a glimpse of the perforated portion at the bottom of the page but didn't have the heart to look at it right off the bat. Instead, he started perusing the paper from the very top. It started out as a thank you letter from the creators of the Tonally website, and then Earl got to the statistics at the middle of the page. 784,913 people listened to the sample of the track. 675,660 liked it. 100,707 people paid Ben's option of a dollar as opposed to the other tiers, and then Tonally subtracted their ten-percent from that figure, with slight interest. Earl's eyes bulged as he finally got to the check at the very bottom of the page, and his whole body became as still as stone as the number internally repeated itself within him. *90,000.....?*

90,000…… cents?

…….90,000 dollars?!

"But… but… huh?"

Earl turned to Ben as slowly as possible, his mind not quite catching up to the moment. As he met Ben's frenetic gaze, who'd done his best to maintain his poker face up until now, Ben yelled at the top of his lungs in triumph. He pumped both arms wildly into the air, and then grabbed Imani and hoisted her up into the air, spinning her around with glee. *"We did it, E! We got 90,000 motherfucking dollars! That's 45,000 between us!"* Earl's mouth remained agape as his mind fought to comprehend what was going on. Even halved, that was more money in a month than his job would've provided for him in the span of a year. "This… this isn't a joke?"

"Nope! You and I can go cash it right now!"

Earl stood, calmly putting the check down at the spot where he'd been sitting. He looked between Imani and Ben who both eyed him cautiously, attempting to gauge his reaction. Suddenly, without warning, Earl's victorious howl greatly exceeded Ben's as he dropped to his knees, unable to support his lower body any longer. Earl tapped into the overwhelming sense of catharsis that had previously only manifested itself in his fantasies, and the feeling was more than he could handle at once as his joy-laden hoots transformed into streams of ecstatic, relieved tears. Out of all the good he felt that he'd done, all the rules he'd been forced to adhere to by one authority or another, the times he'd been censored, ignored or overlooked, it had led to this, something that was his.

Earl's sobs were loud and sloppy with snot leaking from his nostrils, and his eyes were bloodshot red as he bore the sum of his emotions. He felt like he'd been validated after long years of listlessness and protracted uphill battles with his own psyche.

"We did it, man."

Ben had closed the gap between himself and Earl and simply stood near him, his own voice cracking as he too became victim to a few tears. Earl wrapped his arms around Ben heartily. The two didn't even need to exchange words of appreciation; the magnitude of their achievement was relayed in the embrace they'd shared.Earl finally released his impassioned hold, and Imani handed both Ben and Earl tissues to assist them in composing themselves. She'd done nothing but watch the two bask, careful not to intrude where she felt she didn't belong.

"Are you guys alright?" "Yeah, baby. Thanks."

Earl had to take a few shuddering breaths to right himself, but he gave Imani and Ben a thumbs-up, using one of Ben's own infamous gestures to affirm his recovery from his avalanche of raw emotion. "I'm good," he croaked out with a subsequent sniffle. "Dude, I promise you, this next song will be even bigger than that one. I'm going to add a nice little chorus, maybe tweak the beat to make it hotter than it is, we're about to own this! 90,000 dollars is going to be pocket change compared to what we're going to be putting out there and getting back! Are you with me, E? Are you ready to play this game?!"

"Ready?" Earl said with a renewed confidence. "We're going to play the game, win every time and then reinvent it!" "There we go! That's the Big E that I knew was hiding in there all along!"

Earl and Ben did a handshake that ended in them clapping each other on the back, a sign that they were in it for the long haul. "Alright, so how about we take a ride down to the bank?!" Earl was about to agree, but a thought pushed its way to the forefront of his mind that he couldn't shake, and the temptation was too strong to ignore. He took out his phone, checked the time, and a malevolent smile snuck upon his lips.

"Actually, can we make two other stops first? I need you to take me back to Saniya's for a second so that I can pick something up."

--

Earl strolled into the Sub Shack with a comfortable, light gait. He smoothed out his work uniform and adjusted his SS hat, making sure that it was perfectly centered on the top of his head. It was as if the stars had aligned because Thursdays were his days to work one of his two late shifts out of the week. He put his hands on his hips nonchalantly and took in the smell of lunchmeat and gluttony for the last time as he made his way onto the production line where his co-workers resided. Jaiquan's lazy eye shifted off-center, as it usually did. Where Earl would typically feel dejected, exasperated frustration at the flagrant, brazen irresponsibility of his co-workers, he casually shrugged and offered his compatriot a warm smile. "That's cool! Let me get myself together first, and then I'll be right out!" Jaiquan grunted in response as a customer walked up to the counter, ready to satiate their hunger. Earl traveled to the back area where the employee designated for dish-washing resided, trying to find the manager for the night. After a tepid nod from the dishwasher, Earl knocked on the door to the manager's office and stepped back. A minute later, a wide-faced, oval-eyed woman with long, lanky arms came bobbing out of the office, her eyes narrowing when she realized who had distracted her from counting the money in the registers for the cashiers working the morning shift.

"What do you want, Earl? You're fifteen minutes late. I'll let you off with a warning this time, but next time, you're getting written up." Between Jane's thick eyebrows and the space between her two front teeth, Earl wasn't sure which one of her qualities he'd miss the least. He had only been partly paying her any mind, but he'd gotten the gist of her reprimand. "That's fine, Jane. The warning isn't necessary though."

"…What do you mean? You can't show up late with no consequences attached to it! What kind of message would that send to others?"

Earl had to stop himself from giving away his true intention back the vitriol that rose at the back of his throat. Jane never liked him, and he never understood why, not that he cared. Her favorites would call out or be half an hour late all they wanted, and then have the audacity to joke around with Jane or each other in the back while Earl slaved away on the production line. "It's not the best look, Jane, but I did have something that I wanted to bring to your attention before I started my shift." "What is it?"

Earl could hear the irritation in her tone, but hadn't a care in the world as to how Jane felt. He'd braced himself for this, injecting courage into his heart so that he could deliver the farewell that Jane deserved. He cleared his throat and lifted an index finger in the air as if to elongate the theatrics of the situation. "Fuck this job, fuck this hat and shirt, fuck this building and I hope that that fat fuck you like bending over backwards for chokes on that goddamn ham and swiss sandwich one day. Oh, and most importantly, *fuck you.*" Jane blinked a few times.

Earl's delivery of the line had been so suppressed and casual that she wasn't entirely sure if she'd imagined it or not. "What did you say?!"

"You heard me. I don't get paid enough to be the best worker here day in and day out. You can kiss my black ass because I quit!"

Earl backed away and tossed his hat at Jane's feet, which twirled gracefully throughout the air before landing directly between her ankles. His former supervisor's face was fixated in stupefied terror, mortified by Earl's emboldened resignation. "Sayonara, bitch!" The dishwasher couldn't hide his inquisitive stance anymore as he turned around, his mouth in the shape of the letter "O" as he looked between Jane and Earl, confounded at the stunning, one-sided exchange that had happened before him. Earl mockingly saluted Jane before exiting the back area and heading up to the front of the store, leaving as quietly as he'd entered. He could feel the thumping of his heart in his ears, and his hands shook involuntarily.

Nobody will ever speak to you any way they please ever again. We're going to show everyone what happens when you sleep on the kid, one day at a time.

Earl traipsed through the parking lot to Ben's car where he took his place in the backseat and leaned back, carefree. "You actually did it?!" Ben said, looking at Earl from the rearview mirror. "Yeah, fuck them." "You're wild, Earl! That would've been perfect to get on video! I wish I had seen you in action!" Imani stated, turning to look at Earl with her naturally sultry eyes. *Maybe you will one day.* "Oh, dude, Imani and I were talking about something cool while you were in there! We need to properly celebrate us making our way into the big leagues!"

"…How do you mean?" Earl's apprehension couldn't have been clearer as Ben elaborated. "We're going to throw a party next week! Liquor, weed, anything anyone wants to bring will be welcomed!" "You know I hate parties, Ben. I don't do any of that; it's not who I am."

Earl felt his phone vibrate but trained himself to ignore it knowing it was most likely Charlotte. answer any of her calls or listen to the many voicemails that she'd left him. "Dude, please? It wouldn't be right celebrating without my partner-in-crime! Bring Saniya if you want, but you need to come." As Earl opened his mouth to object, Imani

227

added in her two cents.

"Ben's right. You don't have to drink anything if you're not into it, but I'm going to have to throw the peer pressure card at you too. Pretty please, Earl?" All Imani had to do was bat her eyelashes at Earl, and his resolve crumbled instantaneously. "Okay, okay. Saniya and I haven't been speaking a lot lately, but things should settle in time for the party." "Right on!" Ben pumped his fist and started up the car, elated at Earl's answer. Earl looked at the building one last time, resolving never to return to it for as long as he lived. "Thank you, Earl! You can introduce me to Saniya, and we'll have a lot of fun! Don't worry, I'll make sure Ben doesn't overdo it with inviting people. It'll be a night to remember, you'll see!"
Imani punctuated her guarantee with a smile that almost made Earl melt into the leather of the interior of Ben's car.

Anything for you.

Chapter 15

"Sans, please. I promise that I'll talk to Charlotte tomorrow, but can we enjoy tonight?

This means a lot to me."

Saniya looked at Ben's townhouse, peering into the windows at the party within. Earl's pleading voice finally broke her silence as she uncrossed her arms, ending her streak of defiance. "She's been blowing my phone up begging to speak to you. She misses you and wants you to come home. It's been long enough; this grudge that you're holding against her is childish." Rather than refute her point, he conceded, not wanting to strain their relationship further.

"You're right. I've been handling it in the worst way imaginable, and I'll rectify it, I swear. Can I please have my Sans back?" Saniya stared at him for a long time, waiting until she could discern whether his claim was sincere or not. "You'd better do it, and yes, I'll stop being a brat." The small smile that Saniya gave Earl was confirmation enough for him as they both stepped out of his new car. His particular model of Cadillac wasn't exactly the most sensational ride on the market, but Earl had just been happy to be mobile again rather than needing to depend on others for transportation. "You shouldn't have quit your job though," Saniya made sure to emphasize as Earl pressed the button next to Ben's door, remembering the doorbell's existence this time. Earl stifled a sigh as the pair waited, having heard Saniya's spiel constantly over the last week. When he broke the news of his success to her, attempting to quell the persisting tensions from the Charlotte debacle, he thought that she'd be overjoyed. After hearing the unavoidable news regarding the Sub Shack, however, her excitement faded, and she turned on her "mother mode," as Earl defined it.

"Why would you do that?! There's no guarantee that you'll be as lucky going forward when it comes to the ups and downs of the music industry! What happens if it doesn't work out, and you have to go back to working a regular job? If any employer goes to contact the Sub Shack to find out what kind of worker you are, they're going to be told of how you quit and not want to hire you!" On and on and on.

Earl wanted her to be as elated as he was. He thought that she, having an intimate understanding of what he'd been through, would be nothing but enthused and supportive.
Instead, she can't ever be happy for you.

Finally, the door flung open, and Ben's eyes nearly sparkled as he announced Earl's presence.
"Ladies and gentlemen, the man of the hour has arrived! Stop whatever you're doing and give it up for

my man, the lyricist, Earl!" The whole house erupted into cheers and hoots as Earl walked into the house. Before Earl could even register what was happening, Ben had an arm around him and pointed to Imani, who prepared her phone to take a photo of the two.

"Alright, Big E! Say 'Success'!"

Ben smiled as wide as his face would allow him, but all Earl could conjure up was an awkward half-smile as Imani snapped the picture. "That's definitely about to go up on the WeLink page!" Imani said, looking at the results of her handiwork. "Hey, Saniya!" Ben said, acknowledging her as she stepped into the house. "Hey, Ben." Her greeting had been comparatively more subdued as Ben peeked outside, noticing the new vehicle parked in his driveway. He'd put up a sign next to his house that advised people to park close to the curb or at the parking lot a block away from his house, reserving his driveway for Earl and Saniya.

"Dude, is that a new car?!"

"Yeah, I bought it a few days ago."
"Nice, dude! Now, chill and enjoy yourself! Give me five minutes; I have something ready to go that I think that you'll like!" Ben darted off through the thicket of humanity, leaving Earl, Saniya and Imani to get acquainted. "Hi, I'm Imani! Ben's girlfriend! You must be Saniya; I've heard nothing but wonderful

things about you!" Imani held out her hand for Saniya to shake, which Saniya gave a dubious look before accepting. "What have you heard?" Saniya asked, trying her best to power through the night with as genuine a countenance of interest as she could produce. "I hear that you paint and do some kick-ass photography on the side! I might have to pick your brain later so that you can give me some pointers! I'm trying to become a model, so I welcome anything you could offer so that I can go about making the most of my profile!"

Saniya chuckled softly at the compliment, running a hand through her hair to emphasize her humility over her expertise in the visual arts.

"It's nothing professional or anything. I'm more into painting and sketches than I am at photography, but I could look at some of your pictures and throw some tips your way, if you want." "Awesome! We'll have to set a date to link up soon! So, would you like a drink? You can pretty much pick your poison. Anything that Ben doesn't have hidden away, some of our invitees have, but you probably want to be more wary of anything in the latter category," Imani emphasized with a chuckle. "Sure, I'll take something light. I don't want to wake up with a hangover tomorrow, so I'll take a spritzer or a cocktail if you have it." "Gotcha! My mom dated a bartender for about a month, and he showed me a little something-something! Be right back!"

Imani went off to prepare Saniya's drink, and Earl noticed that something about his girlfriend wasn't quite right. She'd usually been the sociable one to compensate for his lack of socialization, but she, so far, had restrained herself. "What's wrong? Not feeling the rum today?" Earl joked, hoping to dissolve some of Saniya's tension. "No, but you see it, don't you?" Saniya deflected, nodding in the direction that Imani had departed in.

"…See what?"

"There's something off about her, and I can't put my finger on what it is. She seems… fake."

Or maybe that's jealousy talking. "I haven't noticed anything too weird about her." "Of course, you wouldn't," Saniya dryly stated. "Men don't have the ability to see women in any sort of objective light; you just see how pretty she is. Maybe I'm jumping the gun a little, but something about her rubs me the wrong way."
You can be judgmental, that's for sure. Imani squeezed through the crowd, carrying two fancy glasses containing a pink, vibrant mixture with a few ice cubes smoothly floating on its surface.

"Here you go, girl!" Imani said, handing one of the two drinks to Saniya, who took it pensively. Imani then raised her glass, keen to make a toast.
"To our successful boyfriends and the bomb-ass girls by their side! Cheers!" "Cheers." Saniya ultimately

indulged Imani, meeting her glass with a clink as they both sipped their drinks. Earl looked around, already exhausted by the partying people surrounding them. Just then, Ben burst through the crowd and leapt on top of his living room couch, holding an empty glass in one hand and a fork in the other. He made a gesture to someone in the distance, and the heavy, pulsating music cut off as he smacked the side of the glass with the fork, doing so until he'd garnered the attention of everyone in attendance. As the last ring of metal with glass reverberated off the walls of the now-quiet room, Ben paused dramatically, letting the anticipation build.

"Alright, everyone, settle down! Now, before anything else, I'd like to get Earl up here with me! Come on down, E!"

The partygoers all laid their eyes on Earl, who wanted to crumble under their scrutiny. Ben began to clap slowly, prompting everyone else to follow his lead until the entire house had joined in. Earl, seeing no other choice, began his trek over to Ben's couch. As he inched closer, Ben reached out his hand, which Earl grabbed as Ben hoisted him up to stand next to him.

"What you are looking at, folks, is the new, musical dynamic duo! I'm Ben, your creator of beats, mixing old school with new, and throwing in a classical, jazzy twist! This is Earl, the lyrical beast, who tugs at your heartstrings and makes you feel what he has to say! Together, we're going to take this world by storm!" The jubilant shouting that followed almost deafened Earl as he winced, watching Ben adore the love he'd gotten from the crowd. "Now, I know what most of you are thinking: What if we're one-hit-wonders who get a little taste of fame and then that's it? Well, allow me to let you listen to something. Play it, Vince!"

The slow, opening notes of a piano echoed throughout Ben's silent townhouse, and it was clear from the first ten seconds that the player of the instrument had known what they were doing. At the fifteen-second mark, the smooth, elegant notes began to transition. What started out as a beautiful stroll through a pristine park became a thundercloud moving in over a nice, breezy day, the gray skies beginning to overpower the blue. The notes became more aggressive, faster; single notes became chords, and soon, it was as if many different pianos were trying to play over one another, battling for dominance.

Around the sixty-second mark, the erratic music came to a crescendo, and then abruptly stopped. Five seconds of silence filled the startled room, then came the powerful advent of the saxophone like a bolt of lightning from the heavens.

"If I told you I grew up poor as hell, abandoned, fending for myself, my grandmother praying for some wealth, stayed worried about my mental health.

Would you believe me?" Earl's eyes widened as his voice blasted throughout the speakers, accompanied by a saxophone in the background accentuated with a harsh, bass-driven beat that complemented the grit of the lyrics. Before the audience had a chance to endear themselves to the song, many of them already broadcasting their favor of it by way of their gyrations and head bobbles, it ended. The unanimous disappointment made itself known as Ben laughed haughtily.

"That's just a taste of the next one! If you want to hear the whole thing, you'll have to wait for it to go live in another day or two! In the meantime, let's really kick shit off properly!"

A random person that Earl didn't recognize in the slightest walked up to the couch with two shot glasses and a plump bottle with a dark liquid sloshing within it. Ben grabbed the two glasses, opened the bottle with his teeth, then poured the contents of the bottle into each glass until they had been about three-fourths full. "This is Pincer Vodka, straight from Scotland! According to the website I bought it from, this will put a person flat on their ass!" Ben tried handing Earl one of the two glasses, who stared blankly at his allotted share, unwilling to put the drink anywhere near his mouth. Looking out into the crowd, he saw Saniya, arms folded, looking on disapprovingly. Then, he saw Imani, who smirked and winked at Earl. Hesitantly, he took the glass from Ben, already smelling the pungent vodka from a distance. "Just this once, okay?" Ben whispered, causing Earl to nod.

"A toast! To money, creativity and opportunity! Killing it one track at a time and making our mark from rhyme to rhyme!" Earl decided to throw caution to the wind, wrapped up in Ben's glorious tribute. Their glasses connected with a clink, and Earl and Ben knocked back the vodka to a hail of encouraging praises. Earl regretted it almost instantaneously as the vodka sizzled against the back of his throat first, then burned at his nostrils. Coughing, he hopped down from the couch and staggered about the room, trying to collect himself. The world became a distant fog as Earl lurched around, bumping into people who offered muffled words of congratulations as Ben called for the club music to come back on.

Earl's hysterical outburst almost seemed like the onset of a nervous breakdown as he felt himself slink to the floor with his back against the wall, laughing maniacally. He'd been so engulfed in hysteria that tears rolled down his cheeks and he struggled to catch his breath, almost feeling like someone was slowly putting their hands around his neck and adding more pressure with every second. Earl threw up in a corner of Ben's house, coughing and heaving as he expelled the contents of his stomach. When he was finished, wheezing and panting heavily as he took a minute to regain his wits, he looked up to see a shadow looming over him, waiting for his recognition. "Get up."

The room possessed a slight wobbling effect, so he cautiously made his way to his feet. He tried to simultaneously reach an equilibrium where he could remain balanced and do his best not to repeat his act of regurgitation.

"What the hell is wrong with you? I've never been more embarrassed by you in the entire time that we've been together. Did you know that people recorded your little presentation? You don't even drink, so what were you thinking taking a shot of vodka of all things?!" Earl's acumen and dishevelment unstably flew across the spectrum from one second to the next as the vodka went from being the worst experience, to being the best, back to being the worst due to Saniya's sobering presence. Apprehension turned into liquid courage, which became something deep and dark. "I... I wasn't..." Earl stuttered, trying to speak slowly as to not trigger any more sudden projectile bile. "What, you weren't thinking? This is what you do; you let Ben take over and you do whatever he wants you to do. I don't understand what possesses you to—" "Shut the fuck up!"

Everything froze as Earl's scream traveled from ear to ear. Games were halted, conversations were stopped dead in their tracks, and the attention of the party seemed to funnel into the impending explosion. "I'm sick of your shit! This is the first time in my life that I feel like I've accomplished something meaningful, and you can't be a decent girlfriend and fucking support me?! Always nagging, always bitching, and then you get on your high horse and try to make me look like this pathetic pussy who can't make his own decisions. Well, guess what? Not everyone has their lives figured out by the end of high school. Not everybody has all these scholarships lined up or has a mother who gets smacked on the ass by the principal and wins a multi-million-dollar settlement! I wrote a beautiful, provocative book, and the fact that I had nothing to show for it was utter bullshit! Meanwhile, claiming 'sexual harassment' can set you straight for the rest of your life!"

Saniya's face said it all as Earl lambasted her, years of unspoken grudges finally coming to roost. "Charlotte was broke, barely being able to pay the mortgage, and Randall is a drug- addled fuck-head who would rather do heroin than help us fucking survive from month to month. I didn't make a deal with my prissy mother to pay for a studio apartment as long as I got good grades in school; we didn't have the money to pay for me to go to school even if I wanted to!

You could afford to fail and try again; I couldn't! All I wanted you to do was support me, but instead, you condescend to me, and I don't need that. So, the next time you try to trivialize my accomplishments, I want you to remember that I busted my ass for this. I earned this moment;
me! You should be congratulating me and sucking my dick, not bitching about me not making up with

Charlotte or quitting a shitty job that made me miserable. If I want to take a single shot one goddamn, motherfucking time during a party that was thrown for something that I did, then I think I'm deserving of it!" Rather than enmity, Saniya simply covered her mouth, horrified at the things that she'd gleaned from Earl's intense, slurred rhetoric. "…I'm leaving. I'm calling a cab, and I don't want to see or hear from you for the next couple of days."

Saniya hastily disappeared into the crowd and all eyes were on Earl as he stood there, forced to weigh what he'd said and done. When the scrutiny proved to be too much for him, Earl walked away, heading towards Ben's backyard where he knew he could be alone. With long, determined footfalls, he was only a few feet from the back-door when Ben caught up to him.

"Dude, what happened?!"

"Just leave me alone for right now, Ben."

Ben didn't bother to follow Earl out the door as he sat down on one of the lawn chairs that Ben had kept in his small yard for lounging when the weather was nicer. Earl laid back on the chair and rubbed his temples, trying to process the multitude of thoughts and feelings that raced through his mind. The party had resumed, and Earl stayed on the lawn chair for the remainder of it, wondering, wishing that he could take back the entire event. Seeing the pain on

Saniya's face made him feel lowlier than he'd ever felt, and soon, the introspection and slight headache that followed caused him to sober up significantly after an hour.

As the festivities died down and people were starting to leave, another hour of self- loathing also went by. An additional half hour passed before footsteps came his way as Ben opened and slammed closed the sliding door that led to his backyard, causing Earl's aching body to twitch out of a fitful nap he'd been stirred from.

Ben stood next to Earl for a while, uncharacteristically quiet. When he spoke, it had no ounce or inkling of humor, but it was still obvious that Ben had been drinking quite a bit. "Ya wanna tawk 'bout it?" Ben said with as much sincerity as his drunkenness would allow. Somehow, this made Earl smirk, knowing that Ben cared about his plight as he looked up at the night sky, seeing the appearance of the first few stars."Nah, Ben. Maybe some other time." "Coo. Liss, ah needa favurr."

"Sure, what do you need?"

"Maddie. Still heer, 'n she needs go-home. Frenn left." Somehow understanding the request, Earl furrowed his eyebrows, not realizing that Madison had snuck into Ben's party as he didn't recall seeing her. He'd wanted to inquire as to how and why Ben allowed her to be there, but he thought better of it considering Ben's present state of mind. "Yeah, I got her."

Earl heard Ben's mumbled words of gratitude as they both made their way back into the now-empty house. "Where's Imani?" "Urpsturs, gone." Earl shook his head, figuring that Imani would be passed out somewhere as he made sure

that Ben's back doors were closed and locked, then made his way to the living room where Madison laid face-down, unconscious, on the couch. "Alright, Ben. You go upstairs and get some sleep. I'll make sure that the door is locked on my way out." "Thunku."

"Close enough," Earl stated as he helped Ben up the stairs, making sure that he got to his room safely before heading down to retrieve Madison. He walked over to her and nudged her a couple of times. After the sixth nudge, her eyes opened halfway, and upon lazily scanning her surroundings, she realized that Earl was standing over her.

"…Url?"

"Yeah, Maddie. It's me. I'm taking you home."

Fighting his own pounding headache and other sporadic bodily aches, Earl positioned himself so that he had most of her upper body propped up over his shoulder, supporting most of her weight as they hobbled towards the front door.

Chapter 16

Earl's car traveled down the dark, isolated road, occasionally dodging any potholes that stood in its way. The cool air of the night whipped against Earl's face as he snuck a glance over at the groaning, writhing figure next to him every so often to make sure that Madison was faring well as they reached the halfway point back to Ben's parent's house. His mind had been raging a violent war within itself, one side believing that Saniya needed to hear what he'd said at the party, and the other side begging him to apologize.

"No. Please."

The squeak of her voice had almost been completely imperceptible. Earl looked over at Madison as his car slowed down to wait for a traffic light to turn green so that he could turn at the intersection, only being six or so blocks from Madison's destination. Madison's eyes shot open and she began blinking rapidly, trying to orient herself to her surroundings. She straightened her posture from the slumped position that she'd been in since getting into the car. Then, she massaged her forehead, futilely trying to ease a torturous migraine. "Don't take me back home, Earl. My parents will kill me."

245

Earl stifled a grunt, wanting to be alone for the remainder of the night so that he could figure out how to restore the goodwill of his relationship after his latest transgression against Saniya. "What do you want to do, go to a friend's house?" "Grace ditched me; I don't even want to look at her right now. Most of my friends' parents like to gossip, so that's out of the question anyway. I'd never be able to explain why I showed up at their house at 11 o'clock at night reeking of booze without it coming back to my parents. Ugh, my head…"

Earl presented an amused huff following her proclamation as she shut her eyes as tightly as possible, trying to mitigate the throbbing agony of her head. "The last thing I remember is Grace and I downing that cheap-ass Bacardi rum, and the next thing I knew, I was out. Do you know how long I was out for? …Some creep didn't try to rub up on me, right?" Earl pulled over outside of a gated community, the gates separating Earl from the condominiums hidden within. He sat in the guise of thoughtful contemplation, minimally aware of the fact that he didn't know the answer to Madison's query. His brain was operating at a sub- optimal level due to the vodka he'd imbibed, shrouding his mind in a mist where it took time to articulate himself. A chill shot down his spine as he recalled his first-time drinking experience, wondering how people could've enjoyed such a toxic beverage.

"I don't know, honestly. I had a shot of the strongest vodka that Ben possibly could've bought, and I'm still kind of feeling the effects of it." "Oh," Madison said, almost sheepishly.

"So, where is it that you were thinking of staying for the night?" "There's a motel like ten minutes away from the house. Before you say anything to Ben, I want you to know that I only know about it because some of my friends went there for their graduation parties." Earl hummed in acknowledgement, doing his best not to judge parents that he didn't even know.

Just because yours were shit doesn't mean that everyone else's is. Didn't you just condemn Saniya for being privileged? Maybe their parents couldn't afford a five-star hotel like Mrs. Clements when you graduated. "Anyway, I can direct you there from here. This light that's coming up? You want to take a right then keep straight, and it should eventually run into a strip mall. Behind that is the motel." A new thought emerged in Earl's brain, and he gave Madison a parental expression of incredulity.

"Do you have money for a motel?"

"Seriously? It's a shit-hole where drug dealers, hookers and people who wasted their talents or potential go to do whatever it is that they do. Any place where you can stay the night that charges hourly isn't exactly going to burn a hole in your wallet. Could you handle that for me? Please? I need a place to sleep for the night so that I can get myself together at home in the morning when dad goes to work. He has the nose of a bloodhound. If he even catches a whiff of alcohol, I'm fucked."

"Don't worry about it; I'll pay for you," Earl said, laughing at Madison's pained expressions.
 The ride to the motel had been brief, the only complications being a dozen police cruisers speeding down the street in response to a big incident happening downtown, and a vagrant that tried to knock on Earl's window for spare change as Earl encountered another red light. Outside of the radio, which had remained at a low volume due to Earl's insistence that radios only distracted him whilst driving, and Madison's directions, there was a shared silence between the two until they'd pulled up in the motel's parking lot.

The building itself looked old and dilapidated, in dire need of major renovations. There was a couple arguing outside of one of the rooms on the right side of the building, a shady figure smoking next to a defunct vending machine, and the parking lot itself had been lined with bits of gravel that could've easily torn Earl's tires to shreds. "I told you it was a shit-hole."

Earl could feel Madison's hubris as she tilted her chin upwards and puckered her lips mockingly at Earl, who rolled his eyes in response. His eyes fell upon the bright neon sign at the front of the motel, indicating the obvious designation of the location, but missing a crucial element. "They can't even find the M in 'motel,' I see. What a lovely 'Otel' this is." Madison snickered at Earl's snide remark as the two of them exited the car. Earl made sure that his windows were all the way up and everything was locked and secured, going as far as to put the safety club that came with the car onto the steering wheel, much to Madison's pleasure. "I didn't know that they sold those anymore! I guess you have to be careful when you're older," Madison joked, poking fun at the age gap that existed between them. "I'm sorry, I couldn't hear you over the jingling of my car keys. You know, for the car that I own." He petulantly shook his keychain in front of Madison's face, whose eyes narrowed at

Earl. "Dad should be getting me one over the summer, but… touché, sir. I'll let you have that."

The pair walked, or in Madison's case, staggered, to the entrance of the motel, making sure to avoid any suspicious or unsavory personalities on the way in. Earl inwardly praised the fact that he hadn't bought an extravagant car, mostly because he couldn't afford it, but he was certain that nobody would steal his new set of wheels as he ensured that Madison was settled in at the motel.

Earl went to the reception desk and checked in for Madison, required to part with only fifty dollars for Madison to stay overnight. Once that was done, they were given a key, the room number and vague instructions on how to get there. They found the room after wandering around the left side of the motel for a while, initially unable to locate it due to the lackluster guidance from the reception clerk. Earl opened the door, almost expecting to come across a crime scene, but was startled by how unremarkable and plain the room had been.

"Expected to see a chalk outline too?" Madison inquired, noticing Earl's bewilderment as she walked in and collapsed face-down onto the bed, exhausted from all the walking they'd done.

"I'm never going to drink again."

Earl raised his eyebrows, knowing that Madison's muffled promises to herself were going to be broken in another week or two. "Alright, Maddie, are you good? I'm about to head out." What's wrong with you tonight?" Madison deflected, raising her head from its spot on the bed, leaving behind a soft indentation. She turned to look at Earl standing in the doorway, who tilted his head curiously.

"What do you mean?"

"Trust me, it's obvious. You have the look of someone who's going through some rough shit. Come, sit, and close the door before you get over here. It's cold outside." "I don't think that's a good idea, Maddie," Earl remarked, feeling as though the disheveled girl had an ulterior motive in her condition of daring intoxication. "Is it Saniya? I do remember seeing her as she was leaving, and she looked pissed." Earl paused, recognizing that being so aloof about the things that bothered him was the reason that he and Saniya were on bad terms as it was.

"...Yeah, but I don't want you to have to worry about my problems." "I'm right here, and you're one of the few people in the world that I can tolerate, so what's the harm? Come on! I promise that I'll let you leave without a fight once you tell me what happened. Venting is good for the soul; it could be just the thing you need!" Earl shook his head, noting his tendency to overthink certain situations. He loved Saniya, and though he thought about being with other women, he knew that he didn't have the heart to cheat on her no matter how grim things had gotten between them. Never mind the fact that it's Ben's baby sister who you have over five years on. He'd lose his shit if anything happened.

Tossing his ridiculous notions to the wayside, he closed the motel door behind him and sat on the bed next to Madison, who remained prone, her eyes fixed on his as she eagerly waited for him to speak. "Saniya and I got into an argument, and I mean a bad one. When you've been in a relationship as long as the two of us have, sometimes, certain issues come up, and you think that they're so small and insignificant that you can ignore them. Then, they reemerge, and you swat them away because you don't want to rock the boat. But, over time, the things that you've chosen to cast aside turn into things that irritate you, which becomes anger, eventually ending at resentment.

I didn't handle my gripes with certain aspects of our relationship very well, and… it spilled out of me at the party while I was feeling the effects of the vodka that Ben gave me. I can't fully blame the drink because I did hold on to those issues that I failed to bring to her attention, and I wish that I had done it in a better way." Madison sat up next to Earl, nodding as he explained the origins of his fight with Saniya.

"What problems do you have with her?"

"…I know that she means well, but I feel as though sometimes she doesn't appreciate me," Earl admitted, trying to shake off the last remnants of inebriation from his system.
"I love her, but I feel like she's too… stringent, maybe. She's all about the right way of doing things, which is cool, but I think she looks at me and sees someone who isn't capable of making their own decisions. I know that my emotions get a little wild, but I'm not a child, you know? I doubt that she feels this way, but I feel like I'm a burden to her. Like she not only doesn't need me, but I'm actively holding her back."

Madison's eyes either fell to the floor in silent meditation or she'd look directly at Earl, not once giving him a look of sympathy. Earl noticed, for once feeling as though someone looked at him with understanding rather than pity or sympathy. "It's funny, we haven't talked about having kids in a while, mostly because she didn't want to reopen the subject until she finished getting her degrees. She definitely has the qualities and mentality of a mother. She'll be ready for it when the time comes. Her mother is very no- nonsense and on top of things too, so it's no surprise where Saniya gets it from. Still, I wish that she would let me enjoy the moments like tonight where I feel like I've finally discovered myself as a creator of something with meaning."

There was a deliberate pause when Earl finished venting his grievances to the younger girl. Earl had to admit to himself that he'd felt significantly better now that he'd had a platform to ease his pressures regarding his relationship properly. You have to find a way to get Saniya to hear you out though. You put on quite a show, and what if she doesn't forgive you? Then what?

"For what it's worth, I think 'Light From Darkness' is the first time that I've cried during a song in a long time. It was wonderful, Earl. You're a real artist, someone who's passionate about what they do." Earl and Madison locked eyes, and in that exchange, he was an underlying admiration for himself as an artist that he'd never known previously. There was an almost tangible degree of intimacy that prevailed in that moment more than anything he'd recalled sharing with Saniya in recent memory. "I've always known what you were, Earl, even when Ben first brought you over to the house. There was something about you that I knew not a lot of people would understand, just like they don't with me. Have you ever felt that way, that there aren't a lot of people in the world who really understand you?"

Earl wasn't sure if it was the leftover buzz from the vodka or the magnetism to Madison's authenticity, but he found himself seeing things about her that he hadn't taken the time to remotely notice before. Her long, sensual eyelashes that fluttered every time she blinked, the slight raspberry perfume that she wore even the way that her pale skin shone in contrast to the darkness of the room. "Yeah. Even though I go to a 'meeting' once a month with other people who share my feelings and thoughts based around anxiety or depression, I feel so disconnected to them." "Well, you have me now. I think that I can understand you perfectly, Earl."

Never breaking eye contact, Earl could feel the heat from Madison, craving him. She was so close to something that she'd desired for so long, and Earl was acutely aware it. Take her. Nobody needs to know; make her yours for the night. You deserve a little treat for all that you've done.

Wordlessly, Earl's arm reached out to Madison, and he traced her forearm with his index finger. When she offered no resistance, he caressed her thigh, eliciting a sigh from Madison. Earl let his fingers dance on different parts of Madison's body, touching and teasing, and her contented sighs became impatient moans. "Stop teasing me," Madison said breathlessly.

Give her what she wants.

Earl, growing restless himself, let their eyes meet one more time before he leaned in and kissed her, feeling the electricity of their lips pressed together prick at his every nerve. It started out slow as their lips met elegantly, but after a while, Madison's longing couldn't be contained. Their kiss became torrid and aggressive as Earl moved Madison onto his lap, never breaking from her as his hands moved all over her body. Madison finally broke away from their battle for dominance, much to Earl's dismay. Her lustful visage foretold her next move as she slid down onto the floor in front of Earl and began taking off his belt, throwing it in a random corner of the room after a swift struggle. Unwilling to wait any longer, she hooked her fingers around his pants and boxers, bringing both down with one downward tug. Earl's girth flopped out freely, ready for Madison's insatiable indulgence. Without missing a beat, Madison wrapped her lips around it hungrily, eliciting a gratified moan from Earl. Her head bobbed, up and down, eager to please with no uncertain amount of expertise, employing techniques that Earl's mind could barely keep up with.

This is what you've always needed, someone to make you feel like the king that you are. Saniya doesn't have that appetite anymore, and besides, isn't it good to have someone else for a change?

Earl ignored the intruder as his legs began to shake with Madison digging her nails into his hips as she brought him closer and closer to release. Before she could take him there, however, she stopped. She wiped her mouth and stood up over Earl, a cocky expression adorning her face.

"That'll teach you to tease me."

Earl liked that, the challenge. It had been a long time since he'd felt such an animalistic need as he snatched his pants from the floor and dug into his pockets, hoping that the back-up condom that he carried with him was still there. Saniya had always joked that he should carry a condom or two around with him just in case they're away from home and feel like having a quickie, but he'd never had an applicable use for them until now. He smirked, pulling out a blue condom wrapper from one of the flaps of his wallet. He unwrapped it and put it on, quickly, hoping that it would hold up during his performance. Madison's intrigue turned into shock as Earl lifted the petite girl off her feet and flung her onto the bed in one quick motion. "Wait! Just... be gentle. I've done a few things, but it's never gotten this far before."

Shit.

Earl's carnal attitude began to subside as soon as Madison informed him of her virginity, and he'd suddenly felt pangs of immense guilt. You can't do this. Don't. You'll prevent her from sharing this with someone that is actually going to want to be with her. Just do it. Take her nice and slow, make her addicted to you. Between his conscience and the intruder, Earl wasn't sure what course of action to take as he froze just above Madison, unable to look her in the eye.

"You aren't having second thoughts, are you?" Madison taunted. "Maybe she was right about you. Maybe you're just a pussy." Earl gritted his teeth, grabbed Madison's legs, positioning them upwards so that her feet were up in the air, and inserted himself inside of her. Madison yelped out in pain as Earl got as deep as he could get, making sure to include every inch of his girth. After a few excruciating moments, he slowly pulled himself out to survey the damage. Much to his surprise, there'd not been a single droplet of blood. "More," Madison stated simply with a look of defiant determination.

Earl indulged her, going at a slow pace until her body acclimated to the new sensation.

When she'd felt as though she could take more punishment, she urged Earl to move faster, harder, begging him to make her his. He had her in all

257

manners of positions and angles with Madison growing more enraptured with him by the minute. She became not only amenable, but willing and enthusiastic, to whatever Earl wanted to do to her.

As Earl held a fistful of Madison's hair in one hand and gripped her hips with the other, thrusting himself into her with reckless abandon, he couldn't hold himself back anymore. With a prolonged, forceful growl, he reached his climax, making his last few plunges within her count. The euphoria of his release traveled throughout his entire body, causing small, involuntary spasms as he collapsed on the bed next to Madison. Both breathing heavily and having their fill of one another, unable to speak from their now-depleted reserves of energy, the pair allowed the shared bliss of their encounter to send them both into a deep sleep.

--

The calming sound of the rushing water lessened the effects of the migraine that Earl had as he splashed some cold water onto his face to wake himself up. He kept his eyes averted from the mirror, unable to look at his reflection as he did his best to forget about what had transpired last night. Don't be ashamed. You're official now, you've proven yourself as a force not to be fucked with. Saniya will only know if you tell her, and you aren't stupid enough to let that slip, are you? The intruder's mocking tone only served to add to

Earl's distress as he heard the rustling of bedsheets from behind the bathroom door. Earl groaned, knowing that he'd have to find a way to deal with Madison. Choosing not to prolong the inevitable, he turned the faucet, curtailing the flow of water to the sink, and opened the door to the bedroom.

Now that Earl had been free from the illusions induced by hard liquor, the room had looked a lot more unclean as it was coated in the rays of the break of dawn.

"Hi, Earl."

The morning greeting was cheery, but subdued as Madison put her shirt back on, which she retrieved from the foot of the bed. After she put on the last article of clothing, smoothing it out as best as she could, her and Earl shared an awkward, knowing exchange of looks.

"Earl, I—"

"Please. Not now. I'm taking you home."

They gathered up their belongings and left the motel room, saying nothing else to one another. On the way back to his car, Earl finally had a moment to check his phone, hoping that Saniya had tried to call him. What met him instead were twenty missed calls, most of which were suspiciously enough from Randall. Earl rolled his eyes, wondering what Randall could possibly have to say to him, but he held off on that call. Right now, his only priority was taking Madison home. The car ride to her house was deathly silent. Earl focused on the road, and Madison stared out of the window, lost deep in thought. When Earl turned the corner to her parent's house, he put the car in park next to the curb and unlocked the passenger-side door, a pronounced cue for Madison to leave. "…I love you, Earl. I know that a part of you feels the same way, and you're having a hard time letting it sink in." If Earl hadn't been so determined to be rid of Madison, he'd have probably laughed. He hadn't expected someone like Madison, who prided herself on her snark and myriad witticisms, to have such a naive outlook on the meaning of their night together. For a moment, he wasn't sure what was worse: the fact that he'd betrayed Saniya, or the fact that he'd enabled Madison's fantasies about the two of them being together further. "Don't tell me how I feel, Maddie. Just… leave."

"Last night was incredible," Madison retorted, putting a hand on Earl's knee. "Saniya doesn't deserve you anyway. I won't tell anyone about what happened, it can be our secret until you're ready for me. In the meantime, if you need someone to 'listen' to you, I'll be here." Earl scoffed, demonstrating that he had nothing to say regarding anything that came out of Madison's mouth. With a considerate nod, Madison opened the door and stepped out of the vehicle, making sure to look back at Earl with a wink before entering her house. You have to tell her. The guilt will eat you alive if you don't.

Earl's conscience made him squirm uncomfortably in his seat as he took out his phone and stared at it, wondering whether or not he should call Saniya and confess to his misdeeds. After a moment of contemplation, his heart racing in his chest, he went to Saniya's name in his phone and prepared to tap it to call her. However, an incoming call from Randall precluded his intentions as he groaned, raising the phone to his ear to answer the call.

"What?" Earl said impatiently.

"I don't know where the fuck you've been at, but I hope you're happy. She's gone because of you."
"...What are you talking about?" Earl said, confused by Randall's gloomy, solemn tone.

"She was stressed over you, and it was too much for her to take. Charlotte had a heart attack last night. The doctors tried to save her, but they had to call it after a few hours." Earl's eyes bulged as he sat up in his seat, panic beginning to overtake him as he gripped his cellphone hard enough to nearly break it. "What are you saying?!"

"Charlotte passed last night, Earl. Whatever you've been doing the last week, I hope it was worth Charlotte's life." Randall hung up, and the phone fell from Earl's hands as he sat dazed. His brain, for once, had ceased its endless production of thoughts. Numb.

261

Earl couldn't believe what he'd heard. He'd wanted to cry, to scream, to hit something, to do anything. Instead, he was helpless. Not just helpless.

Culpable.

May as well have killed her yourself.

Chapter 17

He stood, unmoving, staring at the impersonal box he'd been closely and carefully holding as he waited to summon the courage to knock upon her door. Everything had been a blur during the last couple of days, and Earl refused to endear himself to any of the events that had transpired, largely being on autopilot since the personal confirmation that Charlotte was truly gone.

He'd gone down to the mortuary, being the one who had to decide what to do with Charlotte's body. The building was ice-cold in temperature, but Earl had been too numb to register the hairs standing on his arms. He'd shuffled behind the impassionate diener, who pushed his way through the set of double doors leading to the storage units. As Earl filed in behind him, he could feel her presence. It was faint, but it was as if she'd been standing in one of the corners of the room, watching him silently.

The man walked over to one of the units and pulled it out, and Earl froze as he recognized the gray mane that fell over the side of the slab she rested on. The man agreed to leave the room temporarily to allow Earl a moment to say his goodbyes, impartially informing Earl that he'd be back shortly. Earl stiffly stood next to Charlotte as he heard the man's footsteps get softer and softer until he couldn't hear them anymore. He was mired in disbelief as he did his best to find the mettle to lift back the sheet covering Charlotte's head to remove any lingering doubts. His last glimmer of fruitless hope was swiftly shot down as he pulled at the sheet enough to expose Charlotte's unmistakably lifeless face, discolored from the frigid chamber she'd lain in. That was the moment that Earl couldn't support his lower body any longer, falling to his knees next to her as he bawled, wishing that he'd been a better grandson.

"I'm so sorry."

He repeated the phrase multiple times through his strained, cracking voice, cradling himself, never feeling more displaced from the world around him. In her will, she specified that he, not Randall, were to handle all the necessary proceedings after her passing. Earl tried to forget a lot about his upbringing and past, about the ostracization from family and friends, the constant war waged against the encroaching darkness of his more detrimental thoughts, and all the bridges he'd burned in the chaotic wasteland of his former self-destructive misery before Saniya. But he did remember that yellow folder. Charlotte had given it to him during his freshman year of high school and told him to peruse the contents of it. The more paperwork that Earl had cycled through and skimmed, the more upset he became. It had been nothing but life insurance specifications, who to call if she died unexpectedly at home, and other things that Earl didn't want to think about. "I know it's upsetting, but you have to be ready, just in case. I don't know how much time I have left, and Randy can't be depended on. Put it somewhere in your room, and make sure that you always know where it is."

Earl closed his eyes as Charlotte's words echoed in his head, his grief trudging up memories that he'd done a good job of burying deep inside of himself until now. He'd found it difficult to express any one emotion; the last few days had been such a miasma of tears, self-hate and disgust at himself that his well of emotions had effectively run dry. He'd never felt so tired, barely being able to sleep at the motel that he'd confined himself to while he handled things in accordance to Charlotte's wishes. He hadn't gone back home yet; he couldn't bring himself to. His eyes shifted back to the box, the final punctuation of Charlotte's life. Etched onto one side was her first and last name, the date she was born, and the date that she died. Nothing more. No poetic epitaph, no references to her perennial patience as a daughter or her dedication to motherhood, nothing.

When Earl was initially given the box and had time to scan it over, he was outraged at the terseness of the inscription. In hindsight, however, he knew that Charlotte wouldn't have wanted someone to plaster something ordinary or generic when trying to sum up her life in so few words. "No funeral. I don't want a bunch of people looking stupid over my dead body. It'd just be a bunch of bullshit anyway; the only people who show up to funerals are relatives who hope they appear in the will, and people who want everyone to know how sad they are over an inevitability. Selfish fucks. Earl, when it's time, burn my black ass up and be done with it. If I look down and see a funeral, I swear that I'll hop out of the casket and smack the shit out of everyone."

Earl smirked sadly as he recollected one of Charlotte's many humor-laden, but accurate observations and opinions regarding the subject of existence, and humanity in general. Few understood their bond, not knowing Charlotte much to begin with. She'd curse a lot, was staunchly opposed to lying or skirting around a point, and Earl had seen her deal with insubordination in the least tactful of ways. But that was only the side that people tended to bring out of her. Nobody ever saw her love for interior decorating, heard her dreams of wanting to travel, or observed her adoration for children like Earl had. They never knew her quirks, such as despising the title of "Grandma" and never wanting to hear it. They never saw her fight to do everything to make her mother as comfortable as possible during her last days despite the hell that Charlotte had went through with her during her childhood. She had a tough exterior with a heart of gold filled with tenderness, love and wisdom, but occasionally, there was a hint of depression, loneliness and even regret.

Earl remembered seeing shades of her vulnerability about a month or two after his great- grandmother had passed. He'd went to greet Charlotte to another morning, as was the standard. When he got closer to her usual haunt, the kitchen, he stopped, hearing the distant sounds of a harrowing, soulful song. Concerned, he walked in and saw Charlotte crying with her head buried in her hands. She looked up at Earl, wide-eyed, shaking slightly as she tried her best to quickly hide her sorrow.

"…I miss my mom."

It was rare for Charlotte to outwardly express that kind of sentimentality. It broke Earl's heart because he knew that she'd finally let herself grieve after dealing with all the paperwork, disputes over the will and other issues that came from her mother's passing. His aunt and uncle only added to Charlotte's burdens during that time when they were supposed to unite to put their mother to rest, and Earl never forgave them for making things difficult for Charlotte. Yet, here he was, the last person in the world that she loved and trusted, and he felt responsible for Charlotte being reduced to a pile of ashes in his hands. He'd promised to transfer her to something less impersonal, something beautiful and decorative. He knew she'd like that. Deciding that he'd stalled enough, Earl raised a fist to the door, tapping his knuckles against it. He dreaded the eventuality that he'd have to be there sooner or later, but that didn't
make him any less anxious.

You aren't the one that should be pitied, she should be. You're the one who fucked up, and now you're paying for it. You should be lucky if she decides to open the door at all. The intruder had turned on Earl completely, despite its previous encouragements. Rather than validation, all Earl got was venomous spite and castigation. His conscience had gone silent, as did the part of himself that tried to play internal damage control when Earl had gone too far. Instead, it was just him and the intruder, the one who pushed him and fueled his most malignant thoughts. To Earl's surprise, the door opened, and Saniya stood blocking his entry to her apartment. "What do you want, E?" she said tersely, refusing to give Earl any indicators signaling how she felt about his arrival. Even her eyes, which had typically been one of her most expressive traits, had adopted the same impassive language as her body.

"...Can I come in? Please? I know that I messed up at that party, but can we talk for a second? I need you, Sans."

Saniya's eyes landed at the box in Earl's hands, which had the side with the inscriptions facing her. Reading it briefly, she went from expressionless to horrified. Her eyes met Earl's, and upon seeing the bags settled just under his eyelids and feeling the tangibility of his despair, Saniya knew that she couldn't turn him away.

Stepping out of the doorway, Saniya allowed Earl to enter her apartment, shutting and locking the door behind him. She hadn't shown it, but she herself had been a despondent mess since the events of Ben's party. After catching a taxi home, she'd collapsed onto her bed and cried for what felt like hours, wondering how she'd let someone hurt her so deeply.

She'd considered their chain of recent arguments before the party and wondered if the relationship, as it was, could even be salvaged. As she sat on the couch nearing the back of her apartment, indirectly requesting Earl to join her, a part of her felt guilty for having the mere inkling of potentially ending their relationship. Things had obviously reached a boiling point, and she'd been angry, but she also knew that Earl was dealing with a lot too. She had a lot of time to reflect on the years they'd been together so far, especially the beginning, which had been ensnared in Earl's standoffish behaviors in of itself. She wanted to help him, and came to the conclusion that there had been a lot of pain behind Earl's outburst. She stood by a few of her criticisms against him and his string of reckless behaviors, but could see how she perhaps had been more judgmental rather than appropriately hopeful and encouraging. There were, of course, a few personal digs at her expense that she knew she had to address, but recognized that now wasn't the time or place to bring them up.

Soon, she promised herself.

Earl put the box on the table in front of them and sat down, staring blankly at it. Saniya could tell simply by familiarity that Earl was accusing himself of what happened to Charlotte. She'd have asked about it, but wanted to let him lead the conversation if he decided to speak. The only thing that she knew for certain was that she wanted to be there for him despite her misgivings about seeing him so soon. "New Orleans," Earl finally said, his eyes inertly staring in the direction of Charlotte's remains. Saniya's eyebrows furrowed in confusion, but she dared not interrupt Earl during his reminiscence.

"She always wanted to go to New Orleans. She said that she wanted to eat their 'real' shrimp gumbo, drink a cocktail or two and kick back at the Jazz and Heritage festival that they have every year. When I first started writing, I used to joke that we'd go on a vacation down there when I got my first big book deal. I don't know how expensive the trip itself would've been, but if things with my music had gone well in the next month, I probably could've been able to take her. She had a lot of dreams that she never got to experience, so I kept that one in the back of my mind for when I made my breakthrough. I guess she'll never go to New Orleans now."

Despite his formerly deadened senses, he couldn't help himself as he burst into tears, unable to hold back his bereavement. He leaned over with his head falling into Saniya's lap, and she tried to comfort him by stroking the back of his head slowly and gently. "I've made so many mistakes lately, Sans," Earl choked out through his intermittent sobs. "You were

270

right. I shouldn't have ignored her like I did. I was all that she had left, and now all I can think about is if she died thinking that I hated her."

Saniya said nothing, opting to keep quiet in the event that her occasional impulsive way of speaking will end up further hurting Earl. "When she had that stroke years ago and couldn't drive her car anymore, I was so happy to eventually get my license so that I could help. Instead, I treated running errands as an inconvenience over time, and I think she picked up on that. There's so much that I could've done for her to make her happier and give her the appreciation that she deserved. I know it's stupid to say it now, but I wish I hadn't taken her for granted." "There's nothing stupid about it, E," Saniya defended.

"I don't know what to do, Sans. It's my fault that she's gone, I ruined everything with you. I just feel like I'm spiraling. I know I have no business asking you this, but can I stay here for the night? Please? I don't know if I can be by myself again tonight." Saniya wanted to say yes, but the part of her that was still angry at Earl caused the word to stop short of coming out of her mouth. She wasn't sure if she was ready to accept his request and lead him to think that everything was fine between them only for her to bring up their altercation later and it appeared as though she'd maliciously waited to attack him. On the other hand, she didn't want him to leave the apartment and potentially hurt himself or get into a

271

bad situation due to his lack of clarity amidst his grief. Her indecisiveness, however, alarmed Earl as he got to his feet and stood in front of Saniya, distraught. "Sans?"

After another minute of deliberation, Saniya found her answer, believing that putting off certain conversations was the reason why things had been so stunted between the two of them. "Earl, I just don't think that now is a good time for you to stay here. I want to have a conversation about what happened at Ben's first, and—" "You really want to do this now?" Earl interrupted, instantly changing from mournful to irritated. Saniya, caught off-guard by his reaction, did her best to try and defuse the situation. "No, baby, I'm not trying to—"

"You know what? Fuck it, I'm going back home." Earl snatched up the box he'd entered with and made his way to the front door, incensed at Saniya's failed compliance. She did everything to try and get his attention as he stormed out, even attempted to appease him by offering to let him stay, but he wasn't interested in her pleas. Without another word, Saniya watched as Earl angrily trotted down the stairs and disappeared out of her line of sight. She waited, listening to his footsteps and hoping that he'd turn around, but he marched on until she was forced to take in nothing but the uneasy lull of the empty stairwell.

--

Earl's car screeched into the driveway and he
slammed the car door shut behind him as he fumbled
around in his pocket for his house keys. He'd been so
angry that he hadn't realized that Randall's car was
parked on the curb just outside of the house as he
tramped through the front door. "You've got some
goddamn nerve coming in here, boy." Earl's head
whipped into the direction of the living room where
Randall was sitting, watching the television. His eyes
were bloodshot red, and his head swayed unnaturally
as he stood, planning to confront Earl. "What the fuck
were you doing while you were gone? Your little boy
band meant more to you than your grandmother? You
should be ashamed, coming up in here and thinking
that you're going to reclaim the house. No, you get
back in your car, and you get the fuck on."

Earl's eyes shone with malice, and he gritted his teeth
so hard together that they were in danger of cracking.
Closing the distance between them, Earl reared back
and punched Randall as hard as he could, sending the
old man falling to the floor. Before Randall could act
further, Earl grabbed him by the front of his dirt-
covered shirt, lifted him up and dragged him to the
washing machine just a few feet away from the front
door. Clearly under the influence of drugs, Randall
flailed helplessly as Earl wrapped his hands around
his neck and loomed over him maliciously. "You get
the fuck out, you junkie piece of shit," Earl snarled.
"This is my house, it's in my name. I'm not going to

let you fuck Charlotte's house up any more than you already have, you understand me?" The grip around Randall's neck tightened as Earl emphasized his point, tinting the older man's anguished expression with fear.

"I don't give a shit where you go, but you don't live here anymore. Charlotte should've kicked you out years ago." Earl kicked the door open and tossed Randall out onto the driveway. Randall's nose began to leak with blood as he scrambled to his feet. "And if you ever come back here, I'll have you arrested for trespassing. Go OD in an alley somewhere; you're better off dead." Without waiting for retaliation or a response, Earl slammed the door shut and proceeded to pace around the hallway, trying to calm himself down. He decided to go to his room before he tore the house apart. Entering his room, the first thing he saw, proudly splayed across the bed where he'd dumped it, was Axlam Suleman's book 'The Desperate Sails of Somalia,' taunting him. He felt his body shaking as he stared at the book, a reminder of his failures, of the dreams he'd never accomplish.

"You fucking cunt."

Earl, remembering the manuscript saved within it, picked up his laptop and held it under his arm. He opened the small box atop his dresser that contained the flash drive with his manuscript backed up onto it and grabbed it as well, making sure to snatch Axlam's book in the process. He took all three items to the middle of his living room and tossed them angrily at the floor. The screen of his laptop received a large crack down the middle of it upon impact, the flash drive clattered, but remained largely intact, and Axlam's book hit the hardwood floor with a harmless thump. Enraged, Earl made his way to the utility closet opposite of the front door and grabbed a hammer from the toolbox hidden against the back wall. He went back to the pile of items he'd haphazardly tossed onto the floor, and he began striking all three of them with the hammer. Every embittered swing became gradually more vicious, underlined with deep, primal grunts. The laptop turned into a clump of broken mechanical pieces and loose circuits, the flash drive was misshapen beyond repair, but Axlam's book mocked Earl with the decent condition that it was still in, only hosting a few indentations. Growling in frustration, Earl suddenly thought of something, and he popped back into his room briefly, retrieving an old Sub Shack shirt that he'd written 'Fuck This' on the front of in marker. He laid the shirt out in the middle of the floor, then threw the remains of the laptop and flash drive onto it. He picked up Axlam's book and began ripping it apart, one page after the other, making sure that each page covered the shirt and the wreckage atop of it.

When he was satisfied with his work, he threw the remainder of the book into the pile and retrieved the lighter from behind the clock at the top of the bookshelf in the corner of the living room that

Charlotte would use to light scented candles from time to time. He bent down, flipped the switch on the lighter that produced a small flame from its tip, and held it over a few of the sundered pages until they were engulfed in flames. He made sure to burn the sleeves of his old uniform too, in case the pages didn't catch fire quickly enough for his liking.

The flames slowly covered most of the bundle, becoming an amalgam of melted alloy, singed paper and charred cotton. Earl backed into the chair that Randall had previously occupied, sat down and watched the fires consume his shortcomings. In the burning jumble, he'd found that his heartbeat had settled, and his pupils dilated as fascination overcame him. He felt that he could start over, well and truly this time. No more half-assing and no more appeasement, those days are over and done with. This is a new introduction, a fresh start. Burn it all, and from the ashes, you'll become a musical legend. Fuck waiting, it's time to take whatever you want because you've shown that you're capable of it.

Earl nodded as he watched the fire warp the hardwood underneath and create a layer of soot on the ceiling. Just then, a flash of realization hit him, and he rushed back to his room to retrieve one last thing: his anti-depressants. He went to the bathroom and flushed the remaining pills down the toilet, then came back to the contained fire and threw the bottle in with the rest of his former life. That's right, all of it. Leave no traces of anything pertaining to past misfortunes.

Earl took out his wallet and pulled out the card for his monthly support group meetings. After scowling at it, he ripped it in half and threw it into the flames. The pity party ends here. This, Earl, is your genesis. Your canvas is clear and your brush is poised, ready to create.

The heat from the dying fire had been an odd comfort, but one that garnered a smirk from Earl as he pulled out his cracked phone and scrolled through his contacts, one name popping into his mind as he discarded his support group card. He tapped the name, and the phone came alive, ringing as he awaited a response. Three rings later, he was rewarded. "Hey, Earl! Didn't expect to hear from you so soon!" Kim said cheerily. Earl heard the crying in the background, which he assumed belonged to her baby, but he was far from the point of caring.

"Hey, Kim! Uh, if it's a bad time, I can call you back later!" Earl said, hoping that Kim declined his 'polite' suggestion. "No, no, it's fine! I was about to put Christian to sleep anyway!"

"Cool, cool!"

He understood the irony of his veil of geniality juxtaposed to the small inferno that danced around in his eyes. "So, are you busy? I'm actually kind of bored and wanted to see if you were interested in hanging out!" "Sure! I could always use the company. I'm a bit of a homebody, so you'd be a nice change of pace!"

She knows what you want, and you know what she needs. "You got it! Just send me your address, and I'll be right there!" "Okay, Earl! See you when you get here!" Earl hung the phone up and shoved it back into his pocket, his task complete. He watched the last embers of the fire fade into thin air, turning most of the immolated objects into cinder. Before you leave, grab Charlotte from the car and bring her back home.

In Earl's haste, he'd forgotten about Charlotte, who he left sitting in the passenger seat. Before he went to retrieve her, however, he observed the aftermath of his impromptu purging ritual. The smell was horrible, wafting into his nose and making him scrunch his face up in disgust, but it'd been worth it. You always wanted to be like Epsen Knight, whose books will live on for centuries. Well, immortality awaits. Yours to reap, plus, you'll be the first Veares to ever make a name for himself. Be the man that you always dreamed you'd be.

Chapter 18

Music became an obsession. When Earl wasn't suggesting songs for Ben to listen to, motivating his partner into innovating new kinds of beats, he'd spend hours jotting down lyrics. His visits with Kim also became more frequent over the last few weeks, and he'd ignored Saniya's attempts to regain contact with him. Ben and Earl's friendship had reached a strange plateau; it was clear to Earl that Ben had something heavy on his mind but wouldn't speak about it.

As Earl spent his time perfecting his brand of narrative-based lyricism, sequestering himself either at home or at Ben's studio, his wardrobe had transformed to parallel his new objectives and resolute outlook. From simple clothes to elaborately designed shorts, pants, shirts, and even embellishments such as sunglasses and other lavish accessories. Much to Ben's amusement, Earl had made a habit of wearing ornate half-capes and he would frequently tell Earl he looked like he was about to challenge someone to a duel.

Tzar-Mo was born. Eventually, it came time to unveil their second paycheck, and Ben excitedly sprinted into the living room where Earl was sitting. Today's cape was all-black with a metallic, gold trim and as

Earl rose to meet Ben, the cape swayed elegantly. "Since we have two songs to collect from now, I'm expecting this check to be stacked! We're really going to be on a roll once I finish editing the others next week! At the rate we're going, we should be able to put together a full album in a few months!"

"Yeah, I'm writing another song that should be done by tomorrow, so that'll make, what, six in total?" "Yep!" Ben responded, trying to maintain his air of elation. Earl sighed, attempting to avoid the inevitable conflict, but perhaps today was the day to ask Ben about it. Ben ripped open the envelope and immediately scanned the bottom of the page where their paycheck resided. He put a hand to his chest and pretended to faint but got back up as soon as he dramatically hit the ground. Miles ran to check on his owner, but as soon as Ben revealed his ploy, the black cat went back into his corner. "Earl! We're 250,000 dollars richer! Each!"

The money's nice, but what matters is the fact that your artistry will soon be recognized worldwide if this keeps up. From local luminary to global phenomenon; that's the throne you want to sit upon. Earl extended his fist to Ben to celebrate their success, and Ben hesitated briefly before meeting his own fist with Earl's. *This can't go on. Things are awkward now, and you have to mention it.* "Is there something wrong, Ben? There has to be; we just made a hell of a lot of money, and you don't seem as...

eager as usual. You've been a little off the past few weeks. Are you worried about Imani?" Imani had come down with the flu and was recovering at home for what had been the third day of her illness. Ben put the envelope down on the table next to him with a deep sigh as the concern that he'd been concealing made its way to his outward demeanor.

"It… it's going to sound *really* silly, Earl. I probably should've asked when it first came up because I know you didn't do anything wrong, but I don't know, it's a weird thing I'm about to ask." *Here it comes.*

"Go for it, man!" Earl encouraged, masking his nervousness. "So, do you remember the party we had last month?" "Yeah, what about it?" "You took Maddie home that night, right? I know it's a dumb question, but my mom apparently caught her sneaking into the house the next morning and sensed that she'd been hiding something. While Maddie was in the shower, mom called Monica's parents to thank them for keeping Maddie for the night, and it turned out that they were on vacation in Spain. Of course, I knew that Maddie had lied, as she does with our parents, but then, mom asked her where she'd been without telling her that she already caught her in a lie. She told me that Maddie had again told her that she stayed with Monica and had just gotten dropped off, and I guess she either didn't know or forgot that Monica was gone for a week. I'm not saying you did something wrong because I know you better than that, but where did you drop Maddie off?"

"A motel," Earl stated casually. "On our way back to your house that night, she begged me not to take her home. She told me about a motel nearby that her friends liked to stay at or something. She said that she didn't want to piss off her parents knowing that she'd been drinking so heavily, and I wanted to do her a favor. So, I drove her to the motel, paid for her room, made sure she got there safely, and then I went home."

Ben shook his head at Earl's answer, finally understanding what had transpired.

"She probably had some dude meet her there when you dropped her off because someone had to have taken her home that morning. I'm not angry at you, Earl, but you know how I get about Maddie sometimes. I hope that she just passed out and didn't have time to do much else." Earl slowly exhaled the breath that he'd been holding, relieved as Ben stood there, lost in thought.

"You could've asked me about it sooner, Ben."

"Yeah, but I don't like the idea that Maddie is out there doing the same things that I was. I know how that sounds, but it just doesn't sit right with me, especially with how weird she's been acting since then. Dad's trying to prepare her for college, and she doesn't seem interested. It's like she's a different person now, so I guess she's dating some dude on the low and isn't telling anyone. I was hoping that you were going to tell me that you took her straight home and that I was just being a little dramatic, but I had a feeling about it." "Oh. I'm sorry about that, Ben. I'm sure that Maddie will be fine though; you know how she is."

"Yeah," Ben said, stroking his chin. "But here I am worried about Maddie, and haven't asked you how you've been since… you know." Ben scratched at the back of his head awkwardly, not broaching the subject of Charlotte's death since Earl had informed him two weeks prior. "I'm fine. Really. I hired someone for a day to help me clean up around the house last week, and it's looking better than ever! I'd been sitting around letting everything get dusty, and I realized I was being extremely lazy when it came to maintaining the house. I think the best way to honor Charlotte is to be the best me that I can be going forward, just like she always wanted."

In reality, he'd only cleaned the house up due to the filth, bordering on total squalor, that it had suffered since he spent most of his nights at Kim's. Earl planned on making considerable changes to the house soon, further distancing himself from the person he used to be. "Sounds about right, Big E. I think she'd be proud of you. Wait, you hired someone to clean your house for you?" Earl rolled his eyes, figuring that it was only a matter of time before Ben would find something to comment on. "Look at you, Big

Money Mo! …Can I ask you where you got that from? Not that I don't dig the name 'Tzar-Mo,' it has a cool ring to it, but why?" "I'll say this," Earl said, comically flapping his half-cape behind him. "A true artist never reveals his secrets!" "…I thought that was a magician. You know, 'A magician never reveals his secrets'? It's a little early for us to be stealing lines, isn't it? Running out of ideas already? I mean, it'd make sense, you do kind of look like a magician when you wear those capes." "Fuck you, Ben."

In the middle of their jubilant laughter, a loud ping alerted the two. Ben checked his phone, and Earl watched as Ben's face went from curious to utterly astounded. "Uh… so, I've been getting alerts from some of our fans, and it looks like we've gotten some attention from Lil Grande."
Earl blinked mechanically, not fully understanding what Ben meant. "You mean, the rapper? One of the most… unfortunately adored people in the industry?" "Looks like it," Ben responded, trying to get more information. "There's a video making its rounds online, and it seems like you're the focus of it." "What?!"

Ben gestured for Earl to come over to him so that they could watch the video together. Ben tapped the play icon over the still image of Lil Grande in what looked to be a studio, and the video sprung to life. "'Ey, it's ya boy, Lil Grande, and I ain't worried about no mothafuckin' strike, ya heard? I stay in the studio, stay getting bars, stay fucking ya girl, stay high."

Earl had to bite down the disgust he felt for what he was hearing and observing. Lil Grande, in his opinion, ~~had~~ personified everything that was wrong with entertainment and art. He was loud with no substance, had sloppy, multi-colored dreads to distinguish himself from his competition, had gold fronts to show off his wealth, had teardrop tattoos so that people could see how "hood" he was, and his songs were the highest tier of mind-numbing trash that Earl had every had the misfortune of listening to. That, combined with the droves of fans that insisted on
making him famous in the first place and maintained that he was one of the best artists out there made Earl more indignant towards the boisterous rap personality.

"So, listen, while I was gone, I hear that ya'll found this new mawfucka who call hisself 'Tzar-Mo.' How ya'll let this lame nigga get hot? Look at him, he look like one of those gay-ass niggas from those old R&B groups that was always in the background trying to keep up with the real ones." A still image of Ben and Earl popped onto the screen, the two walking down the street, which made Earl tense up as he heard Lil Grande laugh at him. Over the past month, Earl and Ben had amassed a small, local following and periodically went out to greet and talk to their fans with many of them requesting more music. Earl, making the transition to Tzar-Mo, would travel in the poshest of attires he could put together, his half-capes being a signature style of his. "With his peanut-shaped head, him and his white boy. The two of them probably be fucking each other in the ass. Homeboy real name is Earl, how we let some punk-bitch like him blow up? Nigga probably still has his mother wash his drawers for him."

The video transitioned back to Lil Grande, whose camera caught the studio he was in as he showcased the kind of life he himself had been living. His studio made Ben's look like child's play, comparatively. "I could roast homeboy all day, but this is what it comes down to. This is what's real, and I got a treat for ya'll coming up. It's time for the kings to show these clowns how it's done. If you ain't 'bout the bang, you ain't with the gang-gang. Peace." The video ended, and two opposite reactions occurred simultaneously. Ben looked at Earl with sparkling exuberance, and Earl's contempt was so apparent that he could've set Ben ablaze with the ire he was radiating. "Dude! This is amazing! Lil Grande has millions of fans! Do you know how much of the spotlight he's just put on us?! The mention is enough to get more eyes on our stuff and continue growing our fanbase!"

"That unoriginal, mumbling motherfucker just slandered us! How is that 'good'?!" "People who had no idea who we were know now! It's free publicity!" "No," Earl asserted, "it's bullshit. Who does he think he is, coming at me like that? His style of 'rap' is something that anybody can do, he just got lucky." A bolt of realization shot through Earl as Ben noticed the fresh, determined glint in his best friend's eyes. "You know what, scratch all those other songs for right now, Ben. Give me about an hour, we're about to prove a point."

--

"Are you sure you want to do this?" "Give me the beat, Ben." Ben tinkered with a few dials on his console, and Earl was flooded with an angelic, vocal harmonization alongside a contentious beat that sounded more modern than their signature classical mixtures. Earl swung to the rhythm of the beat and began the song he'd spent the hour working on, titled 'Open Season'.

♪ The gloves are off for a little while, I hear there's been a lot of talk. I'll dial it back to walk the walk, an intermission from my routine style.

♪ Let's talk about rap, the state that it's in, the "bars" are sparse, the message is thin. Depreciated, it's such a sin, mortals boxing with God and they just can't win.

♪ "Entitled," hilarious, guess it's a habit

♪ When you reach for the crown and you just cannot grab it. It's one thing to front, another to taunt, but the comparison's like fast-food to a three-star Michelin restaurant, no détente.

♪ Let's defang the gang and cut through the jive and slang: They brag about liquor, then call up the "shooters," Referring to class, you've flunked out, I'm the tutor, Then it goes to women, and they've got no shame, Say the streets made them "hard," or so they claim.

♪ You got Young This and Lil That, mumbling copycats coming up to bat.

♪ Bottom of the ninth, you think there's no doubt, But you swing on me and you get struck out. I'm all heart and soul, and that's a fact, you're my victim now, call me Zodiac. Not in my nature to follow the pack, A decade from now, they'll blast my soundtrack.

♪ The rest will fade to irrelevancy; a thousand yous, but one of me. The hypocritical bluster isn't my style, Battling ignorance with raw wit and guile. I could do what they do, play tit for tat, But fuck that, I'm known for meat and not for fat. You got riled up for no good reason, Step to me, that's considered treason.

♪ I'm the hunter, you're the rabbit, Take you by the ears, open your throat with one slit, Expose the truth that you're counterfeit.

♪ But I'll let you go, though you poked out your head. If I wanted to kill, you'd already be dead. Go back to your hole, stay buried within, Won't be merciful next time, it'll be open season. ♪

Earl tossed his headphones onto the stand and raised his fists in victory, proud of his work. When he emerged from the live room, however, he saw that Ben hadn't shared his enthusiasm.

"What's wrong? You didn't like that?"

"No, no, it was hot, but... I don't know. I feel like maybe it's too aggressive towards that whole group.

There are a lot of artists like Lil Grande, and I think that someone will take offense to it." "You sound like me, Ben," Earl said mockingly. "What happened to the risk-taker? I thought you of all people wouldn't care if we make a few people mad or not." "Yeah, but you don't look at anything outside of our WeLink page. I know about the stuff that goes on when it comes to beef between rappers. Shit could be deadly. "That's where you have it wrong," Earl commented, raising a hand to stop Ben from saying anything else.

"I'm not a rapper, I'm a lyricist. I don't want to be categorized with rap because most of it is garbage. What *we* do, alternately, is art." The sounds of Beethoven blared throughout the room, startling Ben as Earl smirked, pulling out a brand-new phone. "Desperately needed one," Earl bragged as he checked it, seeing one new message from Kim and another from Saniya. "Hey, baby. Are you coming over? I have a surprise for you." Attached to Kim's message was a picture of her in lingerie, which made Earl gulp. "On my way!" Earl replied, but he had to admit that Kim was beginning to grate on him.

She seemed to think that they were in a relationship, but Earl just needed someone to sate his needs while he was on the outs with Saniya. *You'll have to cut her loose soon, but you can get a fuck or two more out of it before you*

do. Earl moved on to Saniya's message, which he, in his charitable mood, decided to read instead of

290

immediately delete.

"Please, Earl. Can we talk?"

"Sure," Earl replied, but he'd decided it would be after he met with Kim, just to put himself at ease before seeing Saniya. "Alright, Ben, I gotta head out. Saniya wants to talk, and honestly, I've been missing her a lot." "Oh, cool! Do you want me to hold on to your cut then? I'm going to work on this beat, upload the song to Tonally, then head to the bank." "Just don't spend any of it, Ben." "I'll try to keep myself from rolling around in it." "Good! Oh, and when you get the chance," Earl paused as he got halfway up the stairs, looking back at Ben. "Say hi to Imani for me. I hope she feels better soon.

Chapter 19

The sun shone brilliantly in the blue sky, illuminating the parkgoers as they indulged in the nice, summer weather. Amongst the happy-go-lucky crowd sat Saniya, who watched the surrounding merriment from a bench with a faint smile. It had reminded her of the time that her and Earl went to the Moonstone Beach in California with her parents after everything made sense then. They'd laughed, had deep, thoughtful conversations in the dead of night, and she could tangibly feel the love that they'd shared. It was so different now; it had been for quite some time, but she hadn't wanted to acknowledge it. Earl had his flaws in those days too, but she'd provided a haven for him to freely express his thoughts and feelings. She couldn't do that anymore; it just wasn't enough.

She wasn't sure what had changed. Maybe they'd grown too familiar with one another, or perhaps they were merely going through a phase in their relationship, which Saniya hoped to be the case. She peeked at her phone, making sure that she had the right time – 4:30. He was thirty minutes late, but she didn't care. The only thing that mattered was that he showed up, which he promised he would. As soon as she slid her phone back into her pocket, it vibrated, and she felt her heart skip a beat because she knew it was him. "I'm sorry, I'm about a minute away!"

She put her phone away with the same speed that she'd checked the message, admittedly extremely happy for her boyfriend. Though they'd been apart, she'd seen that Earl had done well for himself. She couldn't wait to make fun of his new stylistic choices, inwardly wondering whether or not Earl would make a grand entrance, pyrotechnics and all, waving his cape throughout the air. She never thought him to be the grandiose type, but after everything he'd been through, he deserved it, she figured. A frisbee almost smacked– her head, but her reflexes allowed her to catch the frisbee as it came within an inch of her face.

"Nice catch!"

A small child, who couldn't have been more than eight, came clumsily running towards Saniya. She couldn't hold back the smile that crept onto her face as the boy's baseball cap, too big for his head, bobbed up and down erratically, threatening to fall off his head. "Sorry about that, miss!" the boy said softly, obviously contrite over his mistake. "My mom tells me that I don't know my own strength. She says I drink so much milk that I'm stronger than other boys!"

The kid rolled up his sleeve and grunted, trying to force one of his spindly arms into forming any kind of muscle. He even punctuated the action by puffing out his cheeks, of which Saniya had to hide her mirth. "Those are some big arms! I'm sure your mommy is so proud of you!"

Saniya handed the kid back his frisbee, unable to stop smiling as the child thanked her and ran back towards what appeared to be the boy's father. Saniya had been staunchly of the stance that she didn't want kids until she was ready, and Earl had mentioned the idea of children every once in a while. Nowadays, she found herself more amenable to the idea of having kids of their own. "There's that motherly side again."

She got up from the bench and spun around, seeing the boastful grin and flamboyant attire of her boyfriend. Without thinking about it, she ran up to him and leapt into his arms, which was readily reciprocated as Earl gripped her tightly.

"How have you been, E?"

"Keeping myself busy, throwing myself into my music." "I heard your last track! I gotta say, it was pretty hot!" As much as Saniya had wanted to be stubborn, she had to acquiesce to the fact that Earl had been a surprisingly competent and refreshing change of pace from the type of music that she was accustomed to. "Am I better than Lil Grande?" Earl joked, still riding the high of the track he'd made earlier in the day. "Eh, give it a few more songs and I'll get back to you on that."

Earl sneered, causing Saniya to guffaw in delight. In an instant, however, her giddiness faded as she remembered their last encounter, particularly Earl's headspace. "Is everything alright with you, E?" Saniya asked cautiously, not wanting to accidentally push one of Earl's many buttons. "You mean with Charlotte? Yeah, I'm cool," Earl responded calmly. "I hired a person to help me clean the house last week, and it's looking pretty presentable! I also revamped my stale sense of fashion, as you can see!"

Earl flapped his half-cape backwards theatrically, and Saniya's eyes could've rolled out of their sockets in an exhibition of dissent. "Yeah, I've seen some pictures. How are you dealing with the whole... you know, 'people' aspect of your surge of popularity?" "It's weird, Sans," Earl said, taking a moment to consider the inquiry. "It was Imani's idea to have us go out and meet people. She said it'd be good for our numbers, which was true. Ben does most of the talking, which is less pressure on me. Although, I didn't get too comfortable around fans until I upgraded my casualwear! I'm telling you, it's the best thing that's ever happened to me!"

Saniya couldn't resist any longer, seeing her chance

to make fun of Earl. "You look like you stepped out of 15th century Italy. Don't get me wrong, it's cool, but you need help color-coordinating with some of those things. …Actually," Saniya said, furrowing her eyebrows, "who the hell makes you those? They don't look cheap." "They were cheaper than you'd think! I met this chick at one of my support group meetings named Kim whose mother taught her how to sew and make some cool stuff from scratch! She has her own online shop and everything!" "Oh! I'm glad that you're finally building a wider network of friends, E! It's about time you opened yourself up!" Saniya noticed Earl flinch, but thought that it was an effect of the summer breeze whipping against his face.

"How has your art been doing? Did inspiration strike you yet?" Saniya frowned, realizing that she hadn't painted or even sketched anything since her altercation with Earl. She found herself too upset to explore any of the myriad of techniques that she'd been eager to apply to her canvas. "No, not really," she admitted. "I don't think I've had my head on straight since the last time we saw each other." She knew that she'd broached a topic that she wasn't entirely sure would be received well, knowing Earl's unpredictable temperament. To her relief, Earl exhaled sadly rather than reacting combatively, his eyes landing somewhere near her feet.

"Honestly, regarding our last… argument, I overreacted. I shouldn't have ignored you for almost an entire month. I have to give you a lot of credit though, you didn't leave me." "Of course not, E," Saniya answered tenderly. "I let you have your space because I know that we were reaching a… toxic stage in our relationship. I don't want to break up, I want us to have a fresh start. I was thinking about us, everything we've been up to this point. I don't want to throw that away." "Me neither."

Earl sat down on the bench with Saniya following right behind him, and they watched people playing or enjoying the beautiful weather.

"I've been a real jackass to you, Sans. I shouldn't have said what I said at that goddamn party. It was mean-spirited and unnecessary. I was angry, and I lashed out. That, then Charlotte leaving me afterwards, I lost myself. I felt that familiar sense of powerlessness, and I guess I think about your mom and how things worked out for her, and it upsets me sometimes. I know how that sounds, but I wanted to be acknowledged for once. I don't want to be the shadow looming in the background anymore. Do I want a lot of people in my face? No, but I want to be seen for the talents I feel like I have to offer. It turns out that the thing I needed all along was music, I guess."

Saniya smiled and reached out to grab Earl's hand, squeezing it lightly as she stared lovingly into his eyes. "I know you didn't mean anything by it. I've

297

been a terrible girlfriend too; you were right when you said that all that I focused on was the negative. I was concerned for you, E. I mean that. I think about the place you were at mentally when we first met, then you telling me about how you used to be before I came along. I didn't want to sit back and watch you lose control of yourself. I know you, and I know that you have a kind, generous heart that doesn't want to purposefully hurt me. I shouldn't have turned you away when you showed up with Charlotte either. I know how much she meant to you. She had to carry the weight of two parents and I know that it wasn't easy on her all the time, or you. I should've been there to hold and comfort you, not reject you." Waves of guilt hit Earl all at once as he thought about what had happened with Madison and what he'd allowed with Kim. He sighed deeply, and his legs shook as he tried his best to not outwardly express his sudden deluge of shame. In his mind, Saniya had been an obstacle, not the girl that he'd fallen in love with. Their reconciliation had reminded him of his long-term goals for them that he'd promised not only to her, but himself.

"It'll work out for the best, E, you'll see. A part of me feels like we had to go through the last few months to strengthen us, not break us. We have a shot at a revival better than ever before! As long as we have each other's backs, nothing will be able to tear us down." Her optimism was a breath of fresh air. Kim tried, but she wasn't Saniya. Nobody was. He'd felt disgusting, remembering his romps with Kim while her baby cried in the next room.

Don't you do it. If you tell her, you'll be making the biggest mistake of your life. Just shut the hell up and let it ride. "So, do you have any more songs that you're working on?"

"Yeah," Earl mumbled, feeling small and ridiculous in his ritzy attire. "I have a few things in the chamber." "Well, let me listen! You must have a sample or two of something, or some notes you've taken!" "Ben's actually working on a sample now, but I don't know if he's uploaded it yet." Earl took out his phone, and Saniya oohed and aahed as he checked Tonally to see if the sample was finished.

"All new everything, huh? I'm a little jealous, E! I'll have to start beating those girls back with a stick! Or buy some mace, whatever I'm in the mood for," Saniya said with a facetious shrug. Earl found that Ben had indeed posted a sample of their newest song to Tonally, and before he had a chance to act, Saniya restlessly took the phone out of his hands. "You have to let me listen to the whole thing afterwards though, I feel like a girlfriend should have first dibs on anything new!" As she went to press play, however, a new notification appeared in the middle of the screen, and Earl's life suddenly drifted into slow-motion. Instead of the song, Saniya was greeted to a video of a phallic, vibrating object that massaged the outer lips of an intimate area that Saniya knew wasn't hers.

Captioned below the video was a single sentence. "You wore me out, but you always leave me wanting more!"

Amidst the moaning, Kim's name showed up at the top of the screen, further incriminating Earl as Saniya's face went from confused, to disgusted, to enraged. "Is this how you got that discount on those clothes?" Saniya asked with an eerie amount of collectedness. "Sans, baby, look—" "No, *fuck you!*" Saniya screamed, causing curious heads to turn in the direction of the conflict. "You're worse than Dominic! At least he had the *balls* to own up to his nasty shit! What, were you going to fuck me and then fuck this bitch on the side?! Oh, fuck that."

Saniya threw Earl's phone onto the ground and began to walk away with Earl trailing behind her.
"Sans, I love you! It was a mistake!" Saniya whipped around with her hand primed, and the slap that followed broke the tranquility of the joyful park. "No, pretending that I could deal with all of your bullshit was the fucking mistake! You know what your problem is? You're a self-righteous *asshole* who cries when he doesn't get his way. You're like a child, and I'm done babysitting you. I could tolerate a *lot* of your shit, but cheating? I don't play that." Saniya scowled as she yelled at Earl< who held a hand Saniya had hit him. "I don't know how to help you at this point, but I'm not going to make myself suffer any more worrying about your stupid ass. Just like

with Charlotte, all I've ever tried to do is keep you grounded, and you don't appreciate—"

"Don't you bring Charlotte into this, you *bitch!*"

Saniya quieted down immediately, letting Earl's temper erupt and travel amongst the winds. She nodded, seeing him seething, and made a smooth, final statement to her former love. "Stay the fuck away from me. It's over. Your life can fall apart for all I care." Earl watched as Saniya walked away from him, briskly, not once losing a step of her graceful, adamant gait.

--

He tried calling her again, and this time, he was met with a startling surprise. "We're sorry, the subscriber you are trying to reach is not available at this time." *Blocked.* He nearly threw his phone across the room, but restrained himself before he gave in to the impulse. With a defeated sigh, he flopped down on Ben's couch, emphasizing his failure by throwing his hands up in the air. "She still won't bite?" Ben said as he bit down on a potato chip while watching a basketball game, his favorite team winning by a significant margin. "Maybe it's time to let it go, Earl. I understand that you want her back, but she took the time to put your stuff together and neatly leave it outside of her apartment for you to pick up. If high

301

school taught me anything about girls, it's this: If they're angry, you might have a shot. If they're cool about distancing themselves from you, then that's it."

The past few days were supposed to have been the best of Earl's life as his song besmirching Lil Grande went live the previous week, boosting his fanbase significantly. He existed amongst a sea of positive feedback and adoring fans with Imani subtly changing his social media page from reflecting Ben and Earl as a duo, to promoting "Tzar-Mo" individually. Ben had suggested the change, accepting his role as Earl's behind-the-scenes ally. Rather than celebration when Ben initially called Earl to brag about his latest milestones, Earl had spent that night, alone, trying to find a liquor strong enough to knock him out. Since his break-up, he'd suffered–spells of insomnia, and not wanting to take pills, he opted to have a liquor cabinet built into his home. Through trial and error, he found out that his body wouldn't accept cheap liquor, it passing through his body from one of two exits as quickly as he would imbibe it.

Saniya, much to his dismay, had followed through with her promise to disavow him entirely. In-between his new drinking hobby, which was the only way to fend off the constant numbness he became afflicted with, he would meet up with Kim, trying to whet an empty appetite while giving her the impression that he cared about her. "It'll be alright, Earl. One day, you'll find another girl who can be the second-in-command that you need, like Imani is to me." Earl didn't bother to acknowledge him, knowing that Ben's platitudes would never come to fruition. The two boys were abruptly alerted by Imani, who had bolted into the living room in a panic, wearing an apron.

"What's cookin', good-lookin'?" Ben cooed.

"Lil Grande is here, in Washington! He posted a video of himself getting off the plane with his security thirty minutes ago!" "Good." Both Imani and Ben stared at Earl as if a third eye had emerged from his forehead. He stood up, casually, wearing an expression of stone. "He heard our song, and he was rightfully pissed. He contacted me directly two days ago with some thin threats, so I gave him this address to see if he could support his tough, public persona." Earl's strategy had worked, coaxing the slighted rapper into engaging him personally.

Beyond antagonization and getting him to come to Washington, Earl hadn't had a plan. The only thing that Earl was resolute that he wasn't going to throw a single punch, even if that meant that he'd allow Lil Grande to beat him until the rapper compensated for his easily- wounded pride. Some potential outcomes came to Earl's mind, but he wasn't exactly sure which of them he'd preferred becoming a reality.

"What the hell is wrong with you, dude?!"

Ben's eyes were wide and in search of answers, but Earl showed nothing but apathy regarding the impending confrontation. "It's good for publicity, right?" "When was the last time you've even been in a fight, Earl?!" "Middle school, and it went about as well as you'd think." Before Ben could try to make sense of Earl's train of thought, loud, thumping music blared throughout the neighborhood, a flagrant anomaly within Ben's community. "Speak of the devil." Earl walked past Ben and Imani, opening the front door as a black truck skidded in front of Ben's townhouse. Sure enough, Lil Grande emerged from the back of the truck, catching sight of Earl as he walked onto the lawn to meet the man he considered the bane of the music industry. "I'm gonna knock the shit out of you, cuz. Don't nobody fuckin' disrespect me like that." Lil Grande handed his large, gaudy chain to a man that could only be described as a wall, being big and sturdy as he took Grande's other accessories. "Just shut the fuck up and fight me if that's what you're going to do. That's what's wrong with you incoherent, pointless 'rappers.' You spend all day hyping up bullshit, then can't follow through. You're fragile, and now you're mad because I unmasked you." Earl's inflammatory statements only served to enrage the celebrity who pulled his shirt over his head, exposing his upper body, and threw it to the ground. "For someone who theorized that I like to fuck men, you sure were quick to take that shirt off. Maybe you're projecting some hidden part of your sexuality that you don't want to deal with." "I'm gonna fuck you up."

As Lil Grande advanced towards Earl, who didn't bother to assume any type of fighting stance, Ben sprinted out of the house and stood between the two. "I'm not watching this go down," Ben said, determined to stand up for Earl. "Let him do it," Earl taunted. "It's what people like him do when they realize they don't have the talent to keep their careers afloat; they make a lot of noise in order to stay relevant. Him coming all the way up here just to fight me does nothing but prove my point."

People had come out of their homes to bear witness to the remarkable spectacle taking place. Some of them already had their phones raised, recording the volatile situation. The big bodyguard that had been standing next to Lil Grande had begun walking up too, but Grande turned around and gestured for him to stop. "Nah, Daryll, I don't need you. I'll fuck them up myself. First, I'll kick the shit out of white boy, then I'll shut the punk-bitch behind him up. Can't even fight his own battles." "And you can't create good content, so who's the 'punk-bitch' when it's all said and done? I'm going to be the one that people will remember, and you'll be a pathetic 'Where Are They Now?' half-hour special on some dead network that, like you, are trying and failing to maintain a semblance of importance in the face of certain extinction."

Lil Grande had heard enough and tried to push past

Ben to get to Earl, but Ben pushed Grande away. Grande took a swing at Ben, who ducked the punch, then reared back and connected his fist with Grande's mouth. Earl smirked absently as he watched the brawl, experiencing the same high that he'd felt after recording a song. Grande eventually managed to grab Ben's legs and hoist him off the ground. Ben writhed out of his grasp, which sent both men to the ground as Grande got the advantage, raining a coordinated set of punches down on Ben. Adrenaline coursed through Earl's veins as he vicariously felt the aggression of the fight. Ben began to lose any contending leverage that he had as Grande continued beating him, which stopped as soon as the sirens started sounding. A blur of blue and red lights flew down the street and stopped behind Grande's truck. Two police officers stepped out of the car and ran towards the clash. One tackled Grande off of Ben, and the other lifted Ben off the ground and held him back as he tried to continue their battle. Earl grinned from ear to ear as the officer restraining Grande pulled out a pair of handcuffs and latched them onto his wrists. Lil Grande grunted in discomfort as he was lifted up and pulled in the direction of the police car, casting a steady stream of slurs and profanities towards both Earl and Ben.

Imani ran out of Ben's house and went over to her boyfriend to calm him down and check him for injuries. In the wake of what had transpired, Earl had been elated knowing that one of the better outcomes that he'd foreseen had happened almost to perfection.

306

Of the many ways that he'd hoped the situation had gone, this was the second-best variant as he wanted to show Lil Grande how powerless he truly was against him. "Peasant," Earl muttered to himself as he saw the police car containing the bombastic rapper cruise down the street and zip around a corner, out of sight. *A king doesn't need to entertain the dealings of a jester.*

As soon as the car left, Earl walked over to Ben. He did his best to mimic Imani's concern over Ben's well-being as the cut above Ben's left eye bled heavily. Imani ran into the house to get antiseptic and bandages, and that left Earl and Ben out in the front yard as Ben held a hand against the wound to temporarily stop the bleeding. "Thanks, Ben. You didn't have to do that. I should've jumped in and helped you out; it was my fight, not yours." "No worries, dude," Ben responded, wincing as he gave Earl a thumbs-up with his unoccupied hand. "You're like a brother to me. I wasn't going to let that asshole roll up here and do that to you." Earl smiled warmly, pleased that Ben had played his role in the most ideal manner possible. Him and Imani both. Earl, for the first time, understood the true breadth of his power and influence.

--

"We have a real treat for you guys on the show next!" the energetic man bellowed into the microphone as

Earl sat across from him, smirking as the radio host prepared to introduce him. The "Will Does Washington" radio show had escalated in popularity over the last few years, the Washington-centric broadcast being a candid conversation between Will Brooks and whatever celebrity he'd invited onto the show followed by a few questions from whoever called in. It'd started off humbly, but quickly became tailored towards either celebrity gossip or just as a platform for people to get to know more about their favorite idols. Earl's invitation to the show was a sign that he'd been doing something right. "Joining us today is a Washington native and one of the hottest up-and-coming artists in the rap game! He recently had beef with Lil Grande, and his songs have given Tonally more web traffic than they've ever had! Let me introduce to you, Tzar-Mo! What's happening, man?" "I'm cool, but I want to clear one thing up before you throw more questions my way. I'm not a rapper, I'm a lyricist. Rap focuses on the lowest common denominator to get by, while my fans enjoy what I'm actually saying and how I tell a story in my songs."

"Oh!" Will exclaimed, seeing the perfect opportunity to prod Earl for further insight. "So, is that why you and Lil Grande have been at each other's necks lately?" "I don't know what Lil Grande has against me, but I showed him that there's more to music than who can make the most noise to attract attention. The difference between the two of us is that one made a career from what he believes is 'style' with absolutely

308

zero substance, and the other is me. I don't understand why it's so hard to be talented and sleek." Earl grinned as Will soaked up every word, feeding off the radio personality's proclivity to incite controversy. As Earl saw it, the more publicity he could garner, the better. "Does that mean that we can expect a round two soon?" Earl frowned as Will appeared to have missed every point that had been touched upon, only trying to spin and advance his own narrative. "No," Earl stated dryly. "In fact, his agents reached out to us and apologized, ensuring that we'd never have to worry about any more unexpected fights from Lil Grande."

"His fans have a lot to say about that. They think that you're soft, that you encouraged Lil Grande's label to punish him for what many thought was a warranted response to 'Open Season.' You did throw a lot of shade in that song, did you not?" Earl's face scrunched up, but he tried his best to hide his simmering displeasure regarding the opinions of Lil Grande's fans. He knew that there was a camera nearby that would post the interview online, and he didn't want to give off any signs of distaste.

"He has his fans, and I have mine. I had absolutely nothing to do with his label reining him in. Some people like his brand of entertainment, which is their prerogative, and others like my output where I'm more descriptive, meticulous and empathetic. There's enough out there, music-wise, for the fans to find what they're looking for and enjoy." Earl's noncommittal answer seemed to have pleased Will, who cackled and moved on to his next point.

"Alright, so we'll back off of the topic of Lil Grande and talk about you. Who is Tzar- Mo? Better yet, where the hell did that name come from?" Earl found his mood rise exponentially at the subject concerning himself as he grinned, making sure every tooth was visible. "So, growing up, I was big on classical music. I was one of those weird kids who played classical music if I had a bad day or to mellow myself out if I was feeling anxious. 'Tzar-Mo' is an anagram of 'Mozart,' one of the most acclaimed composers of the classical period. Mozart was, allegedly, a prodigy at the age of five, somehow grasping the concept of writing music to create his first musical compositions. I know it's a high bar to set, but I want to be to modern-day music what Mozart was to music in his era."

"See, you aren't just an average dude because I don't know anyone who would come up with something like that! You're well-spoken, you conduct yourself well, and honestly, I'm kind of shocked that someone like you didn't decide to become a teacher or professor or something."

"I originally had wanted to become a writer, but after a while, I figured I was better suited for music." Earl had hoped that the camera hadn't captured the lightning-fast twitch of his right eye, an indication of the lie that he'd forced out of his mouth. The

310

interview plodded along as Will asked Earl about various other pertinent topics, which began to irritate the rising star as none of it pertained to who he was or the motivations behind his music, but he never let that show in his mannerisms. When Will opened the questions from callers, Earl's patience quickly eroded as he was either asked the most asinine things or was asked a slightly reworded variant of the same question time and time again? If it wasn't Will making a bothersome, trite observation, his fans annoyed him with their lack of variety, only seeing him as a novelty rather than an artist. Earl's first interview and formal introduction to the public eye hadn't been anything like he'd expected, and rather than embracing it, he began actively rejecting it.

Chapter 20

♪ Time to wake up and open the blinds. Time to shed yourselves of the shackles and binds. Time to change the world, time to start the show as you embrace the broad strokes of your maestro.

♪ Easel at the ready, raring to go, My Palette's unbreakable, artistic flow. Conducting the future, nourishing the present, it's lofty, I know, but I'm prepared, unhesitant.

♪ Caress auditorily; humble, rebuke glory,

♪ Now stand for me as we fill the space in this barren repository. I'm a husk, but my lyrics make me whole, Leaving people incited, never focused on bankrolls.

♪ Was dealt a bad hand, but learned to cope. When life buried my head in the sand, touting 'No Hope.' Expanded my scope, stopped being a joke, "I'm not done yet, so forget the rope."

♪ We can take it slow, there's no need to rush, Lead by actions, not words, with the stroke of our brush. Hopelessness is temporary, so pick up a dream and follow my voice.

♪ I lived in my head, sometimes wished I were dead, now I'm telling you there's another choice.

♪ Pick up your pen, your brush, camera or ball, Perfect your vocals, time to install. Ourselves as kings and queens and aspire to have it all.

♪ They say we're the ones that ruined society; lazy, uncaring, no sense of propriety. "Back in my day, the men were men, we had life figured out by the time we were ten. You're weak sexual deviants, no discipline. You can't shoulder our burdens, you've failed us again.

♪ The phones ruined your minds, we're shifting the blame, We're perfectly sane, nothing here to defame. Drunks that tanked the economy?

♪ No, we were holy and clean!" Maybe they're the ones who meet the criteria of "therapist's wet dream." A Neo-Renaissance, we're taking control. We can prove them wrong, we can shine and glow. Fight against the grain, make ourselves a name. Destroy misconceptions, leave no room for false claims.

♪ Transform desperation to emancipation, Children of the nation, march, no cessation. I'll take your hand, guide you if I must, We'll create limitless art with the stroke of our brush. ♪

The packed section of the mall that Tonally had rented out specifically for Tzar-Mo had exploded with sheer euphoria as Ben stood up next to his friend and bowed dramatically. "That was the only song that you guys will be getting for free! If you want more, you gotta line up and support our debut album, 'Neo-Rinascimento'!" He'd been up the street from the mall for all of his life, but never in his wildest dreams could he have imagined any of what he'd currently found himself entrenched in. They were chanting for him, or at least, his alias. People showed up wearing every solid color of the rainbow, representing themselves as a part of what Tzar-Mo referred to as his *Palette*. It had only been last month since the cruise Ben had planned where a lucky group of fans got to hang out with Tzar-Mo and Ben, offered the chance to see the unveiling of the cover of their album. It hadn't felt real then, and it didn't feel real now.

"Now, without further ado," Ben said as he gave the man of the hour a proud look, "I'm going to give the mic over to the myth, the living legend, Tzar-Mo!" He stared blankly into the crowd as they cheered, going as far as to arrange themselves within their ranks so that they created a gradient that resembled an actual rainbow. Ben sat down as Tzar stood, the fans shouting his name wildly as he rose. Kim had tailor-made Tzar's outfit for this special occasion, making half-capes a permanent fixture on his purple suit

314

instead of an accoutrement. His eyes scanned the entire crowd, then drifted to the table where stacks of his albums were ready to sign. However, instead of the enrapturement that he thought he'd be swept away by, he felt nothing. No tears of joy, no happiness, no feeling as though months of songwriting had finally paid off. Only emptiness.

But he had an obligation. He put on the biggest smile that he could and addressed his rabid fans, who doted on his every word. "I can't believe any of this is happening. It feels like yesterday when Ben and I first started this, and we had no idea where it would go. As any diehard fan knows, I'm sure, I'd wanted to become an author." The crowd responded negatively to Earl's former ambitions, which only served to make him feel worse. "Yeah. I'd spent a year and some change working on a manuscript, but it didn't quite work out. In the midst of a creative crisis, I found solace in writing lyrics and bearing my soul through a different kind of medium. I didn't compromise my dreams of becoming a storyteller, I just redirected it."

So many eyes, so many smiles, and yet, how many of them knew him? His heart? His mind? How many of them saw him as a person and not as some kind of idol? "'Neo-Rinascimento' isn't just a catchy name, it's not just an assemblage of songs, it's a movement. It's a story about the millennial era; the trials and tribulations that each and every one of us have been

315

through at one point in our lives. The song that you heard, 'Stroke Of Our Brush,' is one of many featured songs that embody how we're perceived and how we're expected to act. It's a lesson in never giving up on your heart's desires or conforming to the burdens imposed on us by a malignant, indifferent society."

Are you trying to convince them, or yourself?

"I know that everyone came out here to support me, and I appreciate you, truly. Without you guys, there's no telling where I would be. You created me, and it's only fair that I give back to you." Tzar's rally went on for a few more minutes, having practiced the script multiple times over the week so that he wouldn't fumble-over any words. He let his mind wander as he mechanically went through the main bullet points. Gratitude. Meaning. Purpose.

Are you the decorative, exalted knight that thought the world of himself yet?

After he spoke, it was time for the album signing, which was just one face after another. The occasional girl would slip him their number, which he collected in his back pocket, but it became routine to the point where he thought he was at the Sub Shack again, serving customers. The fans loved him. He now had more money than he knew what to do with.

None of it mattered. None of it had given him the

purpose he'd been chasing. It was a dumb question here, a "You inspire me!" there, all of it was so ordinary. *You know, don't you? You know that four months ago, you turned away your heart. You did, nobody else. Bitter one day, vengeful the next, arrogant the week afterwards. Even songwriting is a chore now, but you're too far in to give up now. Cling to the legacy that you wanted because it's the only thing that you have left.* Long after his hand stopped cramping from the sheer number of signings, long after the specks in his eyes from the flashing cameras faded, he knew he'd still go home and crawl into bed, alone, regardless of who laid beside him. "Do you got time for me?"

Tzar clicked his pen and signed the inside cover without thinking about it, but when he looked up to give the album back, he'd froze. His voice hitched in his throat and he blinked rapidly, thinking that he'd finally crossed the threshold into utter insanity, He'd aged poorly since the last time Earl had recalled seeing him, but there was no mistaking him. Their similarities matched up far too much for it not to have been him. "Dad...?"

--

Earl Sr. was covered with tattoos, most of which Earl

assumed had been from his stretch in prison. Each looked as if a different person had tried their hand at branding his father. The outline of his hair had started a few inches higher than the average person's, and Earl tried to distract himself by wondering what age the unfortunate genetics would curse him with dying follicles. The older replica wore tattered pants and a faded shirt riddled with tears, streaks and holes, making him indistinguishable from a homeless person. If it had been anyone else, Earl might've felt sorry for them. The man sitting across from him looked as though he had to fight hard to survive and Earl didn't want to imagine the things his father had to do to keep himself alive.

"You've done well for yourself, Junior. I can't tell you how proud I am of you. I'm so sorry that it took me so long to see you, but I got out of jail about a month ago. Then, I heard about ma. I feel so bad. I should've been there, for the both of you. I saw that you were having the album signing, and I knew I had to use that to own up to all the shit." Earl stared at the cheeseburger in front of him, his father offering to buy him a cheap meal while they spoke in the mall's food court. "I know the life that I chose back when I was young and stupid. I wasn't ready for fatherhood. I didn't understand how precious the life of a child was, neither me nor your mother did. We failed to nurture you when you needed us the most, and I know that there aren't enough apologies to make up for what you had to go through." His son looked everywhere but, in his eyes,, opting to stare at the center of the table when he'd run out of things to focus on. "...Junior, please. Say something. I want to give you the life that I should've given you from the moment you were born." "You're ready to be a parent twenty-three years later?" His voice had been cold and distant, cutting his father with an ominous glare. "Do you know how many nights I spent wondering if I'd ever get to see either you or my mother? Yeah, you showed up, what, three times during my childhood, and now you want a gold medal for parenting because you finally felt bad about being a shitty father?"

"Look, Junior, I—"

"My name isn't 'Junior,' and you should be lucky that I haven't had my name legally changed. How you name something after yourself and then make the decisions you made is beyond my comprehension, Earl." The impersonal way the name slithered from his son's lips was like a punch to his gut, but he persevered, expecting there to be a lot of retaliation before he could get through to his son.
"You're angry, I understand that, but—"

"You understand?" Earl angrily retorted. "You understand the feeling of having to listen to your grandmother talk about how much potential her son had, then squandered? The fact that you chose a life of drug-dealing and imprisonment is something I don't think she ever fully recovered from. She blamed herself for you being the person you were. I remember the story about the first time that the police busted into the apartment that you used to live in, and she got to watch as the police dragged your sorry ass out of there in handcuffs. She didn't know why, but she said that somehow, she could look into your eyes and knew that somewhere down the line, she'd ruined you." Earl Sr. was rendered speechless as he considered Earl's words.

"I was the anomaly. She didn't know how to deal with me at first because I wasn't out there like you were. I got Charlotte after you had disappointed her, when she had spent every weekend drunk for years until she got herself right. As a kid, I had to stand by and watch her stumble around the house after she'd argue with her mother, who suffered from early-onset dementia and spent all her money, money Charlotte was supposed to have, falling prey to online scams. We almost lost the house because of that. Not only did Charlotte have to figure that out, fearing homelessness herself, but then I came into the picture with all the issues I had. It took us years of struggling, month after month, day after day, to build the rapport and love that we had have together. Where were you then? Charlotte loved me, but never knew how to talk to me. I went through all of that by myself. Without you. But you were too busy running the streets to give a fuck, right?" "…There's no excuse for putting you through any of that. I want to make it right now, so could we try to start over?" *"Start over?"*

It had come out with such underlying outrage that it caught Earl Sr. by surprise ~~as~~ Earl leaned forward to address his father, making sure that nobody else heard him. "When you can find the time machine that allows you to go back and will yourself to becoming a halfway decent human being, you come find me." Earl leaned back into his seat, smirking mirthlessly as he beheld his father. "Look at you. Pathetic. Tattoos over almost every inch of your body, thin as a stick, and now that you've survived jail, you want to swoop in and be Super-Dad! I'm supposed to be grateful of the fact that your conscience caught up with you! What a coincidence, by the way, that you turn up when I finally have something of my own and have money and a platform!" It was his father's turn to be indignant, having had just about enough of his son's attitude. "I'm trying to make things right, and all you have to say is how much you don't like me?"

"What else is there to talk about?! We sure as shit don't have anything in common! Here I am, independent after clawing, surviving, trying to make sense of my place in the world, and then what happens? You emerge from whatever shit-hole ~~jail~~ you came from. You had over twenty years to get me on that wagon, to convince me that you're just this flawed, beaten person who's trying his best. Guess what I see? A joke. A waste of my time. I don't need you anymore; my faith in having a united family vanished when I was a teenager and reality taught me

321

otherwise."

Earl's anger had begun to fade into a melancholic resignation, the situation catching up to him as he let out years of frustration towards his father. "I used to wonder if I was just crazy and imagined seeing you those few times when I was younger. If the promises were real or not. You'd leave before I could tether myself to the idea that you were ever there to begin with."Earl shook his head, seemingly lost in his own thoughts. "I think as a kid, I was too ignorant to grasp the concept that neither you nor my mother wanted to be there. Honestly, I don't even know why I'm so angry at you now. You're a stranger. You don't deserve to be referred to as 'dad' or anything akin to that title. Maybe it was better this way, the fact that you never raised me. Charlotte did more for me than you or my mother could've, and she's the person I'm the most grateful for in this life. As for this notion you have of us cultivating a relationship? Some father/son bonding? I can't do it. I just can't. You don't get to waltz into someone's life and decide that you're ready to be a part of it. That's not how it works."

Earl stood up and reached into his pocket, producing his wallet. After fumbling around within it, he pulled out and calculated a certain amount of money before tossing it down in the middle of the table. "That's fifteen-hundred dollars. I don't care what the fuck you do with it, but don't contact me ever again. At least the other one had the sense to stay away from me." Earl Sr. sullenly stayed seated as he watched his son walk away, leaving the older man to shake his head before pocketing the money that Earl had given him.

Chapter 21

He'd run out of ideas, experiencing the worst creative dearth he'd had yet. Seeking inspiration, he went to the one person that he knew he could depend on and rung his doorbell, awaiting his appearance. Madison had disappointed him, proving to be nothing more than another anticlimactic entry in his black book.

"Talked about her journalistic dreams and told me that she was willing to be mine. I guess the encore performance did wonders for her. She's improved a lot since the last time." He recalled what he'd written in his notes with a frown. That's what his life had boiled down to, cataloging his trysts in a book, a futile attempt to create a purpose. The campus students had been the most aggravating part of his visit to Madison's university. "When's your next song coming out?!" "Can I have your autograph?!"

If it wasn't a pen or a phone being shoved in his face, it was a deluge of requests to be either featured or mentioned in one of his songs, or visit them personally and "rap" for them, or other pointless observations. Unfortunately, such interactions had been par for the course when it came to his fandom. It'd almost made his journey there fruitless. Ben's door swung open, and instead of his usual cheery, goofy demeanor, Ben had been fuming. His rigid, erratic breathing and clenched fists were enough to almost intimidate Earl, who considered his next words carefully. "…What's wrong?"

Ben slammed the door behind him and got directly in Earl's face. "What the fuck were you doing at WSU yesterday?" *Oh. Shit.* Ben had been very acquainted with Earl's "hot streak," going as far as to actively approve of it.

"It's been a long time coming!" Ben had said regarding Earl's acts, believing that it'd help loosen him up and provide needed inspiration. This time, however, Ben had known something was terribly wrong, feeling a sense of discomfort that he hadn't felt in months. He'd known that the campus had been out of Earl's way, and he wouldn't have gone up there if there wasn't some ulterior motive present. Ben had initially reasoned that Earl had to have been visiting someone else, refusing to believe the alternative, but when pictures of Madison and Earl together at a coffee shop made their rounds online, Ben's worst fears were all but confirmed.

The tense silence between the two lasted for longer than Earl could come up with a feasible lie, so he stood there, mouth agape, trapped. "Don't tell me that you weren't there because there are pictures of you with some of the students. Actually, you just have to answer one question for me, and that'll tell me what I need to know. You better tell the truth too." Earl could do nothing but nod, his mind trying to decide if he should deny the impending accusation.

"That night that we had the party after Tonally cut us our first check. You said that you took Maddie to a motel. The two of you spent the night together there, didn't you?" Ben knew the answer, but he wanted Earl to admit it. Earl's heart pounded against his chest, trying to escape the dire situation. With a gulp, Earl gained the courage to answer Ben. "…Yeah."

No sooner than the word had fallen from Earl's mouth did Ben's fist connect with his jaw, dislocating it as Earl tumbled to the ground. Earl howled out in pain and gave his chin a quick tug, realigning his jaw. Ben cursed and rubbed his knuckles, putting all his strength into the punch as he stared Earl down.

"She's eighteen! What's wrong with you?!"

Getting to his own two feet, Earl did nothing but shrug his shoulders, unwilling to hold any brand of accountability for his actions. "I don't know what I was thinking, Ben. I'm sorry." "Sorry?!" Ben had started to continue his assault on Earl but stopped short of a couple of feet away from him and put his hands on his hips, ambivalent as to what to do next. "Look, I—" "Just shut your mouth, Earl. In fact, I can't look at you right now. Get back in your car and get away from me before I do something that we're both going to regret." Earl didn't hesitate to turn around and get back to his car as Ben disappeared into his house, furiously slamming the door shut behind him. Not knowing what else to do, Earl put his keys into the ignition and pulled away from Ben's house. It was only halfway back to his own home that Earl had realized how badly he'd been shaking.

--

Epsen Knight. His literary hero. "Death Dies Once." Earl's favorite. Earl sighed, remembering his ideal self, the aspiring author. Nothing felt better than the creation of his book, which now seemed like a distant memory. It was as if it had never happened as the manuscript had been forcefully erased, now a footnote amongst Earl's timeline. He wasn't sure what made him want to read Epsen's book after being separated from literature for so long. Maybe it was nostalgia, the fact that the book was the only thing that sent Earl to a place where Charlotte was still alive, Saniya was still his, and his friendship with Ben had never been better. He'd had a habit of reading what he considered to be Knight's magnum opus whenever he'd had writer's block and felt like he lacked the talent to be a credible author, feeling Knight's passion for his own works bleed through every character, every page. There had been punishing lows during Earl's writing stint then, but nothing compared to what he felt now. An absence of feeling when he desperately wanted to.

His reverie was broken by the ringing of chimes, indicating that someone was waiting for him at his front door. The chair screeched across the hardwood floor as Earl rose and shuffled towards the door, expecting Ben. It was the perfect time for him to belt out the profuse apology that he had planned for his old friend. It was always when he thought that he couldn't sink any lower that life surprised him, reminding Earl of his shortcomings.

I wonder what Dr. Tommen would say?

Earl's bitter reminiscence ended the moment that he opened the door, and his body became as still as a statue. Before him was the object of his desires, the dream that dissolved his steadfast apathy. "Hey, Earl! Do you mind if I come in?"

There stood Imani in the shortest pair of denim. "Ben was so upset that he turned me away when I got there, but I figured that it gave you and I a perfect opportunity since we never get the chance to hang out! I bought some wine!" Imani said, revealing the bottle that she'd been hiding behind her back. "I know that you got it like that now and probably have a more refined palate than this, but I hope that you like it! It used to be one of my mom's favorites, and I guess I inherited her tastes in fine wine. Earl, realizing how long he'd been staring at Imani without speaking, opened the door with an embarrassed greeting and led her to the living room where he'd

328

previously been brooding. He made sure that she was situated on the couch before heading to the kitchen and retrieving two glasses for the wine Imani had brought. "How have you been, Earl?" Imani yelled from the living room. "Fine!" The lie stung at the tip of his tongue as he returned, glasses in hand as she smiled sadly at him. "I can tell that you're still processing a lot of things. It's written all over your face." "…I guess. I'm just tired." Imani handed Earl the bottle of wine, and the liquid fizzled and bubbled as Earl filled both of their glasses about halfway before putting the bottle down in the middle of the table. "Do you want to talk about it? I don't mind, I'm interested to know where your mind has been lately! You may need someone to just sit back and listen, and I'm more than ready to slide into that role!"

Imani crossed her legs as she took a sip of the wine, patient and supportive. Earl was taken aback by her willingness to hear him out as he'd felt as though there had been nobody else he could speak to. "I don't know if I can stand this lifestyle anymore. Tzar-Mo was supposed to be this lyrical champion; an outlet for me to not only bring light to difficult topics, but to inspire those minds brimming with potential that don't have the support system to flourish on their own." "And you feel like you don't do that? 'Neo-Rinascimento' was amazing, especially for a debut album." "I feel like nobody hears me though." It was Earl's turn to take a swig of the wine, recoiling as he registered how different it had been from his typical choices of liquor. Imani, smirking, beat Earl to his impending question, seeing curiosity lining his face. "It's called 'Apfelwein.' It's a wine from Germany, and it's basically apple cider with alcohol in it. This particular bottle has some kick to it though, it has a higher alcohol content than the brand usually does. I guess you could call me a kInd of connoisseur, but without the snobbish attitude." Earl chuckled, then downed more of the tart, but sweet liquid. It was smooth, almost as elegant as Imani. The wine was a perfect match for her. "But, continue! Is it the fame? The fans?"

"It's a little bit of everything. The life of a 'celebrity' is a pain in the ass. You can't breathe without someone trying to record it. I can't shop anywhere, I can't pump gas for my car in peace, I can't even walk down the street without people screaming at me from their car windows or running up to me and asking me a thousand questions like I'm some robot created specifically for their entertainment. I feel the monotony that working at Sub Shack used to make me feel, but at least when I left that building, nobody harassed me on the street.

And don't get me started on the internet aspect of it. Between the constant flood of messages, I get to see pictures of myself that people take without me even noticing and then send them to gossip websites like that's a cool thing to do! Then, I have everyone ask me 'What's next?' ad nauseam, day after day, hour after hour, not giving me time to orient myself for my next track. I don't have any room to create anything because people consume my music so fast, then want more immediately afterwards without taking in what they've heard. When they feel like I don't give them what they want quickly enough, they lash out and get pissed off at me for not being the 'artist' I presented myself as." He poured himself more wine as he paused to take a break from his rant. Imani took a minute to scan the room lost in thought from Earl's account of his popularity. "Everyone wants to be the one that makes millions and is bathed in the adoration from the public. Even though I haven't technically hit the big leagues as a lyricist, I already feel as though it's not the life for me. If I have to deal with shit like this now, I can't begin to imagine what it'll be like if I went from local celebrity to being noticed nationwide.

Most days, I can't distinguish myself from Tzar-Mo. Money and fame haven't fixed my life or made me happy; I'm miserable. Hell, I feel worse now because it feels like I'm not in charge of what I do half of the time even when I have more space to make moves than most people! This is the only moment in months where I've felt like a real person. The second you become a celebrity; you stop being human. You don't have feelings because you have money. You don't have legitimate opinions because you aren't attuned to the strife of the everyday person anymore. You must become the avatar you made, this false representation of success, for every waking moment simply due to expectation. If you aren't, you're a fraud, a joke, and nobody takes your work seriously. You honestly want to know what I spend most of my days doing?" Imani responded with a simple nod. "If I'm not fucking something, I'm trying my damnedest to get drunk so that I can forget about the fact that I wanted this, and it's not what I thought it'd be. I sacrificed everything to get here, and the opulent lifestyle is the only thing that affirms for me that it meant anything. I do these things that I don't enjoy anymore because it feels like the only thing someone in my position can do. I can't sleep, I can't eat, I'm so stressed that I haven't written anything in weeks. I'm tapped out. I wanted to be great. I thought it was owed to me after spending so much of my life taking orders or being unheard and unappreciated. Now, I'm about to lose Ben, the last semblance of a world I'll never know again, because I fucked Madison. I don't know what to do. I'll go to Charlotte some days and try to find solace there, but all I'm reminded of is how terribly I treated her in the end."

Earl pointed across the room to a stand with an ornate urn resting atop of it, his exasperation evident in his animated gesticulations and irritated, forlorn intonation. "I don't know anymore. About anything." Imani had almost finished her glass of wine in the midst of Earl's diatribe, and Earl, noticing, refilled her glass with an appreciative smile serving as his reward. After meditating on everything, Imani finally found the words to address Earl's woes. "I understand everything that you've just said more than you'd know. For me, though I'm nowhere near as big, the nature of my modeling setup means that I always get some kind of unwanted attention. If it's not opening my messages to a sea of male genitalia or other disgusting advances, it's being threatened when I fail to post as regularly as I do. Just like how you feel about never having any peace of mind. Girls hate me because they're either intimidated by how I look or see my free depiction of sexuality as an indication that I'm a slut. Guys hate me because they want to fuck me, and when I'm not interested, they reveal themselves as chauvinistic assholes by talking down to me and telling me that I'm 'just a tease.' A few even threatened to rape me if they ever saw me out in public." Imani scoffed mirthlessly, and Earl felt horrible listening to her as clarity engulfed him. He was just as bad, if not worse, than those guys who would see Imani as nothing but something to fuck. The only difference was that they were bold enough to make their intentions known.

"I don't want to be that kind of person, but I feel as though this era of men are among the most parasitic and irredeemable that they've ever been. At least back in the day, they were honest about how they viewed women as less than they were. Now, it's hidden beneath these schemes, games and ulterior motives. They think that we're stupid enough to wander into their bedrooms like living, breathing sex toys that they can brag to their friends about when they're done using us. Sadly, most of us are. We fall for the bullshit, and then cry ourselves to sleep wondering why some insecure jackass who can't find his own worth didn't see ours." Earl was taken aback by Imani's indignation and anger, seeing her shake slightly as she spoke.

"That's what happened to my mother. I told you that my dad only popped up every so often. He was a lot nicer when I was little; he'd be dad of the year for a day, long enough to ease his way back into my mom's good graces, then he'd control her. I didn't know at that time - being so young. He was my hero, and I was happy that I saw him maybe four or five times out of the year until he got bored of us. ...I didn't tell you the whole truth about my mother." Earl's eyes widened as he involuntarily leaned forward, entrenched in Imani's story. "I didn't exactly leave home voluntarily. I didn't have a choice once my dad had my mom institutionalized. He'd randomly came back after not showing up for the entire time that I was in high school, claiming he'd changed. Of course, mom believed him. He knew she would. She always did."

Imani gazed listlessly into the center of the table where the bottle of wine sat and took a longer gulp from her glass than she usually did, tilting her head back to get every last drop. "He fucked her, as he had many times before, and when he tried to give my mom the cold shoulder the morning after, she finally snapped. She kept this case of sharpened pencils on the stand next to her bed, and while he was getting dressed, she took one and without being too graphic, made sure that he wasn't going to be manipulating her anymore. As you can imagine, my dad won the court case that came afterwards, and my mother was sent away." "...So, how did you come around to modeling?" Earl asked quietly, trying to add substance to the stiff silence that followed.

"At first, it was the only way that I could sustain myself since the waitress job I had, barely paid me anything. Then, I found out that I was good at it. Like, *really* good at it. All the annoying things about modeling that I told you I go through now used to get to me back then. Most nights that first year I cried myself to sleep because I couldn't handle the backlash from people. After a while though, I owned it. I accepted and that's where I think you are now."

"How do you mean?"

"People like to throw the word 'greatness' around. The have-nots will always find some way to try and discredit those who have simply because they have nothing else to do with their lives. Their self-esteem is rooted within you as they try to scrutinize what you say, do or how you think, and that's a power that not a lot of people realize they have. Greatness isn't a burden, it's a blessing. If you can bring out that kind of love, or even hate, within people, you've already won." Earl began to feel the stirrings of motivation; a dormant sensation being revived.

"Just like your dad popping up recently? Mine already tried about three months ago when he saw that I was associated with you and Ben. I cussed him out and told him to go back to whatever woman would take his mangled, punctured private bits. One of the great things about coming-up these days? We don't need 'heroes' anymore when we can be our own. Don't let your fan base dictate your happiness. If they want to take pictures of you buying groceries, let them! If they want a reminder of the talent, they won't put in the work to achieve themselves, then let the fans, the media, or whoever else do what they need to do as long as it doesn't directly affect you.

If you aren't the 'hero' to some people that they wanted you to be, then fuck them! You aren't here for them, they're here for you! They pay to hear you, not the other way around. You busted your ass to get to where you are! You deserve this! As for Ben, don't worry about that. He'll calm down after another day or two, I'll talk to him." "...Thanks, Imani. You have no idea how much I needed you today," Earl said, genuinely moved by her endorsement.

"No problem! In fact..." Imani took the bottle of wine, which had now been halfway empty, and filled their glasses until they were at the same level. She raised her glass in front of her, urging Earl to do the same. "A toast! To success, to good friends, and, most importantly..." Imani paused dramatically, letting the moment linger before giving Earl a radiant smile, showing him all of her perfect teeth. "To the

336

death of heroism!" "To the death of heroism!" Earl repeated, meeting her glass with a clink as they drank in unison. She'd been the inspiration that he'd been begging for, her words being the gasoline that his dying fire needed.

Chapter 22

"Tomorrow's a big day for me. Probably the biggest of my entire life. I wish you were here, but I know that you can see me. I'm not exactly proud of all the decisions I've made. But I hope that you're looking down and you see something that's worth being proud of." Earl took a sip of the canned soda he held as he looked at the blue, floral patterns that garnished Charlotte's urn. No more drinking, no more empty sex, no more sitting around feeling sorry for himself.

"I'm going to make a difference, a real one. Tzar-Mo won't just be a bandage, he'll be the stitch that will bring people together, especially those who've lost their hope and need an advocate that understands their pain. I'm changing my outlook; instead of focusing on the things I don't like about fame; I'm going to target the good that I can do. No more pettiness, like the whole Grande debacle. I'm going to do everything right from now on, I promise you." Reminded of the lessons that she'd done her best to impart upon him. For so long, he'd been tangled in so many bad situations, either self-inflicted or otherwise, but his confessions to Charlotte had been the closest he'd been to bringing himself back from whatever darkness he'd been mired in. His mind shifted to Ben, remembering the two justifiable punches he'd received for his past indiscretions. He couldn't help but find a slight, albeit morbid humor about the whole thing, mostly directed towards himself. "I think a part of me was always jealous of Ben. He was the handsome one that all the girls wanted. Our school loved him. Even his dumb yearly pranks made the teachers laugh. I blamed my recent predilection for having sex with all those girls—sorry, Charlotte—on the most ridiculous of reasons. First, it was because I was trying to fill the void that you and Saniya made when you two left me, which was bullshit. Then, he sighed, almost feeling the heat from Charlotte's glare that he knows she would've given him if she were physically present. "Then I said I thought that all of this… promiscuity was a symptom of my popularity. The truth is that I was envious. When I saw Imani that first time, I was so angry. Mad at Ben for having her, at Saniya for not being her, and at myself for unable. I spent so much time locked away from the world, not wanting to interact with anyone.

It wasn't even something that was forced on me, I chose to be guarded and irrational. I chose not to socialize and allowed myself to be awkward and asocial. That's not Ben's fault, it was mine, yet I vilified him for it. I used Maddie, I manipulated Ben, lusted after his girl, and Saniya…" Earl's voice trailed off, and an unexpected tear ran down his cheek. "I didn't deserve her. I was stubborn and vain. I looked at everything she wasn't rather than everything that she was. She was kind; she had a bigger heart than anyone I'd ever known. I loved her sense of humor. I liked the way her smile highlighted her freckles.

She stuck by me when I'd shut down and refuse to speak to her. She was patient with me when I was writing my book and would go through every single emotion imaginable. I miss her. It's a shame that we never appreciate anything until it's gone. But I hope that she's in a better place, with someone that can give her what I refused to." Using the back of his hand, he wiped his tear away and shook his head, refusing to get too emotional. "More importantly, I'm so sorry that I wasn't there for you. I don't think I can ever forgive myself for being so ignorant. I try not to, but I end up thinking about you every single day. I miss your wisdom. I miss hearing you laugh when you got a game show answer correct. I even miss you threatening to smack me if I didn't do something that you wanted."

Regardless of his wishes, more tears trailed down his cheeks as his voice began to crack. He gave himself a moment to weep, something that had been building up for months without him ever being aware of it. "I love you, Charlotte. You'll always be in my heart. I can't guarantee that I'll do everything right, but I can guarantee that I'll try." A soft rattling at the door confounded Earl, who wasn't expecting any guests. He slid the chair back into its position in front of the television, then made his way to the door. "Hi, again!" Imani said cheerily as he walked into her visual periphery, holding up a stout bottle with a very thick bottleneck. Earl gulped, not knowing whether he should turn Imani away or not. He'd already done enough to Ben and didn't want his reluctant friend to think that anything was going on between the two of them. "I know I was just over yesterday, but I thought that you deserved a small celebration!

She rotated the bottle of brandy in a playful motion teasing Earl with two of the vices that he'd tried to swear off, liquor and the girl enticing him with it. "I know brandy is a very formal drink, but hey, I think that after something as big as potentially being signed to a record label, it was just what the situation called for!" "I… I…" Earl stuttered, unable to force himself to turn Imani away, though he'd wanted to. "Aren't you going to let me in?" *You aren't some feral animal; you can control yourself. Besides, it's one drink! After this, you can swear off the stuff all you want!* Imani's eagerness combined with his internal assertions caused Earl to open the door for her, an invitation she accepted merrily.

After watching silly movies, playing Charades exchanging stories about the most embarrassing moment of their lives having more brandy than either had intended on drinking, Earl and Imani laid on the couch, giggling. "I think I'm ready to break up with Ben," Imani stated casually, which got Earl's attention. "What? What happened?" Earl slurred. "I can't see a future with him," Imani admitted. Imani looked "I want a man with big ambitions. Someone who isn't afraid to be himself and knows how to treat a woman. Someone like you." Earl, whose eyes widened in total disbelief. After letting the moment drag on, Imani began laughing loudly, kicking her feet in amusement. "I'm kidding, Earl! You should've seen your face!" Earl laughed along, but felt a pit of disappointment that he tried to shrug off. "Oh, oh! I need some new pictures for my page!" Imani stood up and straightened out her pants, which generously hugged the lower half of her body. Earl turned his head and shut his eyes as Imani adjusted her bra. She took out her phone and handing it over to Earl as she stood a few feet in front of him. "I don't— I'm not—" Earl stammered, his nerves getting the best of him. "I'm no photographer." "That's fine!" Imani retorted gracefully flipping her hair which was styled into two long pigtails.

"Don't worry about being professional, just do the best you can!" With that, Imani puckered her full lips seductively and posed, the tasteful mounds protruding from the back of her pants being accentuated the most. Earl tried to gulp, but found that his throat and mouth were both bone-dry he centered the frame to get as much of Imani as possible before snapping the picture. "Cool! Now, another one!" Imani bit her lip and bent over in front of Earl, staring at him with a smoky, sultry look. Earl did his best not to look at her cleavage, which threatened to slip out of her sports bra. As he took the photo, he could feel himself sweating.

"One more, and then we'll be done!" "Okay," Earl said nervously as Imani turned her back to him and put her hands in her hair while looking back at the camera, sticking out her tongue playfully. Earl shakily took the picture, but then something caught his eye afterwards. Imani's shirt has hiked up slightly as she posed for the last picture, revealing the bottom of something embellished on her back. "What's up? See something you like?" Imani inquired as she watched Earl squint his eyes, trying to focus on the furtive, vibrant design. "Huh? Oh, no, no!" Earl said, realizing what she was implying. "I'm not creeping on you; I was wondering what's on your back." "Oh, that? It's a tattoo that I got about two weeks ago." Imani said, lifting her shirt so that Earl could catch the full scope of the majestic display. It was a butterfly covered a good portion of her lower back. Its wings. Earl's eyes the most; they started black at the body of the insect, then gradually turned to grey as they spread outward, finally coming to a touch of

"Wow," Earl said. "I know, butterflies aren't the most original but this one is special! It's called a pipevine swallowtail. The males are cool, but the females tend to be more colorful. They're easily the most gorgeous species of butterflies, subspecies that share similar colors as a part of mimicry to fend off predators." "Oh? Why?" "The species evolved to be highly poisonous," Imani said with faux-intimidation. "The wasps, flies and even birds know not to mess with them. The bright, orange spots are there as warnings." "Oh, shit. Are you trying to tell me that you're dangerous?" Imani turned back around and smirked at Earl. "I don't know. Do you think I'm dangerous?" Imani advanced on Earl and lowered herself onto his lap, not once taking her eyes off his. Earl unable to process what was going on until Imani leaned in and kissed him. Once her lips separated from his, he looked up at Imani with horror outlining his features.

"I—I—but what about Ben?" Earl asked, trying to gather up the last remnants of his self- control.

"He's not you."

That, combined with Imani's soft voice, was enough to erode Earl's newfound fortitude as he kissed Imani tenderly. Earl slowly wrapped his arms around Imani and pulled her deeper into their kiss, which became slow and methodical. As soon as Earl would become too enthusiastic, Imani nibbled on his bottom lip, a sign that she had no intention of letting Earl take charge. She would sunder their tangled lips only to torture Earl, biting and licking his earlobes while running her hands down his chest and nibbling on his neck. Earl's eyes rolled into the back of his head, enmeshed in a fit of utter ecstasy. After a while, she stopped completely, much to Earl's chagrin. She then ground her lower body against his crotch, making his legs shake involuntarily as she leaned into his ear and whispered.

"Make me yours."

Imani slid away from Earl, who got up and led her into his bedroom. Once inside, their lips became one again as Earl lowered Imani onto the bed. She allowed his hands to caress her smooth body, but as he went to unbutton her pants, he froze. Condoms. He never had sex with anyone without condoms. As if reading his mind, Imani grabbed at the bulge in his pants, eliciting a pained moan from Earl. "It's okay. I'm on the pill." In his elevated state of arousal, he didn't dare give the issue a second thought as he unbuttoned her pants, eager to pay her back for torturing him on the couch. He slowly slid her pants and underwear off, revealing a tantalizing pink slit, more delectable than he'd ever imagined. He admired it momentarily before slowly easing his face towards her, dragging his tongue from the bottom of her slit to the top, garnering an approving moan from Imani.

She tastes heavenly.

He went on to orally enjoy her for a little while longer, using his hunger to humble her in ways she'd never had a man utilize before, his eagerness to please permeating every flick, lap and dip of his tongue. When she couldn't take it anymore, she brought him up to her eye level. He could see it, that she yearned for it as badly as he did. The two of them saw the depths of the other's cravings, their mutual greed.

"Fuck me. Please." Upon Imani's breathless request, Earl quickly snatched his own pants off, ready to fulfill the needs of his goddess. His room became a portrait of scattered clothes, sheets and other items as Earl had Imani in every way that he could. His unfiltered, raw access to her only served to heighten his already overloaded senses as he used every last iota of strength, he could muster to satisfy his long-coveted appetite. Their lust-fueled contest seemed to go to every square inch of his bedroom as he pinned her up against walls, bent her over his desk and even broke one of his chairs with their combined weight, which afforded the pair a moment of amusement before reverting to their rapacious struggle.

After what seemed like hours, he managed to get one final, emphatic thrust deep inside of Imani as they reached a mutual peak, shockwaves of passion throbbed throughout every inch of their bodies. Earl's body gave out beneath him as he collapsed next to Imani on his bed, his ragged, irregular breathing trying its best to stabilize. He'd never expended his energy like that before and doubted he would ever be able to again. His legs and arms were sore and throbbing and his back had been scratched up courtesy of Imani's nails. Yet, as he passed out, the last thing he saw being Imani's sweaty, elated visage, he knew only one thing. It had been the best experience of his entire life, one that he knew he'd never regret or forget no matter how hard he tried.

--

He opened his eyes, slowly, cognizant of the empty space next to him. Bleary-eyed and groggy, Earl sat up, his entire body still aching. If it wasn't for the fact that his body so worn, he'd dismiss last night as one of his more involved, vivid dreams. But it was all real. Smiling, he positioned himself on the side of the bed and hoisted his body upwards, using his bed as leverage to keep his feet steady. He wondered where she'd went to, his vision of perfection. He hoped that she would be right where she'd been before he passed out so that he could wrap his arms around her and never let her go, but he posited that she had things to do and rushed out.

Or maybe she realized what she'd done and regretted it Earl searched his bed for his cellphone, finally finding it on the floor next to his bed a few feet away from the pants. He checked the time, and was horrified when he saw 8:30 PM in bright, white lettering. *How long have I been asleep?!*

Panicking, he ran to his closet, putting together a halfway-competent outfit. He checked his messages as he bolted out of the front door and surely enough, five new messages from Ben. As he got into his car, he dialed Ben to ensure that the agent hadn't left. "Dude, where are you?! We've been here for over half an hour!"

"I'm on my way, Ben! I overslept!"

"It's late! What, did you sleep through the entire day?!" Afraid of accidentally divulging information reaffirmed that he was en route. He hung the phone and drove wildly through traffic to get to the restaurant. *Do you even feel bad? What about your promises to Charlotte? Was that all just to make yourself feel better?* Earl ignored his internal commentary as he eventually found himself skidding into a parking spot outside of Nobel's at 8:45. He sprung out of the car and scanned the outdoor eating area any sign of Ben or the agent.

"Over here, E!"

Earl turned his head towards the source of the shout, seeing Ben waving his arms. He walked over, the eyes of the patrons of the eatery falling squarely on him as he sauntered over to Ben, inwardly breathing a sigh of relief when he saw that Ben hadn't dressed up for the occasion either. "Good evening, Mr. Veares! I'm Joel Rivers, the representative from Paradise Records here to talk to you and Mr. Wiggins about bringing you two over to our label!" The man sitting across from Ben stated with no uncertain amount of charm. He, unlike the pair he was trying to impress, dressed to the nines. His regal, three-piece suit appeared to be freshly pressed with not an ounce of dirt or lint present anywhere on his attire. His smile revealed rows of straight teeth, almost blindingly white, and he had a distinctive part in his hair, accentuating his opulent status. *He looks like he came fresh off an assembly line of suits.* Joel extended a hand to Earl, who pensively accepted the handshake.

"Would you like something to eat before I give you the rundown of the contract? My treat! We already had a meal before you showed, but I'll gladly foot the bill for a talented gentleman of your magnitude!" "Uh... sure," Earl said warily, warning sirens sounding off within him. Something was very disingenuous about Mr. Rivers. "I'm sorry that I'm so late, by the way. I've been having trouble sleeping, and I guess my body chose last night to try and catch up on some rest." "No problem! Mr. Wiggins informed me about how two of you operate to create such an impactful sound that your fans clearly adore!"

Joel pointed out the people surrounding them that had taken their phones out to snap a quick photo. "Can I borrow Earl for a second, Mr. Rivers? I want to talk to him about what to expect when you go over the contract with him."

"Of course! When you return, Mr. Veares, you can choose whatever you'd like on the menu!" Nodding to Joel's, Ben got up from the table and walked Earl o~~ver~~ to the parking lot, which had been a decent distance away from both Joel and Nobel's customers. "You sense it too, right?" Ben whispered, eliciting a nod from Earl.

"Definitely. Guy is shifty as hell."

"Dude, I feel like they're trying to sign us up for something that we've been good at by ourselves. The more I listened to him, the more that I realized that we honestly don't need a big record label supporting us." Earl agreed, noting that Ben had come into his own as it pertained to the music industry and its internal workings. He'd slowly obtained a savviness for the business that Earl had lacked. "Well, how do you want to do this? Do we go up and tell him that we aren't interested?" "I don't see why not!" Ben replied with a smirk. "But, wait until you finish your food first. Throw some oohs and ahhs his way to make it look like you care, then we can give him the bad news." "I like that! What would you recommend in terms of food?"

"Oh, the steak, most definitely! They cover it in this sauce that I can't pronounce, but goddamn, it's delicious. Plus, it's one of the most expensive things they have, but it's not coming out of your pocket, so you may as well take advantage of the offer!" The chortle that the pair shared almost seemed familiar, as if nothing had ever strained their friendship in the first place. "Alright, let's do it!" Earl said, extending his fist for Ben to bump with his own, which Ben reciprocated enthusiastically. As they began their trek back over to their table, Earl's phone began chiming, and shortly afterwards, Ben's started pinging as well.

"Yeah, what the hell is going on?" Earl took out his phone and was immediately brought to his WeLink page. At first, Earl thought it was a mistake with the restaurant's WiFi , but as he took a closer look, he noticed that he was being directed to a photo by his followers. Confused, Earl clicked on the small version of the picture, causing it to expand to its full size.

What the fuck?

It was actually a set of pictures, and he recognized the first one instantly as he was the one who held the phone up and snapped the lewd photo. As he scrolled through the photos, his body froze as the horror set in. The last photo of the set proved to be more damning than the others combined. It was a picture of himself and Imani, taken whilst Earl was sleeping. Imani's tongue was poked out defiantly with her head on Earl's shoulders. "Feeling inspired after fucking a true artist!" was the emboldened caption beneath the photo, and Earl stared at his phone with his mouth agape for what felt like an eternity. He could feel the heat from the figure that stood before him, knowing that Ben had seen it too. Knowing that he couldn't escape the wrath that was surely headed his way, he turned his phone off and slipped it into his pocket before looking up at Ben, who'd been fuming silently.

"Go ahead. I deserve it."

Earl winced at his own words, not entirely convinced of them, but willing to take the punishment. Ben, ready to oblige, stomped towards him, but just as he was ready to throw the first punch, he stopped. His head turned towards the crowd that had assembled outside of Nobel's, and they watched the impending altercation with bated breath. In an instant, Ben's rage deflated, and he turned to look at Earl not with anger, but with a somber resignation.

"That's what you want, isn't it? You're that fucked up that you'd let me kick your ass so that you can find a way to spin it afterwards?" Ben chuckled humorlessly as a tear fell to the ground, unable to comprehend Earl's actions. "I should've known something was up when she kept defending you after I told her what you'd done to Maddie. Did the two of you plan this together to make me look stupid? Would you at least have the balls to own up to that?" Earl's eyebrows furrowed in bewilderment as he watched someone who he'd only known to be pleasant and humorous shatter to pieces before him. "I don't know what you mean," Earl said softly. "I didn't plan for any of this, Ben. I promise you." "Then why did you do it? You knew that I loved her, and you felt the need to take that away from me?" Ben's voice began cracking as he attempted to stifle his sullen sobs. "I don't know," Earl repeated, knowing that nothing he said would be of any solace to Ben.

"There's something seriously wrong with you. I don't know who you are anymore, but I know that I don't want to be around you. I can't. We're done. You can do whatever you want, but leave me out of it. If you ever come to my house again though, I promise you, I'll go to jail for what happens to you if you show up." With that, Ben walked towards his car and got in, speeding into the descending night as Earl did nothing but watch. With a gulp, Earl shook off the discomfort he felt and made his way back to his table. He'd been played for a fool, Imani had ensured that he'd been left with nothing but himself as he sat down across from Joel with a blank, dark expression. "Give me the contract. I'll sign it. I'm not in the mood for the rundown; let's just get this over with so that I can leave." Joel quietly obliged Earl, neatly putting the binder in front of the distressed artist and handing him the pen that would seal his fate. Without Ben, he needed a system behind him, and he knew that the music was all that he'd had left.

Chapter 23

He could feel his heart sink into the pit of his stomach as he slumped back into his chair, wanting nothing more than to disappear altogether. The plump, amiable man used his pinky to slide his glasses to the top of the ridge of his wide nose, his face marked with pity over his client's misfortune. "...There's absolutely nothing that I can do?" Earl asked desperately, hoping that the answer would be different.

"I'm afraid not," Mr. Gross replied, taking a ragged, deep breath. "The one good thing is that it isn't a lifelong commitment. However, it appears that you do have a set of obligations to fulfill to Paradise Records for the next few years. I just wish that you had contacted me prior to signing it." If it hadn't happened to him, it might've been tragically hilarious. What about mentioning that I signed it when I wasn't in my right mind? What about duress? How about the fact that the agent didn't actually go over the contract with me?" "I've considered those options. Due to the nature of your occupation and notoriety, there likely isn't a shortage of footage to sift through concerning your signing, but that's still a long shot. Plus, I'm not sure if you're familiar with Paradise's history with lawsuits, but they have a damn good reputation simply because their usage of legalese is so meticulously esoteric that they're always within legal boundaries. We could meet them in court, but if we lose, you stand to lose quite a bit. Your best bet, honestly, is to just tough it out and hold steady for at least the next five years, and then we can revisit this. Just to be sure, I'll scan and copy your contract for my own perusal, but beyond that, there's little that I can do."

Earl rapped his fingers against the side of the chair and took a trembling, unstable breath before nodding, accepting his defeat. "Okay. I appreciate you trying to help, Mr. Gross."

"I wish that there was more that I could do for you, Mr. Veares." The hefty lawyer's chair screeched against the floor as he got up with a grunt and made his way to the copier in the corner of the room, next to his bookcase. "I would keep myself in the goodwill of the public if I were you. Paradise usually folds to anything that attracts enough negative publicity against them. At the five-year mark, when you're ready, we can use that to our advantage."

"Thank you for the advice."

--

He slammed his front door, causing the glass panes to shake. He tossed his copy of the contract on the kitchen table and pace throughout the house, hoping to calm himself down.

How could you be so stupid? Who signs anything like that without consulting a lawyer first? What were you thinking? They basically own you now!

He couldn't stop thinking about the moment he'd offered himself to Paradise without so much as a second thought. He felt the brisk air of the night against the back of his neck as he hunched over the table, signing where he was directed to sign, and then the slick agent disappeared into the darkness with only terse parting words to extend. He stood in the middle of his living room, shaking, his hands covering the top half of his face as he tried to escape from his volatile thoughts. *Don't do this now. You wanted this. The spotlight is all yours.*

His eyes snapped open, and with an enraged growl, he suddenly kicked at the sixty-inch flat-screen television that rested on the long stand in front of him, sending it tumbling down to the ground with crash. The chair used for viewing the television had been his next victim as he grabbed it by its arms and tossed it into the cocktail table that had placidly existed in the house for as long as he'd lived there, breaking the tempered glass into large fragments. Candles, books and coasters sat in the heap that the heavy chair had created while Earl turned his attention to the bookcase that had been just behind the chair previously, containing photos of Charlotte's favorite relatives that had long-since passed. Earl got behind the bookcase and pushed it, screaming as he did. Veins protruded from his forehead, neck and arms as the bookshelf toppled over, sending books flying in every direction and cracking the frames of many of the old pictures, if not breaking them completely. The force from the landing of the bookshelf caused the delicate urn settled upon its thin, extravagant stand to shake before unseating itself, exploding into shards as it connected with the floor. Earl's fit of rage cooled once he noticed the remnants of the urn that he'd spent so much time picking out for Charlotte. Wordlessly, he walked over to the shambles and lowered himself to the ground, beginning to pick out the ceramic pieces from the ashes, but some had been so microscopic that he soon discovered that what he was doing was an exercise in futility. After ineffectively picking out one of the bigger shards in the sea of ash-coated ceramic, he gave up as he sat inertly in front of the wreckage. He brought his aching hands out in front of him, seeing nothing but a thin layer of what remained of Charlotte combined with blood that had been the effect of Earl recklessly digging his hands into the mess of his own doing.

Helpless and hollow, the only thing that he could think to do was sob, his wailing echoing throughout every empty room of the house.

--

He hadn't known where else to go or who else to consult. This had been his last hope, trying to find any modicum of comfort that had remained for him. He stood in front of the apartment door that had once been open to him with loving arms, but was now a subject of his despair and remorse. *You did her so wrong. She's never going to take you back.* Not wanting to risk the possibility of backing out, he knocked on the door and waited. Waiting.

Waiting.

Finally, the door opened, but instead of who he'd expected to be there, he'd been face-to- face with a man that he hadn't been the least bit acquainted with. His need to regurgitate contrasted with the man's animated frenzy once he was able to mentally piece together that he'd been visited by none other than Tzar-Mo. "Holy shit, you're Tzar-Mo! You have no idea how many times I've listened to your album!" Earl had to hold back an exasperated sigh as he readied himself to ask the question that he'd been dreading.

"Is Saniya here?"

The strained breath he'd been holding exited from his mouth as soon as he witnessed the confused wrinkles in the forehead of the stranger with the prominent moustache. "I don't know who that is. I just moved in here about three months ago." *There's still a chance.*

An idea made its way to the forefront of Earl's mind as his eyes lit up, eager to see if it would work. "I know this is going to sound weird, but can I see your phone for a second?" "Of course, man!" The stranger handed his phone over happily without a question. Earl went to WeLink through the stranger's phone and typed Saniya's name in. Sure enough, her profile popped up among the list of people sharing her name, and he couldn't have been happier to tap the picture she'd set as her profile photo to allow himself a glimpse into her life. That was, until he realized that the photo his ex-girlfriend kissing someone that wasn't him in front of what had been one of the most elaborate, eye-capturing paintings that he'd ever seen.

She's gone.

"Is there something wrong, Tzar?" the stranger asked, seeing Earl's crestfallen, sunken expression. "Nah, it's fine." Earl handed the phone back to the man, ignoring the subsequent pleas for an autograph as he refused to accept that Saniya had moved on without him. Determined, he only knew of one more place where he could go to regain the heart of the woman who'd loved him the most and knew that he could convince to come back to his side. There had been a lot of missteps, but not this one. He parked outside of the house, which he hadn't been to in quite some time, and looked upon it with a faint sense of happiness and nostalgia. They used to come here for

359

holidays and he'd make jokes with her dad and tease her mother about her penchant for spicy foods.

Resolute, he stepped out of the car and began his ascension up the stairs leading to the humble two-story abode. He was ready to be the person that Saniya needed him to be. He was going to abscond with her heart, as he did once before, and together they were going to see him through his upcoming sentence with Paradise and be at peace with one another when the dust cleared. He'd needed her, now more than ever before, and he knew that he had some things to fix and tweak regarding his methods and mindset, but he was willing to be the change that he'd previously fought so hard against. He rang the doorbell. The door opened a few moments later and standing before him was an older version of his ex, beautifully aged as if the two could've been sisters. "What are you doing here?" she asked sternly, staring him down as though she was trying to melt him down into a fine paste.

"Good evening, Ms. Shirley. I wanted to know if Saniya had been through here lately. I would like to talk to her, if that's possible." The confidence and swagger that he had approached her home with had evaporated as soon as she laid eyes upon him. "What's that cute new name you go by now? Tar-Zo?" "...Tzar-Mo," Earl mumbled. "Well, listen, Earl, you should just be fortunate that Robert didn't come answer this door because he wouldn't have had much to say to you, not verbally, anyway. Truth be told, I don't want to have this conversation either. You're disgusting." Earl winced at the venom and force that Ms. Shirley made sure complemented the word "disgusting." Rather than plead his case, he figured he stood a better chance taking the verbal lashing first before trying to make amends. "I'll give you one thing; it took some real temerity for you to walk your sorry ass up to my house after what you did to my daughter. That, or delusion. Let me ask you something, what did you hope to accomplish by coming here?" "I... I wanted to apologize to Saniya," Earl affirmed, his gaze wandering as he couldn't look at Ms. Shirley without his nerves being rustled.

"I know that I wasn't in the best—"

"Let me stop you right there," Ms. Shirley interjected. "Save that spiel for whatever poor, unknowing soul decides that you're worth a good goddamn and fools herself into thinking that you're a decent person. Lord knows that Saniya fell for it, but she wised up and found herself a real man that actually supports her and her dreams. My baby's art is selling by the bundle, and she even has her most recent sale hanging up in a museum! She's so much happier now than she ever was with you, and I'd have to be one of the worst mothers alive if I so much as entertained any requests you have to try and poison her again." Earl had never felt as lowly and deplorable as he had hearing Ms. Shirley ream him for what he'd put her daughter through. Not even his conscience had done the job that Saniya's mother was doing, leaving Earl to do nothing else but absorb the criticism. "The fact that you somehow thought that showing up here was a shadow of a good idea means that your little musical venture isn't panning out, right?" Earl remained silent, which was all the confirmation that Shirley needed.

"That's what I thought. You want to know something? You and men like you always have been and always will be wastes of God's plentiful resources. Your unfulfilling, empty lives aren't good enough, so you try and drag other people down to where they can join you in misery. I heard about what you said at that party, and honestly, that was all the proof that I needed to let me know who you really were. A drunken mind releases a reservoir of buried truths." A debilitating chill shoot down his back as he listened, ashamed. It took all that he had left not to drop to his knees, crying and groveling. But he knew he needed to maintain what was left of dignity had endured, barely clinging to his personage.

"I'd wish you the best of luck, but it wouldn't be an entirely authentic gesture. It's obvious that you aren't capable of being honest, to yourself or anyone else. I won't debase myself to your standards of conduct for your peace of mind. Now, I'll make my next point once, and only once."

Shirley's eyes emitted a fire that threatened to scorch

him as she leaned forward to meet Earl's tepid, humiliatedstare. "I don't give a damn what happens to you. You could jump off a cliff with bricks strapped to your back for all it matters to me. Know this, however: If you so much as attempt to reach out to my daughter in any way again, there isn't a God existent amongst any religion that will want to involve themselves in the Hell that I'll personally ensure comes down on you without sympathy or mercy. Do you *understand* me?"

Earl responded with a meek nod, understanding Shirley concisely and definitively. "Good. I hope it was all worth it." Shirley stepped back into her house and shut the door, sending Earl back into the cold night as he made what felt like the longest journey back to his car. He sunk into the driver's seat and sat there for what felt like hours, unable to think, unable to process. Eventually, his body retrieved the car keys from his pocket and thrust them into the ignition, bringing the vehicle to life with a turn of the wrist. He backed out of the Clements' driveway and made his way back home, not taking the risk to check either of his car's side mirrors for fear of catching any sight of his own reflection.

Chapter 24

"Tzar-Mo! Tzar-Mo! Tzar-Mo!"

The raving of the crowd that came to the concert had reached a fever pitch. Earl stayed in the expansive room that his producer had affectionately called "the green room." He sat listlessly, staring at the catering table at the opposite end of the room that the venue had provided for him containing various types of salads, snacks and other accoutrements for his benefit. "Only ten more minutes, and everything will be ready for you!"

Earl nodded at Jerry, his producer, who disappeared after poking his head in to update Earl on his timetable. Earl slammed his eyes shut as the chanting prevailed, growing to loathe his own creation. What used to carry so much meaning and potential now meant absolutely nothing. Tzar-Mo was no longer an outlet, he was a costume that Earl was forced to fit into and perform as. His team had spent the last month or two preparing him for this, his big spectacle. They tailor-made Earl a flashy suit complete with his signature half- cape that he now hadn't been a fan of, but forced himself to approve.

He'd had to rehearse a multitude of times, the routine becoming indoctrinated within him.

"Good luck on your first big event!"

Earl distinctly recalled the generic first line of the "correspondence" between himself and the CEO of Paradise Records. He'd never even bothered to come and address his newest vassal directly. Instead he sent Earl a bureaucratic email that he'd been too busy, or too indifferent, to personalize in the slightest. Earl's posture shifted as he leaned back into his seat with his head tilted backwards, failing to convince himself that it'd all been for the best.

"It's an adjustment period! You'll get the hang of things the longer that you're here, I promise! We're a family now, and everyone does a pretty good job of looking out for each other!" Miz Terry's mouth curled into a trained smile as she stated that to Earl during his first month, being as transparent as the wordplay in her stage name.

Earl's head swiveled to the right, a full-body mirror meeting his gaze. He stood, walked directly in front of it, and stared at himself. He was every bit the product that they'd wanted him to be from head to toe. His hair had been cut into decorative stripes to "expand his visibility," his 'updated' half-cape had more frills than Kim's used to, and even when he'd rehearsed one of the songs he'd chosen for his concert, nobody understood him. If they weren't dogged yes-men, they were people who looked at

Earl and tried to maximize the profits he'd brought in, not remotely considering anything he'd truly wanted to add to his music. His life, as he presently knew it, became rife with the falsehoods that he'd promised himself would never happen to him.

He thought he was smarter, savvier. Yet, there he was, an exhibit reliant on his audience to clap, cheer and enjoy the show. Then, they'd go home to their families, friends and loved ones, having gleaned nothing more than before they'd came to see him. Earl's new residence was the closest thing to a palace that any ordinary person would've killed to live in. Paradise had given him the most luxurious mansion befitting his stardom as a gift for signing his talents over to them. Instead of a loving home, Earl lived within a lavish tomb. He was required to throw ritzy parties to maintain his relevancy, he only stuck around for obligation, and rather than cycle through his ardent female fans, he'd shifted to nascent female celebrities looking to use his name to elevate themselves. Otherwise, he spent his nights in a cold bedroom, lying in a king-sized bed. He was barely able to sleep as his mind replayed every mistake; he'd made to get the life he thought he wanted. But as he ran a hand across the seams of his half-cape, he wished that he'd been back at Saniya's studio apartment, complaining about literary agents not liking the concept of his book as she assured him that patience would net him the rewards he'd spent so long working towards.

Interrupting his solemn reverie were increasingly loud, vicious yells coming from just outside of the green room. Curious, he poked his head out of the door, seeing the security staff trying to block someone from reaching him. As soon as he put a face and name to the intruder, his eyes widened, barely able to comprehend the sight. "That's the father of my child right there, so let me through!"

Earl got a complete look as she pushed through one of the smaller guards, revealing the bump in her abdomen. One of the bigger members of his security team went to grab her by the arm, but Earl intervened. "Stop! She's… with me. I know her." Earl nodded, an indication for the guards to leave the distraught woman alone as she straightened herself out and walked up to Earl, beaming. "I bet you weren't expecting to see me again, were you?" "…No."

He wanted to hate her for what she'd done to him, but a part of him couldn't bring himself to. She'd been more radiant than he'd known her to be, the ringlets in her long, ebony hair never losing their sheen. Her body was also as fit and taut as ever, despite the noticeable bump. He waved her into the green room and closed the door behind him, then the two looked at each other, no more secrets between them. Earl looked down at the protrusion, then back up at Imani, who nodded in confirmation of his nonverbal question. "I guess I have some explaining to do, huh?" The producer's head emerged through a crack in the door.

"Is everything alright, Tzar?!"

"Yeah. You think you could give me about another five minutes?" The producer looked between Earl and Imani before acquiescing to the request. "Fine, but we can't keep the crowd waiting any longer than that." The producer disappeared, leaving the two to stare at each other before Imani finally spoke.

"I thought that the last six months would give me enough time to get over you, but I guess not."

"Why'd you do it?"

Imani's eyes danced around, trying to find the words to describe her actions. "When I first met Ben at the bar, I'd saw an opportunity. I recognized him because he was one of the bigger online personalities, so when he offered to buy me a drink, I knew I couldn't say no. I wanted to be associated with him to keep my modeling numbers up so that WeLink could continue paying me decently because I didn't want to go back to waitressing; I couldn't tolerate supporting myself like that again. Then you came into the picture, and initially, I just wanted to keep things friendly with you. But… things changed." "What do you mean?" Earl asked firmly. "We would have… moments. Conversations that made me wonder. Ben took everything as a carefree joke, but you'd listen to me and we had something that I never had with

anyone else. After a while, I realized that you were the star out of the two of you, and it worked out because Ben had become more than annoying. I never felt anything for him. I wanted you, but I also needed a failsafe."

Imani pointed to her stomach, then clarified the implication amidst Earl's confounded expression. "I wanted you to knock me up that night, but I was hoping that I'd get over you so that I could give you an ultimatum. I had planned to find you and tell you that we were going to be a couple, and if you disagreed, I'd bleed you dry with child support. Either way, my numbers would stay up and I'd get more money." Confusion turned into indignation as Earl heard Imani's twisted endgame, wondering how someone could rationalize such methods to themselves. "I don't understand!"

"I promised myself that I'd never be like my mother. She gambled on 'love' and lost, big- time. Instead of that, I chose a more… unconventional route where I had certain guarantees in place. I still want to be with you, and I know that you need this, your career. I don't want to ruin that for you, but if that's what it comes down to, I'm not afraid to prioritize what I want over what you want."

"What the fuck is wrong with you?!"

369

Imani narrowed her eyes, almost puzzled at Earl's reaction. "You're a bit of a manipulator yourself. Don't think that I forgot about the Lil Grande situation. I always thought that something about that seemed off, but I figured you out. You knew that Ben was going to defend you. It was smart. That's why we're good for each other." Earl couldn't believe what he was hearing. Imani had sounded crazier by the minute, and he'd tried to come up with a solution, but nothing presented itself. "So, you want me to accept you as what, my girlfriend?"

"That's the gist!" Imani chirped. "I know that entrapment isn't the best way to show you that I care, but I promise you, I'm here for you, for us. I can help you reach your full potential and make sure that nobody takes advantage of you. I think that we'll make amazing parents too! I'm not saying it's going to be an easy start, but I will say that I'll be in your corner, completely, just as I know you'll be in mine." Imani stroked Earl's cheek lovingly, then held up a finger as if she'd remembered something crucial. "Oh, one thing though: No more fucking other women. I can keep your bed warm; you won't have to worry about that. You won't have to spend a lot of money on me either because I can pretty much hold my own. I want to have my own business one day, but I'm still trying to figure out what I'd want that to be. Anyway, how are you feeling about everything? I know it's a lot, but I want you to be honest with me..."

Earl's eyes fell onto one of the knives over by the catering table, seeing it gleam from the bright lights of the green room. A dark thought entered his mind, leaving as quickly as it came as he stowed the horrific fantasy into the deepest recesses of his brain. "...I... I think that—"

The producer suddenly burst through the door, his mouth in a thin, serious line.

"I've stalled for long enough. Ma'am, you have to go. Tzar, you can have a minute in here, but when I come back, we have to get the show going." Imani sneered at the interrupting man before turning to Earl with a soft, intimate glance. "Come find me after the show, okay?" The producer waited by the door for Imani to leave, and as she walked across the door's threshold, she turned her head back to Earl. "By the way, that night we had together was one of the best I've ever had. Good luck, baby." Smiling, Imani disappeared down the hallway, escorted away by the producer. That left Earl in the green room, alone, trying to process the new information that Imani had sprung on him. Breathing heavily, Earl stomped over to the catering table and grabbed the sharpest knife he could find. He put his hand atop the table, the palm facing upwards, and held the knife right up against his wrist, ready to fatally slice it.

Fear gripped him harder than it ever had as he stared at what would've been his end, shivering.

"It's showtime, Tzar!"

Earl turned around, startled, and was motioned out of the room by his producer, who he followed into the hallway and towards the stage. Every footfall echoed as he began to hear the opening notes of the live pianists that would accompany his performance. When they got to the steps that would lead Earl to the stage, the producer handed him a microphone and gave him one last thumbs-up, telling him that he was good to go. With a deep breath, Earl strode up the steps and was immediately met with the loudest reaction he'd ever gotten, followed by the constant flash of cameras. He looked out into the crowd as Tzar-Mo strutted around the stage, hyping up his fervent fans. It had been almost like an out-of-body experience as Earl beheld the crazed fans while Tzar-Mo waited for the pianists to finish their wondrously adept prelude so that he could take over.

Tzar-Mo wanted Earl to be heard, but knew that the crowd showed up to see him, not his reflection. So many starry eyes to contrast Tzar's abject vacancy. Just perform… "Just… Perform…"

Open the book, Look it took, A blackbird Cold, dark and alone, disgraced, Hanged of his fading, at the page. See what locked inside a cage. no escape. A king symbolically raped. own design, eyes

Visions been chased the hear me? me? of lofty goals he'd craving, Foolishly divine. Who can really Who can really see

Who can still wish, could be me? look in my eyes and daily, that they

Took it for granted, raw ambition implanted, Greed became my God, thought I was almighty, but I was flawed...

Lost sight of myself, now nobody can help, What stands before you? A toy on the shelf. Woke up wanting to be great, Fueled by wrath, swallowed by hate.

♪ Narcissism took my eyes, tried to deny what I rightly deserved Thought it was destined to be mine, a legacy, immaculately preserved.

♪ I wonder if she's looking down at me, A jester laid bare for all to see. Praying I'd come back before I chose to pay, With a signature, sold it all away.

♪ Held the world in my hands, could've been dogmatic, Palette went from vibrant to monochromatic. If you envy this, I would be remiss If I didn't tell you that instead of bliss

♪ You're staring into a dark abyss Karma's sweet promises turned into a hiss. It's not all as it seems, on the surface, might mistake it for a dream. Torturously undone at the seams, No more schemes, no more teams, Emitting silent screams.

♪ Regrets, I've had a few, but the biggest yet is the implosion of a rising star, Seeming hopeful and bright from afar, but death is conclusively all that it met. I had it all, but was too dense to see it,

♪ Now I have it all and if you can believe, I wish that I could acquit it. The best part of living is the simple pleasures, But once you take certain measures, It's a matter of burden, not leisure.

♪ They say the road to Hell is paved with good intentions, But if this isn't Hell, then it's an honorable mention.

♪ Along the path to gaining self-sustainment,

♪ A glowing prospect became a puppet for your entertainment. Doing his damn dance from day to night, And nobody gives a fuck if the strings are too tight. It's not all as it seems,

♪ Plagued by nightmares, plenty of pain to spare.

♪ You hear without hearing, applaud, when you should be jeering, It's my cross to bear, instead of joy, I'm scared. Not a game of kings or queens, just affluent, broken machines, … It's not all as it seems.

♪

Made in the USA
Middletown, DE
25 July 2019